the Road Back to Me

the Road Back to Me

SIX SACRED TOOLS
FOR QUEER HEALING
THROUGH SHADOW, BREATH,
AND TRUTH

Peter J. Cervantes

W. Brand Publishing
NASHVILLE, TENNESSEE

W. Brand Publishing is committed to publishing works of quality and integrity. In that spirit, we are proud to offer this book to our readers; however, the story, the experiences, and the words are the author's alone and portrayed to the best of their recollection. In some cases, names have been changed to protect the privacy of the people involved.

Copyright ©2026 Peter J. Cervantes

All rights reserved. No part of this publication may be reproduced, distributed, or transmitted in any form or by any means, including photocopying, recording, or other electronic or mechanical methods, without the prior written permission of the publisher, except in the case of brief quotations embodied in critical reviews and certain other noncommercial uses permitted by copyright law. For permission requests, write to the publisher, addressed "Attention Permission Request" at the email below.

j.brand@wbrandpub.com
W. Brand Publishing
www.wbrandpub.com

Cover design by JuLee Brand / designchik
Photography by Stephen Cervantes

The Road Back to Me / Peter J. Cervantes —1st ed.

Available in Paperback, Kindle, and eBook formats.
Paperback ISBN: 979-8-89503-038-7
eBook ISBN: 979-8-89503-039-4
Library of Congress Control Number: (applied for)

CONTENTS

Introduction 1

Chapter 1: Working Through the Shadows 7

Chapter 2: Breaking Generational Chains 59

Chapter 3: Tapping Into Healing 109

Chapter 4: Writing Myself Back to Me 167

Chapter 5: Searching for Faith 203

Chapter 6: The Magic of Breathing 253

Chapter 7: The Road Back to Me 297

Chapter 8: A Love Letter to My Community 331

Epilogue: The Work in Real Time 355

About the Author 375

To my Abuelito, Roberto Duran

and my husband, Stephen Hallburn, for being my rock

INTRODUCTION

I almost died at thirty-seven from trauma I didn't even know I was carrying. Not from drugs, not from violence, not from any of the obvious dangers one might expect growing up gay and Latino in Long Beach—instead, it came from the weight of generational pain I inherited and never learned to heal.

I'm not writing this to get sympathy or tell you some sob story. I'm writing it because if I've figured out how to transform decades of trauma into actual healing, maybe you can, too.

This isn't another "I survived, and so can you" story. This is about the difference between surviving and actually living—between carrying trauma and transforming it, and between living someone else's version of your life and becoming who you truly are.

We're all products of our environments, walking around with limiting beliefs our families shoved down our throats before we knew we had a choice. Being first-generation, Latino, and gay? That's playing life on expert mode while everyone else gets the tutorial. Growing up the youngest sibling with immigrant parents in Long Beach barrios during the '90s—with a father who carried toxic machismo like sacred tradition—created a perfect storm of trauma that almost killed me decades later.

The streets didn't get me, but the pain of being gay with an alcoholic father nearly put me in the ground when I was thirty-seven. That's when I realized I had two choices: figure out how to heal or die trying to numb the pain.

LIFE REALLY DOES BEGIN AT FORTY

Carl Jung said, "Life really does begin at forty. Up until then you are just doing research." At thirty-five, drowning in depression and addiction, I would have told Jung to fuck off with his consolation prize bullshit. Now that I'm forty-two, I finally get it. All those years of pain weren't evidence I was broken—they were research. Brutal, necessary research that taught me everything I needed to know about what doesn't work, what hurts, what heals, and what it truly takes to transform pain into wisdom.

Everything that happened before—all the pain, mistakes, searching, falling down and getting back up—that wasn't my life. That was me gathering the raw materials I'd need to build a real life worth living.

It took me nearly four decades to learn this, but it's never too late to want better for yourself—and never too late to build the life you actually want, instead of the one everyone else thinks you should have. The research phase doesn't mean you wasted time; it means you earned every single tool you're about to use to build something extraordinary.

MY PURPOSE: HEALING FOR EVERYONE

My purpose is to share the tools necessary for healing generational trauma and growing up queer. You don't need to be of color—generational trauma affects everyone, especially those in the queer community. My purpose is to spread this knowledge and get you to a place of healing no matter what age, race, or sex.

While my story comes from a specific intersection—Latino, gay, first-generation American—the trauma patterns are universal: family rejection for being different; religious shame about sexuality; the exhaustion of hiding who you are; and the self-destruction that comes from believing you're fundamentally flawed.

These experiences don't belong to any single community. They apply to anyone who has ever felt like they had to choose between their authentic self and their family's love. Whether you're a bisexual woman in rural Texas navigating evangelical parents, a trans teenager in suburban New Jersey hiding from conservative grandparents, or a gay man in his sixties finally coming out after a lifetime of marriage—the specifics differ, but the path to healing is the same. You don't need my exact story to use my tools, and you don't need to wait until you're forty-two to start doing this work. Healing is available to you right now, exactly where you are, with whatever resources you currently have.

THE SIX TOOLS THAT SAVED MY LIFE

Here's the thing about healing—it's not a straight line. It's more like stumbling through a dark forest, falling in holes you didn't see coming or climbing mountains that seem impossible, and somehow finding moments of grace in the midst of chaos.

I've been through addiction, toxic relationships, and mental health crises that had me planning my own funeral. But I've also found love with someone who saw past all my damage, met a therapist who helped me understand the generational shit I was carrying, and discovered that my purpose is to help other people navigate this same terrain.

I'll share six tools that quite literally saved my life: shadow work, generational trauma healing, EMDR, journaling, meditation, and breath work. These aren't abstract concepts but lived practices—tools that pulled me back from the edge and taught me how to transform inherited pain into inherited wisdom.

Shadow work taught me to reclaim the parts of myself I'd been taught to reject—my sensitivity, my creativity, my emotional depth—and recognize them as gifts rather than flaws. Generational trauma healing helped me understand that I wasn't just carrying my own pain, but the unhealed wounds of my ancestors. Healing myself meant healing my entire family line.

EMDR gave me a way to process trauma that lived in my body, not just my mind. Trauma that therapy alone couldn't touch. Journaling became my daily practice of truth-telling, helping me excavate authentic thoughts and feelings from beneath layers of performance and people-pleasing.

Meditation showed me that beneath all the noise of thoughts and emotions was a vast, peaceful awareness that trauma could never actually touch. Breath work became my bridge between the conscious and unconscious, allowing suppressed emotions and memories to surface safely so they could finally be released.

You'll get frameworks for understanding generational trauma, especially how it shows up for LGBTQ+ people—but these tools work for everyone. You'll learn how to reconnect with your body when anxiety or addiction has disconnected you from yourself. Most importantly, you'll gain permission to create your own path forward—one that honors where you come from but refuses to be limited by it.

THE RESEARCH PHASE IS OVER

The biggest revelation? Most of my suffering came from killing off the creative, authentic parts of myself to make other people comfortable. Every time I tried to follow my artistic dreams, my family shut it down. If an acting agency wanted to represent me? "No, mijo." If I got accepted to the Art Institute? "We can't afford it." If I wanted to go to beauty school? "Men don't work in beauty"—as if my sexuality weren't already proof I wasn't their version of a man.

All of that rejection and pain, all of those years of feeling like I was living someone else's life—that was my research. I was learning what happens when you abandon yourself to make others comfortable. I was discovering the cost of performing instead of being. I was gathering data on what it feels like to slowly suffocate your own soul while carrying the unhealed wounds of the generations who came before me.

Writing this book is my reclamation of all that research and putting it to use. This is the artist I was meant to be before trauma and cultural expectations convinced me I had to be someone else. Every page is an act of rebellion against everyone who told me to be smaller, quieter, more acceptable.

This is about what becomes possible when you stop running from your pain and start listening to what it's trying to teach you. It's about breaking the cycles that have been fucking up our families for generations. It's about claiming your right to joy, peace, and wholeness—not despite being queer or traumatized or different, but because of everything that makes you exactly who you are

THE TOOLS WORK TOGETHER

These six tools don't work in isolation—they dance together, each one informing and enhancing the others. Shadow work might reveal a rejected part of yourself, while generational trauma healing helps you understand how that rejection originated within your family. EMDR can help you process the emotional charge around these discoveries, and journaling allows you to integrate those insights.

Meditation provides the spacious awareness to hold everything with compassion, and breath work offers a way to release what no longer serves you—and to embody change at a cellular level. Together, they create a comprehensive approach to healing that addresses trauma on every level—mental, emotional, physical, and spiritual.

If you picked up this book, something in you is ready to move past the research phase and start actually living. Ready to stop surviving trauma and start transforming it. Ready to break the cycles that have limited your family for generations.

The trauma stops with you. The healing begins with you. These six tools will show you exactly how to make that transformation real—not someday, and not when you're "ready enough." Right fucking now.

Your ancestors survived so you could heal. Future generations are counting on you to break the patterns your ancestors couldn't. Let's do this work together.

CHAPTER 1

Working Through the Shadows

The spaces that fuck you up as a kid follow you everywhere. That's just the truth. But sometimes, if you're lucky, you find one space that saves you. For me, that was my abuelito's workshop—a place where love smelled like sawdust and Vicks VapoRub, where broken things weren't thrown away but transformed into something beautiful.

His hands were rough as hell from decades of working with wood and leather. They were cracked and calloused from years of honest labor, but when he'd guided mine across a piece of unfinished pine, teaching me to feel for the grain, there was something infinitely gentle about it. Something that made sense in a way nothing else in my chaotic childhood did.

"Mira, mijo," he'd say, his voice soft with the kind of patience I never experienced anywhere else. "Every piece of wood has its own story—its own structure inside. You have to listen to what it wants to become, not force it into something it's not."

I thought he was just talking about wood. It took me thirty years and a shit ton of therapy to realize he was talking about people too. About me.

THE SACRED WORKSHOP

That workshop was tucked behind his small house in Tijuana. It was a garage that had become something between an art studio and a sanctuary. Tools hung in perfect order on pegboard walls—chisels, planes, sanders—each one worn smooth by decades of use, each one an extension of his weathered hands.

The smell was intoxicating in the way only sacred spaces can be: fresh-cut wood mixed with the Murphy's Oil Soap he used to clean everything, Vicks VapoRub from the jar he kept on his workbench for headaches, and always, *always*, the lingering aroma of Folgers coffee.

This wasn't just where my abuelito worked—it was where magic happened.

Where discarded furniture found new life.

Where broken chairs learned to hold weight again.

Where scratched tables discovered they could be beautiful once more.

I'd watch him approach each piece like a detective solving a mystery, running his hands over every surface, testing joints, examining the damage with the kind of attention most people reserve for precious things.

"This one has good bones," he'd murmur, as he examined a chair someone had thrown away because one leg was wobbly. "Just needs a little attention, a little love. Nothing that can't be fixed with patience."

I didn't yet know the world outside was going to spend the next few decades trying to make me smaller, trying to convince me that the parts of myself that didn't fit into neat little boxes were problems to be solved rather than gifts to be treasured. Abuelito's workshop was the one place where I could take up space, fuck up spectacularly, and exist without having to apologize for every impulse, every expression, every way I moved through the world that marked me as different.

What made this relationship different from every other one in my life was that it had no conditions. He never flinched when my voice cracked in ways that sounded too soft, too melodic, too much like the girls in my class. Never got uncomfortable when I moved my hands in animated gestures that other men would later tell me were "too feminine." And he never corrected me when I got excited about colors, textures, or the way the light fell across a piece of wood he was sanding.

Instead, he showed me a different kind of masculinity—one that came from fixing broken things gently, from listening to stories without interruption, from always having extra *pan dulce* in his pocket *por si acaso*—just in case his grandson needed sweetness in a world that often felt bitter. His strength wasn't loud or aggressive or dominating. It was as quiet, steady, and unshakeable.

Even now, thirty-three years after his death, when I need to remember what unconditional love feels like, my mind goes straight back to that workshop. The way afternoon light would filter through the single window, illuminating speckles of dust that danced like tiny spirits around us. The satisfaction of running sandpaper across rough wood until it became smooth as silk under our fingers. The way he'd nod approvingly when I'd hold a tool correctly or laugh—not mockingly, but with pure delight—when I'd get so excited about a project that I'd start bouncing on my toes.

THE BORDER CROSSINGS

Every weekend, we made the drive from Long Beach to Tijuana. I'd start getting excited the moment I could see the border checkpoint in the distance. Those weekends belonged to us—my abuelo and me. My parents would disappear into their own adult world of friends, drinking, and whatever drama they'd cultivated that week, while my abuelo loaded me into his beat-up Ford pickup truck. It was sacred time with him.

He used the same truck for work during the week, hauling materials and tools to construction sites where he helped build other people's dreams—for wages that barely covered his own modest needs. But on weekends, that truck transformed into our chariot to freedom. It was our vehicle for crossing not just international borders, but the invisible boundary that separated who I had to be in Long Beach from who I was allowed to be in his presence.

On the American side of that border, I was constantly forced into some narrow-ass box of what boys should be—how they should move, speak, think, dream. Every day was a lesson in conformity: in making myself smaller, in monitoring every gesture and inflection to avoid the inevitable corrections:

"Don't walk like that."

"Stop moving your hands so much."

"Boys don't get excited about pretty things."

But crossing into Tijuana meant entering a world where different rules applied. Where the expectations that felt like chains in Long Beach loosened just enough for me to remember what it felt like to breathe deeply. We weren't just crossing the border between countries—we were crossing into a parallel universe, where I didn't have to perform masculinity for anyone, where my abuelito's love created a protective bubble around us both.

The drive itself became a weekly ritual of self-transformation—a liminal space between the person I had to be in Long Beach and the person I was allowed to be in Tijuana. I'd get in the car as Peter who was 'too sensitive,' 'too emotional,' 'too much,' and somewhere between the border checkpoint and his driveway, I'd shed those labels like old skin. As we waited in the long lines of weekend traffic, my abuelito would tell me stories about his own childhood in a small village, about his father who had also worked with his hands—about traditions and skills passed down through generations of men who understood that true strength came from creation, not destruction. Those stories weren't just entertainment—they were teaching me that there were other ways to be a man, other ways to be Mexican, other ways to exist in the world than what I was learning everywhere else.

"In Mexico," he'd say, "a man who can make beautiful things with his hands is respected. It doesn't matter if he's building houses or carving toys—if he can take raw materials and turn them into something useful, something beautiful, he has value."

I soaked up these stories like a desert soaks up rain, storing them away for the harder times— when I'd need to remember that there were places in the world where being different wasn't a curse, but simply another way of being human.

THE TIJUANA CIRCUS

The circus was our favorite destination but calling it a circus doesn't really capture the raw magic of what we experienced there. These weren't the sanitized American productions with corporate sponsors, safety inspectors, and carefully managed risk. This was something older, wilder, and more honest—a traveling show that had been crossing back and forth across the border for generations, carrying traditions that predated the artificial lines humans had drawn on maps.

The performers danced with a casual intimacy with danger that would have given American parents nightmares. Fire-eaters passed their torches to children in the audience just to see their eyes light up. Trapeze artists in their sixties still flew through the air like gravity was just a suggestion they'd decided to politely ignore. Clowns had painted faces that were works of art— elaborate and slightly unsettling in ways that suggested they understood something about the thin line between comedy and tragedy, a line most entertainers never dared to explore.

And the elephants—Jesus, the elephants. These massive, ancient creatures moved through their routines with a dignity and intelligence that made it clear they were partners in this enterprise, not just trained animals. You could see decades of relationship between the elephants and their trainers—a wordless communication developed through years of mutual respect and understanding.

But what I remember most wasn't the spectacle itself. It was my abuelito watching me watch the show. While other adults in the crowd spent the evening managing their children's reactions—"Sit still," "Don't point," "Stop making so much noise"—my abuelito encouraged my amazement. When I gasped in wonder at a particularly impossible-seeming act, he'd gasp right alongside me, his eyes dancing with the same delight bubbling up in my chest.

Sometimes I'd catch him watching me instead of the performance, and I'd see this look on his face—pure pride mixed with something that felt like recognition, as if he was seeing my uninhibited joy—something he'd been hoping to find there all along.

He knew these nights were healing for me— that watching people who made their living by refusing to accept conventional limits was feeding something in my soul that got starved during the week in Long Beach.

"¿*Ves, mijo?*" he'd whisper during the more spectacular moments, leaning down so his words were meant just for me. "There are no rules about what's possible. The only limits are the ones we accept."

Between acts, he'd tell me stories about the circus that came through his village when he was a boy— stories about strongmen who could lift entire carts, about women who danced with snakes and were rumored to be part-serpent themselves, about acrobats who seemed to have made personal peace treaties with gravity. These whispered stories connected us across time and culture, making me feel like I was part of something bigger than just my own small, confused existence.

Those stories also carried an implicit message that took me years to fully understand: the world was full of people who chose to live outside conventional boundaries—people who had decided that being extraordinary was worth the risk of being misunderstood; that there was honor in refusing to accept limitations others took for granted.

When the shows ended and we spilled out into the warm Tijuana night, I'd hold myself differently—like my body had remembered something essential it had temporarily forgotten. Like the possibility of magic was real and accessible, not just something that happened to other people in other places.

THE LESSON HIDDEN IN PLAIN SIGHT

What my abuelito was creating for me wasn't just entertainment or even an escape—it was a form of education that no school could have provided. Every weekend trip was a master class in possibility—a demonstration that the boxes the world tried to put people in were human constructions, not natural laws; that difference could be celebrated rather than corrected; that there were places where being unusual was an asset, not a liability.

This was revolutionary thinking for a kid growing up in the early '90s—especially for a kid who was already beginning to understand that he didn't fit the mold that had been prepared for him. Without ever using words like "acceptance" or "authenticity," my abuelito taught me that the parts of myself that felt most natural were also the parts most worth protecting and nurturing.

The contrast between my weekend freedom and my weekday performance was stark enough that even my then-child's mind could recognize it. In Long Beach, I spent my days monitoring every gesture, every vocal inflection, every expression of enthusiasm—for fear it would mark me as different in ways that brought unwanted attention. In Tijuana, in my abuelito's presence, I could exist without editing and respond to beauty and wonder without calculating whether my responses were appropriately masculine.

This wasn't lost on him. I could see it in the way he created little moments of freedom throughout our time together—encouraging me to touch fabrics at the market because he noticed how I responded to different textures; stopping to watch street performers because he'd seen how music made my whole body want to move; letting me spend long minutes examining the way light played across buildings because he understood that I saw things differently than other people—and that this way of seeing was a gift, not a problem.

"Tienes ojos de artista," he told me once—*you have the eyes of an artist*. The way he said it made it clear this was high praise, not just casual observation. In his world, seeing beauty where others saw only ordinary things was a superpower, not a sign that something was wrong with me.

Years before I had language for concepts like *internalized homophobia* or *cultural conditioning*, my body was learning liberation. Just being allowed to exist without constant correction taught my nervous system what safety felt like—and what it meant to be seen and accepted, rather than analyzed. That feeling became a compass I didn't even know I was carrying, something I'd spend decades trying to find again in relationships, in cities, in creative work. Every time I felt truly safe later in life, it was because someone was offering me what my grandfather had already shown me was possible.

A DIFFERENT KIND OF STRENGTH

Most importantly, my abuelito showed me a completely different version of masculinity than I encountered anywhere else. While the world around me taught that real men dominated through force, that strength meant emotional suppression, and that vulnerability was equivalent to weakness—his workshop demonstrated something revolutionary: the deepest strength could be quiet, patient, and focused on repair rather than destruction.

I'd watch him approach a broken piece of furniture the way other men might approach an enemy—but instead of conquering it, he'd study it, understand it, and work with its existing structure to restore its original beauty. His tools were extensions of his hands, not weapons. His power came from skill and patience, not aggression.

There's one memory that captures this perfectly. It's burned into my consciousness with the clarity that only comes from moments of profound recognition. I'd been helping him sand a table someone had abandoned because the surface was scratched and water-damaged. I was maybe seven years old—eager to help but clumsy with excitement—and I knocked over a jar of stain he'd been mixing to match the wood's original color.

The dark liquid spread across his clean workbench and dripped onto the concrete floor, ruining several hours of careful preparation. I froze, my small body already bracing for the explosion of rage I'd learned to expect from adult men when their work was disrupted by a child's carelessness. In my house, accidents like this resulted in yelling. I was sent away in disgrace, and my clumsiness was analyzed and criticized until I felt ashamed of taking up space at all.

But my abuelito just sighed—not with anger, but with the kind of acceptance that acknowledges the basic unpredictability of life. He put his hand gently on my shoulder.

"*Ahora sabemos lo que no debemos hacer,*" he said calmly. *Now we know what not to do.* Then he handed me a rag and showed me how to clean up the mess safely—turning my disaster into a lesson about handling mistakes without shame and learning from errors instead of being paralyzed by them.

In that moment, he taught me something that would take decades of therapy to fully integrate: real strength isn't about domination or control or perfection. It's about how you respond to vulnerability—your own and everyone else's. It's about creating space for human imperfection while still maintaining standards of excellence. It's about understanding that gentleness and strength aren't opposites, but complementary aspects of the same mature masculinity.

This was a revelation that contradicted everything I learned about how men were supposed to behave. In my house, mistakes were evidence of inadequacy. In school, errors were marks against your competence. But in my abuelito's workshop, mistakes were simply data points—what didn't work that could inform better choices next time.

He modeled emotional regulation in ways that seemed almost supernatural to a kid accustomed to adult volatility. I never saw him lose his temper, hear him raise his voice, or witness the kind of emotional explosions that were routine in my daily life. But this wasn't just emotional suppression, it was something much more sophisticated. He felt everything fully, yet responded from a place of conscious choice rather than reactive impulse.

When I got frustrated with a project that wasn't going the way I'd envisioned, he'd sit beside me and share stories about his own learning process—about pieces he'd ruined through impatience and the years it took him to develop the skills that now seemed effortless. These weren't lectures about persistence; they were demonstrations of humility and acknowledgments that mastery is a lifelong process requiring self-compassion and discipline. In those moments, my frustration would dissolve—not because the problem was solved, but because he'd made me feel like I belonged in the mess of learning.

THE QUIET PROTECTOR

My abuelito was gentle and soft-spoken in ways that might have seemed weak to people who measured masculinity by volume and aggression. I never heard him raise his voice or let anger transform his weathered face into something frightening. His quietness wasn't the silence of suppression; it was the calm of someone who had learned to choose his words carefully and to speak only when he had something valuable to contribute.

This gentleness masked a fierce protectiveness that became evident whenever my father's volatility threatened to spill over onto me. My abuelito never confronted my father directly—too much cultural respect for hierarchy and family roles to challenge another man's authority over his children. Instead, he created distractions, diversions, and invisible safety nets that appeared exactly when I needed them most.

"Ven conmigo, mijo," he'd say quietly, his hand light on my shoulder when he sensed tension building in the house. "I need help with something in my room."

Just like that, I'd be guided away from whatever storm was brewing and led to safety before the emotional weather turned dangerous. These interventions were so subtle that I didn't fully recognize them as protection until years later. At the time, they just felt like invitations to spend time with the one adult who seemed genuinely interested in my company.

His bedroom was simple to the point of austerity—just a dresser and a bed he'd built himself, furniture that would have looked plain in a magazine but radiated the kind of integrity that comes from craftsmanship over ornamentation. The bed frame fit together with joints so precise you couldn't slide paper between them. The dresser drawers moved smooth as silk on runners he'd sanded and waxed until they achieved a kind of perfection that modern manufacturing couldn't replicate.

To my eyes, that simple room felt grand—not because of luxury, but because of the absolute safety it represented. These weren't just pieces of furniture. They were tangible proof of what care and attention could create—demonstrations that broken things could be made not just functional, but beautiful again.

Sitting on the edge of that perfectly-made bed, sometimes he'd tell me stories about Mexico. About the village where he'd grown up or his own father, who had also worked with wood. Other times, we'd sit in comfortable silence, his presence alone enough to restore whatever equilibrium my father's anger had disrupted.

"Your great-grandfather," abuelito told me once, "could take a piece of wood that looked like nothing special and turn it into something so beautiful people would weep when they saw it. He had magic in his hands, but the magic wasn't mysterious—it was just love and patience and paying attention to what the wood wanted to become."

These stories planted seeds that wouldn't sprout until decades later, when I'd finally understand that creativity wasn't an impractical luxury but essential expression—that the impulse to make things beautiful wasn't weakness, but one of the most fundamental human drives.

LOVE WITHOUT BORDERS

What I couldn't see then—and what I wouldn't understand until years of therapy helped me excavate the foundation of my own self-worth—was that my abuelito offered me something revolutionary: love without conditions. Acceptance that didn't require performance and belonging that wasn't contingent on my ability to fit into predetermined categories.

In a world determined to put everything into neat little boxes—boys versus girls, strong versus weak, normal versus different—he created space for complexity, for the gray areas where real humans actually live. He loved me not despite my sensitivity, but with it woven seamlessly into his understanding of who I was. He encouraged my artistic impulses not because they were cute childhood phases, but because he recognized them as authentic expressions of my essential nature.

After years of therapy and shadow work that felt like an archaeological excavation of buried authenticity, I realized what abuelito had given me had been with me all along. It was dormant, but not destroyed—buried but never erased. I'd just lost track of it as layers of conditioning piled up, each one pushing me further from that workshop sanctuary and deeper into the performance of acceptability.

Through years of family and cultural conditioning, I became a shell of who I'd always been—the authentic kid who squealed at circus performers, who arranged wood scraps into imaginary worlds, who moved through life with the kind of unguarded enthusiasm that mirrored his grandfather's approach to existence. That child got buried under increasingly thick armor because he was taught to see his natural expressions as problems instead of gifts.

The journey to finding myself—which wouldn't begin in earnest until my late thirties—wasn't really about becoming someone new. It was about remembering who I was before I learned to hide so well that I forgot that version of myself was even there. The healing work ahead was about integration—about reclaiming the memories of my abuelito's workshop and the sense of inherent worthiness that had flourished there.

The lost child who had been allowed to exist without apology in that sacred space? He wasn't gone. He was waiting—with all the patience his grandfather had taught him—for conditions safe enough to emerge again. It would take decades of destruction and rebuilding before I could create that safety for myself. But when I finally did, he'd be right there—dust-covered and a little wounded, maybe, but still holding those artist's eyes and that capacity for wonder my grandfather had recognized all along.

WHEN PERFECT FALLS APART

I was nine years old when my abuelito passed in his sleep. Just like that, my safe space vanished into the night without warning, explanation, or the chance to say goodbye. The one person I thought would always be there for me—and the only adult I could run to when my father was losing his shit again—was simply gone.

The day it happened, I was playing outside with my cousins in my aunt's backyard in San Diego, California. The sun warmed our shoulders as we chased each other around in whatever game kids invent when they're too young to understand that happiness is temporary, safety is fragile, and love can disappear between one breath and the next.

Whatever game we were playing stopped mattering the second I saw my father's car pull into the driveway. That familiar weight dropped into my chest—the automatic dread of going back to Long Beach. Back to walking on eggshells and the constant vigilance of living in my father's unpredictability.

"Time to go," I muttered to my cousins, already mentally packing my little overnight bag and preparing for the shift from weekend freedom to weekday performance.

But I was wrong.

Through the screen door came a sound I'd never heard before. My mother's voice transformed into something primal and terrifying—a wail that seemed to come from somewhere beyond human language, beyond the carefully controlled emotional register she usually maintained. My body reacted before my mind could catch up. I bolted toward the house, my heart hammering against my ribs, my small fists already clenched for whatever fight awaited inside.

I thought my father had finally crossed the line, that he'd actually hit her, instead of just threatening to. "Enough is enough," I whispered to myself as I ran, though what the hell a nine-year-old kid was going to do against a mountain of a man, I had no idea. But something fierce and protective rose in my chest, something that felt connected to the quiet strength my abuelito had modeled.

When I pushed through that screen door, the scene inside wasn't what I'd expected. Violence would have been easier to understand than what I actually found: my mother—who never so much as checked the mail without her face "put together"—was on her knees in the middle of my aunt's living room, completely destroyed.

This was a woman whose beauty routine was like religious ritual. Every weekend, she moved through the world like she was starring in her own telenovela—big blonde hair teased and sprayed into architectural perfection, outfits coordinated down to the last detail, makeup applied with the kind of precision that suggested her appearance was both armor and art. Her presence was carefully constructed—a fortress of femininity that announced her worth in a world determined to diminish women like her in countless small ways.

That fortress was crumbling in real time. Her face was buried in her always-decorated hands, long red acrylics gleaming like warning lights—each nail filed to perfection and adorned with tiny gold accents that caught the afternoon light streaming through the windows. The seven gold bangles that usually announced her movement now punctuated her sobs with broken, discordant sounds. Rings clutched every finger. They were inherited pieces, gifts from my father, and jewelry she'd bought herself as symbols of self-worth—all pressed against her mascara-streaked face.

Her hair remained perfectly intact, as if the devastating news had hit so suddenly that even her body's collapse couldn't disturb the careful architecture she'd built that morning. She wore one of her weekend outfits—a jewel-toned silk blouse that had probably drawn compliments earlier in the day, a mini skirt that showed off legs she was proud of, and gold embroidery that caught the light like tiny stars.

But all that carefully-constructed beauty was helpless against this blow. The perfection that usually felt like power had become irrelevant in the face of grief. It couldn't be managed, controlled, or made presentable for the public.

I approached cautiously because my child's instincts told me that whatever had happened was bigger than anything I'd ever encountered. I tapped her shoulder gently and moved her perfectly curled hair away from her face with the careful reverence I'd learned from watching my abuelito handle delicate things.

"Mami, what's wrong?" I asked, my voice smaller than I'd intended, already sensing that the answer would change something fundamental about how the world worked.

When she looked up, her makeup was completely destroyed. Her mascara ran in black rivers down her cheeks, her lipstick was smudged beyond recognition, and her foundation melted under tears that seemed to come from a bottomless well of loss. I'd never seen her face so naked, so vulnerable. Even during the worst fights with my father and moments of sadness or stress, she had always maintained the mask of her carefully applied face. But this grief stripped away every defense, revealing the raw human being beneath the performance.

"Your abuelito," she said, her voice breaking on the word like shattering glass. "He passed away last night in his sleep."

THE TSUNAMI

First came the shock—a blank moment when the words bounced off my consciousness like skipping stones on water—my brain simply refusing to process information that would fundamentally alter the landscape of my existence. Then the emotional tsunami hit: grief, confusion, fear, and an overwhelming sense of abandonment crashing through me in waves that made my small body shake like a leaf in a hurricane.

I couldn't hug my mother any harder than I did in that moment—my arms wrapped around her neck, breathing in her familiar Chanel No. 5—that signature scent she claimed as part of her identity, now a jarring contrast to the salt of her tears and the devastating reality she'd just shared.

There was something particularly devastating about watching my mother's perfect beauty destroyed by grief. She'd always wielded her appearance as a form of power in a world that limited women's ways to assert control over their circumstances. Seeing that power rendered useless by this loss revealed something terrifying—the fragility of all our defenses and the inadequacy of any armor when real tragedy strikes.

I found myself trying to comfort her even as my own world collapsed. Some instinct told me that her pain was even greater than mine—that she'd lost her father, but the one man in the family who had always treated her with consistent respect and kindness. My abuelito had been a sanctuary for both of us—a calm presence in a household that often felt like an emotional war zone.

Holding my collapsed mother, I understood something far beyond my nine years: this loss hadn't just taken away my safe space. It had revealed how fragile all our defenses really were—my mother's beauty, my father's strength, and my own childish belief that anything good was permanent. The comfortable illusion that the people who love us will always be there had just been shattered beyond repair.

The workshop where I'd learned what unconditional love felt like was now just an empty room in a house I might never visit again. The hands that once guided mine across the wood grain, teaching me how to fix what was broken, would never touch anything again. The voice that told me stories about possibility and potential had been silenced forever.

In that moment, my childhood ended. Not gradually, not with the gentle transitions some lucky kids get, but suddenly and completely—like a door slamming shut on a room I would never enter again.

GROWING UP IN AN INSTANT

Something fundamental shifted inside me in that moment—something that would take decades of therapy to fully understand and integrate. The protective innocence that had allowed me to exist as a sensitive, creative, trusting child evaporated like morning mist under harsh sunlight. No more sanctuary. No more gentle hands guiding mine. No more quiet presence standing between me and my father's disappointment. No more weekend escapes to a world where I could exist without editing myself.

I knew I was different—I had always known it in some wordless way that I couldn't place for many years. At age nine, in 1992, I still couldn't name what that difference was or what it meant for my future. Innocence was still fiercely protected back then, especially for boys like me growing up in Latino families straddling two cultures. There were no YouTube videos explaining gender expression, no vocabulary accessible to a nine-year-old that could name the ways I didn't fit the narrow box assigned to boys in my community.

Just the constant, low-grade awareness that I was operating in a world whose rules had been written by someone else, for someone else, with someone else's survival in mind.

My abuelito had created a parallel universe where those rules were temporarily suspended—where my difference wasn't named, it was simply accepted as part of who I was. It was folded seamlessly into his understanding of how much variation was possible within the category of "beloved grandson." With him gone, I stood fully exposed to a world determined to correct me, to reshape me into proper manhood—to prepare me for a future I couldn't even imagine for myself.

That afternoon, watching my beautiful mother reduced to ruins by grief, I made a silent decision that would shape the next three decades of my life. Instead of becoming smaller, less visible, less troublesome, now that I wasn't protected anymore, I decided I would become that protection for myself. If gentleness was interpreted as weakness, I'd develop edges. If sensitivity was seen as a deficiency, I'd learn to be hard.

Anger rose from the ashes of my grief like some ancient creature awakening in the depths of my chest. Not the explosive, unpredictable rage of my father—something colder, more focused, more deliberate. A rage that whispered promises of self-protection, of never again being vulnerable enough to feel a loss this devastating.

If the world wouldn't make space for me as I was, I'd carve that space with my own hands, using whatever tools I could. If my father's version of toxic masculinity was the standard I'd always be measured against and found wanting, I'd create my own definition of strength and forge my own weapons of survival.

The trust that once made it possible to exist without armor began to calcify into a protective cynicism—one that kept others at arm's length and left me isolated for decades to come.

What I didn't understand then—what I couldn't have understood at that age—was that this transformation wasn't strength. It was survival masquerading as power, trauma disguising itself as agency. I thought I was choosing hardness, choosing invulnerability, choosing never to be hurt like that again. But I wasn't choosing anything. I was reacting, the way any wounded animal reacts when it learns the world isn't safe. The boy who'd felt everything so deeply didn't disappear because he wanted to—he went into hiding because staying visible had become too dangerous. And in protecting myself from ever experiencing that level of pain again, I also locked myself out of experiencing genuine connection, real intimacy, or the kind of love that requires you to be brave enough to stay soft. That anger didn't make me stronger; it made me smaller, harder, lonelier. It would take decades to understand that the real courage wasn't in building impenetrable walls—it was in learning to be vulnerable again despite knowing exactly how much it could cost.

THE CHANGE

In the months that followed, my mother noticed the transformation happening inside me, but she didn't have words for what she saw. "What happened to my sweet boy?" she asked once, reaching to smooth my constantly furrowed brow, trying to touch some trace of the child who had once been openly affectionate and demonstrative, before grief taught him that love was dangerous.

I pulled away from her touch. It was something I'd never done before, but the tenderness I'd once accepted easily now felt like vulnerability I couldn't afford. The grief was still too raw, the sense of abandonment too fresh. If someone as permanent as my abuelito could disappear without warning, how could I ever feel safe in anyone else's affection?

"He grew up," I said, the words coming out harder and flatter than I'd meant them to— already edged with the emotional distance that would become my primary defense mechanism for the next quarter-century.

My abuelito passed, and I welcomed something that would later work through me like slow poison, trying to destroy me from the inside out with surgical precision. A silent companion emerged from the ashes of my grief—not the comfort of my grandfather's memory, but the cold company of rage, determination, and a resolve that would eventually harden around my heart like emotional scar tissue.

The protective walls I built felt necessary—wise, even. They seemed like a mature response to an unreliable world, a practical adaptation to the reality that people leave, love hurts, and trusting in permanence is foolish. I didn't understand then that what feels like protection can become a prison, that what starts as healthy self-preservation can end up suffocating the very self it was meant to protect.

Everything shifted after he passed—but not in the direction I'd unconsciously hoped. I thought things at home might calm down. That maybe my father would soften in the face of collective loss. That maybe our family would come together through shared grief. That the magnitude of what we'd lost might put our daily dramas into perspective.

I was wrong again. His death wasn't an ending but a beginning—the first domino in years of chaos that would unfold not just in my family dynamics, but inside me, in places no one else could see or help me navigate.

The anger that felt like fuel—something that seemed to give me strength when grief might have paralyzed me—became both salvation and curse. It carried me through the immediate aftermath, giving me something harder than sadness to hold onto when sorrow felt like quicksand. But that same protective rage eventually consumed other essential things: my ability to be vulnerable, my willingness to trust, and my capacity to receive love without suspicion or testing.

UNDERSTANDING GENERATIONAL TRAUMA

I didn't learn the term *generational trauma* until years after my abuelito passed, well into my thirties when I was finally desperate enough to start excavating the psychological archaeology of my own family system. Back in the early '90s, Mexican families didn't use words like "trauma," "toxic cycles," or "intergenerational transmission of wounding." We just lived with whatever dysfunction we'd inherited and called it normal—called it family—called it the way things were.

My home was fucked up long before my abuelito passed away, though his presence had created a kind of buffer that made the dysfunction more bearable—and less absolute in its impact. Looking back now with the benefit of therapy, education, and painful self-examination, I can see that my parents were doing the best they could with what they knew. What they knew wasn't nearly enough to break the cycles they'd inherited from their own traumatized caregivers.

But here's the thing that took me decades to understand. My parents never healed their own trauma and brokenness because no one had ever shown them that healing was possible. They didn't know that patterns could be interrupted, or that the wounds passed down from previous generations weren't permanent features of reality. They were changeable conditions—addressable with the right tools and support.

How could they heal if they'd never been taught to recognize wounds? In their world, trauma wasn't a psychological condition requiring attention—it was life. Pain wasn't seen as pathology. It was just the human condition—the price of existence. Something to be endured with whatever combination of stoicism, substances, and aggressive determination they could muster.

They both came from broken families, but the type of brokenness was different enough that they'd spent their courtship years believing love could overcome the statistical inevitability of recreating familiar patterns. My grandmother on my mom's side had her when she was just fourteen fucking years old—fourteen, an age when most kids today are worried about algebra tests and whether their crush likes them back.

My abuelo was twenty-one when he became a father, which might sound more reasonable until you consider the context. It was rural Mexico in the 1950s, where education beyond childhood was luxury, where survival meant taking on adult responsibilities as soon as you could contribute to the family economy, and where emotional maturity mattered less than the ability to work hard and provide the bare necessities.

Back then, this wasn't considered scandalous or tragic—it was expected. Celebrated, even. Evidence of fertility and God's blessing. The quinceañera, which today marks a girl's fifteenth birthday as a celebration of becoming a young woman, was originally a cultural announcement: this girl was ready for marriage and childbearing. Ready to take on the responsibilities of adult womanhood, whether or not she was psychologically prepared for such massive life changes.

Early motherhood was the goal in my family's generation, the marker of successful femininity. Proof that a young woman was fulfilling her primary purpose in life. Larger families were equated to a blessing from God, evidence of the father's virility and the mother's proper submission to divine will. Nobody gave a shit about what this did to young women's bodies and spirits, or how it compressed childhood into a few brief years before adult responsibilities made play and development impossible.

By the time my grandmother was twenty-six—an age when many people today are just starting to think about settling down—she had five kids all under twelve years old. The math alone is staggering—pregnancy, birth, recovery, repeat—with no consideration for spacing, family planning, or whether the parents had developed the emotional resources necessary to nurture multiple small humans simultaneously.

In Mexican families of that era, this was considered success. Evidence of God's favor and proper adherence to cultural expectations. The more kids you had, the stronger you were presumed to be—the more blessed your household, the more proof that you were living according to divine plan rather than selfish personal desires.

WHEN CHILDHOOD ENDS

My mother was forced to quit school at twelve years old, not because of pregnancy or marriage, but because of abandonment. That's when my grandmother decided she was done being a wife and housewife—done with the demands of caring for five children, done with the life she'd never chosen but had simply accepted as inevitable.

She left, taking only my baby uncle with her—the youngest, the one who still needed constant care and couldn't yet contribute to household maintenance. Just like that, my twelve-year-old mother became the de facto parent to her remaining brothers and sisters, and the caretaker of an entire household, responsible for cooking, cleaning, and raising children when she was still a child herself.

Her childhood ended that day, not gradually, but immediately. Like a switch being flipped from innocence to responsibility without any transition period or preparation. The twelve-year-old girl who might have spent her days learning and playing and discovering who she wanted to become, was replaced overnight by a child-mother who had to figure out how to keep a family functioning—with no manual, no support, no choice in the matter.

Cooking became a survival skill learned through trial and error. Her younger siblings depended on her ability to figure out how to make food stretch, how to create something nutritious from whatever ingredients were available, and how to manage household resources that were always inadequate. Cleaning became an endless cycle that had to be maintained while also caring for children who were mourning their mother's absence and looking to their sister for comfort that she barely knew how to provide for herself.

She never called it trauma because she didn't have that language or framework for understanding what had happened to her. It was just life, just duty, just the role that had fallen to her. "Suck it up and move on" became her philosophy because there was no alternative, no safety net, no adult stepping in to protect her from responsibilities that should never have been placed on a child's shoulders.

But I can only imagine her crying herself to sleep every night during those early months—missing the mother who had abandoned her, grieving the childhood that had been taken from her, and trying to figure out how to be strong enough for everyone else while still being a scared kid herself. The weight of keeping a family together while processing her own abandonment and loss must have been crushing.

My father's story paralleled my mother's in fundamental brutality, though differing in its specific details. He was the oldest of sixteen children—sixteen human beings his parents had brought into the world without adequate resources to feed, clothe, house, or emotionally nurture. His childhood ended even earlier than my mothers, disappearing as soon as he was big enough to contribute labor to family survival.

While other kids his age were learning to read or playing games or discovering their interests and talents, my father was working—on cars and in pharmacies, wherever his small hands could contribute to the family's desperate economic situation. Education was luxury that families like his couldn't afford; childhood was an indulgence survival made impossible.

His parents weren't just struggling—they were dysfunctional and abusive in ways that normalized violence as a parenting strategy. Daily beatings weren't considered abuse; they were seen as discipline—preparation for a harsh world that would show no mercy to children who hadn't been toughened through pain. Emotional nurturing wasn't just absent—it was actively discouraged as weakness that would make their children vulnerable to exploitation.

Like my mother, my father entered adulthood without ever getting to be a child, without developing the emotional skills that come from feeling safe and loved and valued for who you are rather than what you can contribute. Neither of them had models for healthy relationships, healthy communication, or healthy ways of processing difficult emotions.

They met as teenagers who had both been forced to grow up too fast, both carrying wounds they had no language for—both desperate for love but equipped only with survival strategies that often made genuine intimacy impossible. Their relationship was built on shared trauma rather than genuine compatibility, held together by mutual need rather than conscious choice.

THE SCIENCE BEHIND THE DAMAGE

Here's something that blew my mind when I finally started learning about trauma in my thirties: it doesn't just affect the person who experiences it directly. It literally changes how genes express themselves, how nervous systems develop, and how people respond to stress throughout their lives. My parents weren't just carrying psychological scars—they were carrying biological adaptations to danger, embedded in their very DNA.

The research on Adverse Childhood Experiences (ACEs) and epigenetic inheritance makes it clear that trauma isn't just about individual psychology—it's also a form of biological programming, passed down through generations like some kind of cellular memory. My parents' bodies had been shaped by chronic stress, by hypervigilance, by nervous systems that had learned to expect danger at any moment.

In Mexican culture specifically, generational trauma takes particular forms that reflect the specific historical and cultural contexts our families survived. Machismo demands that boys become men too soon. It equates masculinity with emotional suppression and physical dominance, and it teaches that vulnerability is equivalent to weakness—something that makes you a target for exploitation.

Marianismo traps girls in patterns of self-sacrifice, teaching them that their value comes from serving others at the expense of their own needs and desires, that good women endure suffering silently rather than advocating for themselves or set boundaries.

The cultural mandate that family business stays within family walls prevents anyone from seeking help or even naming problems, creating environments where dysfunction can flourish without outside intervention or accountability. The idealization of suffering—*la vida es dura*, life is hard—normalizes pain instead of challenging the systems that create unnecessary hardship.

What I couldn't understand as a child but see clearly now is how these early disruptions shaped my parents at the most fundamental neurological levels. During those critical years, when a child's brain is forming basic patterns of attachment, emotional regulation, and trust, my parents were experiencing chronic stress and premature responsibility instead of the consistent nurturing that supports healthy development.

My mother's brain developed during years when she should have been playing and learning, but instead she was managing a household and raising siblings barely younger than herself. The parts of her brain responsible for hypervigilance—constantly scanning for threats, preparing for crisis, managing everyone else's needs—became overdeveloped, while the areas responsible for emotional regulation and healthy trust remained underdeveloped.

This wasn't a character flaw or conscious choice; it was biological adaptation to impossible circumstances. By the time she became my mother, her nervous system was wired for anxiety—for love that felt conditional on performance, and for emotional responses that seemed disproportionate to whatever triggered them but made perfect sense when understood as reactions to decade-old training in survival.

My father's childhood marked by poverty and violence had created similar adaptations. During the critical period when children should be learning that the world is fundamentally safe and adults are reliable sources of protection, he was learning the opposite. His brain formed around expecting danger, around believing that vulnerability invited harm, and around understanding manhood as dominance—because any other version felt like a luxury he couldn't afford.

The neural pathways that enable emotional intimacy and gentle parenting never had the chance to develop normally, because his childhood environment demanded different adaptations just to survive each day.

HOW IT PLAYED OUT

These neurobiological impacts weren't visible to me as a child, but they shaped everything about how our family functioned. When my father exploded in rage over seemingly small issues, it wasn't just a bad temper—it was his amygdala, the brain's alarm system, triggering fight responses that had been developed and reinforced throughout his childhood as necessary for survival.

When my mother withdrew emotional connection whenever I failed to meet expectations, it wasn't calculated cruelty—it was her attachment system functioning exactly as it was programmed to do: withholding love as a way to motivate behavior change, because that's what had been done to her.

The chronic stress that filled our household, the walking on eggshells that became second nature, the emotional volatility that made home feel dangerous—all of it was the logical result of two traumatized people trying to create a family without ever having learned what a healthy family looked like, felt like, or operated like.

The science of developmental trauma explains what I witnessed but couldn't name: how early traumatic experiences get embedded in the body's responses—in stress hormone regulation, and in unconscious beliefs about the self and others that operate below the level of conscious awareness. Research confirms what my family demonstrated—that early trauma doesn't just create emotional scars, it actually shapes brain architecture, immune function, and even gene expression in ways that get passed down through generations.

In Mexican families like mine, these neurobiological impacts became entangled with cultural expectations that often reinforced trauma responses instead of healing them. The cultural value of *aguantar*—to endure, to bear whatever life brings—discouraged acknowledging pain or seeking help. The emphasis on respect for authority made questioning dysfunctional patterns nearly impossible. The gap between public presentation and private reality created a dissociative split that became second nature.

When cultural values align with trauma responses, families can spend generations recreating the same patterns while believing they're honoring tradition, maintaining strength, and preserving cultural identity. The survival strategies that helped previous generations endure genuine threats can become maladaptive when applied to contemporary situations—situations that might actually be workable with different approaches. This is why healing generational trauma in immigrant families is so complicated—you're not just working against individual dysfunction; you're working against entire cultural systems that have codified trauma responses as virtues. Breaking these patterns requires distinguishing between cultural practices that nourish you and trauma responses that masquerade as tradition.

MY ABUELITO: THE PATTERN-BREAKER

In our context of multigenerational trauma and cultural conditioning that reinforced, rather than healed, family dysfunction, my abuelito was a fucking miracle. Somehow, through a combination of natural temperament, different life experiences, and conscious choices, this man had figured out how to break the cycle.

I don't know if it was simply how he was wired, if the specific traumas he'd experienced were different enough from my parents' to lead to different adaptations, or if he made conscious decisions to be better than what he'd inherited. But somewhere along the way, he'd learned to be consistently present, emotionally steady, and capable of love that didn't come with conditions or performance requirements.

His workshop wasn't just a place where broken furniture got fixed—it was like a neurological reset button for my developing brain. While my house was a minefield of explosive anger and conditional love, where every interaction felt like a test I might fail, his space created patterns of safety instead of fear, and worthiness instead of constant evaluation.

In his presence, my nervous system could actually relax and learn what secure attachment felt like—before the rest of the world taught me that love always comes with strings attached. The consistency of his acceptance, the reliability of his presence, and the way he treated my mistakes as learning opportunities rather than evidence of inadequacy—all taught my developing brain that safety was possible, that I was inherently worthy of love regardless of my performance.

That's why losing him didn't just hurt emotionally—it fucking destroyed me in ways I couldn't understand at nine years old. This wasn't just missing someone I loved, though that was devastating enough. I'd lost the one person who was actively helping my brain learn healthy patterns, the one relationship teaching my nervous system that safety and trust were possible in human connection.

When he died, I didn't just lose his presence—I lost the calm, steady energy that had been co-regulating my chaotic internal world. I lost living proof that another way was possible, that men could be strong without being violent, that love could exist without conditions.

The rage that took over after he passed wasn't just me being dramatic or going through normal grief. It was essentially my brain saying, "Well, if vulnerability gets you abandoned and hurt gets you nowhere, let's try anger and see if that keeps us safer." The walls I built, the emotional distance I learned to maintain, the way I started performing instead of just being—all of it was my nervous system trying to create external safety after the internal regulation he'd been teaching me was suddenly ripped away.

I became my own fortress, because the one person who'd shown me I didn't need to be one was gone—leaving me to navigate a hostile world with the emotional equipment of a traumatized nine-year-old. That nine-year-old would make every major decision in my life for the next three decades—choosing relationships, career paths, coping mechanisms—all from a place of terror disguised as self-protection. And because I looked like an adult on the outside, nobody—including me—recognized that I was still operating from that childhood wound, still trying to solve a problem that couldn't be solved with more armor.

WHY UNDERSTANDING THIS MATTERS

Understanding generational trauma from this neurobiological perspective was like finally getting the fucking manual for my own brain. It helped me realize that healing wouldn't happen just because I understood, intellectually, what was wrong with me; because I wanted it badly enough; or because I applied enough willpower to the problem.

Willpower and insight are valuable tools, but they can't rewire a nervous system that learned to expect danger around every corner before I was old enough to walk—a system that developed stress responses based on survival needs that were real for previous generations but were killing me in contemporary contexts where different skills were needed.

My brain and body needed new experiences—actual, repeated, consistent experiences of safety and connection that could literally create new neural pathways. I needed to teach my nervous system what regulation felt like, what it meant to feel safe in relationship, and what it was like to receive love without having to earn it or perform for it.

This is why all those years of just knowing what was wrong never fixed anything. Knowledge is powerful and necessary, but trauma lives in the body. It has to be retrained through experience, not just understanding. The nervous system doesn't respond to logical arguments—it responds to felt sense, to repeated experiences that slowly teach it new patterns of response.

My abuelito's legacy wasn't just those beautiful memories of sawdust and circus visits, although those matter deeply. What he really left me was proof that another way was possible, even in families drowning in generational trauma. His example became the seed that would eventually grow into my own healing—evidence that strength could be gentle, that love could be offered without strings attached, and that broken people could be restored with patience and the right tools.

This shift in understanding changed everything for me. Instead of seeing my parents as the villains in my story—which felt satisfying, but kept me stuck in resentment and victimhood—I could finally see them as wounded people passing along wounds they'd never had the chance to heal.

Their parents had traumatized them, and their parents' parents had traumatized them—generations of people doing their best with the tools they had, which weren't nearly enough for the complex work of raising healthy humans. This didn't excuse the damage they caused, make the abuse acceptable, or minimize the impact on my development—but it explained it in a way that freed me from the prison of bitter resentment where I'd been living.

More importantly, it showed me that the cycle could be broken—that I could be the one in my family line who said, "This stops here." Who chose healing over repeating destructive patterns, who developed the tools my ancestors never had access to.

I could be the pattern-breaker my abuelito tried to be. I had better resources, more support, and the understanding that breaking generational cycles isn't just possible—it's the most important work any of us can do—not just for ourselves, but for all the generations that will come after us. This isn't about blaming previous generations for what they couldn't give us—it's about accepting responsibility for what we can change now that we know better. The pattern ends when someone finally says 'enough' and does the messy, uncomfortable work of becoming something different than what they were taught to be.

UNDERSTANDING MY SHADOWS

After my abuelito passed, everything about my home environment became a series of disappointments that taught me to expect very little from life and even less from the people who were supposed to love me. Our family dynamic shifted into pure survival mode—existing instead of living, enduring instead of thriving, getting through each day instead of building toward a better future.

The baseline of my daily experience changed from "What might bring joy today?" to "What can I tolerate without breaking?" and "How do I just get through this without drawing unwanted attention?" The emotional weather in our house became unpredictable and often dangerous, requiring constant vigilance and the ability to make myself invisible when storms were brewing.

I didn't understand any of this psychological complexity at the time. Words like "trauma," "generational patterns," and "developmental impact" were foreign concepts that wouldn't enter my vocabulary for decades. It wasn't until my late thirties that everything in my life came crashing down around me, and I started recognizing these family patterns for what they actually were—not personal failures or character flaws, but inherited wounds and adaptive strategies that had outlived their usefulness.

I'm sharing this story because I know that my generation—especially those of us raised in Latino households—still doesn't talk about this stuff openly. Mental health and therapy are often still treated as luxuries for the privileged, or weaknesses for people who can't handle life's natural difficulties. In our families, especially for men, emotional struggles are still frequently dismissed with phrases like *no seas débil* ("don't be weak") or *los hombres no lloran* ("men don't cry").

These messages aren't delivered with malice—they're passed down with the genuine belief that emotional toughness is survival gear in a hostile world. That teaching children to expect and endure hardship without complaint is preparing them for the reality they'll face as adults. But what this actually creates is generations of people who are experts at surviving—but have no idea how to thrive.

Every day, I meet gay men carrying levels of shame and self-hatred that would be heartbreaking—if they weren't so common. Men whose stories sound exactly like mine, whose eyes hold the same shadows of unprocessed pain I carried for decades. Gay men who spent years running from their own reality, numbing themselves with substances, achievements, sex—whatever temporary relief they could find from the unbearable tension of being, in their families' eyes, both too much and not enough.

The pattern is depressingly consistent:
1. Grow up different in families that demand conformity.
2. Learn to hide essential parts of yourself.
3. Develop elaborate coping mechanisms to deal with the cognitive dissonance of loving people who can't fully love you back.
4. Eventually burn out from the exhaustion of constant performance.
5. Turn to whatever numbing strategies are available.

REAL TALK ABOUT GENERATIONAL TRAUMA

Generational trauma is no fucking joke. I believe we all need to examine it more closely, regardless of our individual backgrounds. Science now confirms what our bodies have always known: the unhealed wounds of our ancestors don't just disappear when we reach adulthood or move away from home or try really hard to be different.

They transform—showing up in different forms but carrying the same essential pain. Through epigenetic changes that alter how genes express themselves. Through learned behaviors passed down like toxic family recipes. Through cultural expectations that reinforce trauma responses. Through disrupted attachment patterns that make healthy relationships feel foreign and dangerous.

Queer people, especially queer people of color, inherit generational trauma with multiple layers of added complexity. Beyond whatever patterns our families already carry from their own historical and cultural wounds, we also bear a broader cultural legacy of exclusion, pathologization, and systematic efforts to convince us that we're fundamentally broken at our core.

Coming out doesn't just mean revealing who we are—it means challenging generational patterns, disrupting family narratives that may have remained unquestioned for decades, and often becoming the identified "problem" who forces all the unspoken family dynamics into harsh light. We become lightning rods for dysfunction that predated our existence but gets projected onto our difference, as if our authenticity were the cause of problems that were actually there all along.

WHAT SHADOW WORK ACTUALLY MEANS

This is where shadow work becomes essential. Let me be clear about what I mean by this, because it's not some mystical bullshit or new-age spiritual bypassing. Shadow work is the practical, necessary process of reclaiming the parts of yourself you've been taught to reject, hide, or be ashamed of.

Your "shadow" isn't some evil twin living inside you. It's all the aspects of your personality, your desires, and your natural responses that were labeled "unacceptable" by your family, culture, religion, or society. For queer people, this often includes:

- The parts of you that were "too feminine" or "too masculine" for your assigned role.
- Your natural emotional responses that were deemed "too dramatic" or "too sensitive."
- Your authentic desires and attractions that were called "sinful" or "wrong."

- Your creativity and self-expression that were shut down as "impractical" or "inappropriate."
- Your anger at injustice that was dismissed as "being difficult" or "making trouble."

Shadow work means having conscious conversations with these rejected parts instead of pretending they don't exist. It means asking questions like: "What was this part of me trying to protect? What gifts does it actually contain? How can I integrate this aspect of myself in healthy ways instead of either suppressing it or letting it run wild?"

For me, integrating Shadow work meant recognizing that my "drama queen" tendencies weren't character flaws—they were my natural emotional expressions trying to survive in a family that demanded emotional numbness. My "sensitivity" wasn't weakness—it was empathy and intuition that had been pathologized because they didn't fit masculine expectations. My "rebelliousness" wasn't just being difficult—it was my authentic self refusing to be erased.

THE DEEPER HEALING WORK

For me, this intersection of personal healing and generational healing became the foundation for understanding that my recovery was never just about me. Every pattern I interrupted, every cycle I refused to continue, every moment I chose conscious response over an unconscious reaction contributed to a healing that reached backward through my family line and forward into whatever legacy I might leave.

The child who lost his safe space with my abuelito's death—who spent decades trying to recreate that sense of unconditional acceptance through external sources—slowly began to understand that the real work was learning to become for myself what he had been for me—a presence of unwavering love, a workshop where broken things could be restored, and a sanctuary where authenticity was welcomed rather than corrected.

But first I had to learn how to find and reclaim all the parts of myself that had gone into hiding during those years when survival demanded performance—when being real felt too dangerous to risk. This is where shadow work became essential, not as some esoteric spiritual practice, but as the practical work of integration: the calling home of all the exiled aspects of my identity that had been waiting patiently for conditions safe enough to emerge again.

THE UNIVERSAL APPLICATION

This shadow work isn't just for people who look like me or share my specific trauma. Whether you're a white trans woman who was told she was "too aggressive," a Black gay man shamed for being "too soft," a Latino non-binary person rejected for being "too weird," or anyone else who has been told that essential parts of who you are must be fixed or hidden—this work is for you.

The shadows we carry aren't just personal—they're ancestral, cultural, and collective. But they also contain gifts: the resilience that allowed our families to survive impossible circumstances; the creativity that emerged from a constant need to adapt and problem-solve; and the capacity for fierce love that sustained us through generations of hardship.

Learning to work with these shadows rather than against them, to reclaim the gold that had been buried along with the pain—would become the most important work of my life. Not just for my own healing, but for all my ancestors who never had the chance to heal—and for all the generations yet to come, who deserve to inherit possibility rather than mere survival strategies.

The journey ahead would require tools I didn't yet know existed, support systems I hadn't yet learned to access, and a willingness to feel everything I'd spent decades avoiding. But the foundation was there—laid in those early years in my abuelito's workshop, where I learned that broken things could be beautiful again, that patient attention could transform damage into wisdom, and that love without conditions was possible—even in a world seemingly determined to prove otherwise.

My abuelito showed me that broken things could be beautiful again with patience and the right tools. He taught me these things. The rest of this book outlines the tools I wish I'd had at nine years old—the practices that went into hiding when he passed.

BUILDING YOUR OWN SACRED WORKSHOP: RECLAIMING YOUR HIDDEN SELF

After losing my abuelito—and the only unconditionally safe space I'd ever known—I spent decades trying to recreate that sanctuary through external means: relationships, achievements, substances—anything that might make me feel worthy of love without forcing me to confront the rage and grief I'd been carrying since I was nine years old.

It wasn't until my late thirties that everything came crashing down around me—and that I finally understood what he'd been trying to teach me in the workshop: that broken things could be beautiful again, but only if you were willing to examine the damage with patience instead of judgment, to work with what's actually there instead of forcing it into something it's not.

This shadow work practice isn't some mystical bullshit—it's the practical, necessary work of reclaiming the parts of yourself you learned to hide for survival. Think of it as creating your own internal workshop, a space where you can examine all the parts of yourself you were taught to reject, not to fix them or make them acceptable, but to understand the gifts within.

SIMPLE AT-HOME SHADOW WORK PRACTICE

Real Talk First: Shadow work brings up shit you've been shoving down for years. Start slow and make sure you have someone you can call if things get intense. If you feel overwhelmed, stop and ground yourself or reach out to your therapist. This isn't about becoming perfect—it's about becoming whole.

WHAT THE HELL IS SHADOW WORK?

Shadow work is about making friends with the parts of yourself you've been hiding, rejecting, or pretending don't exist—often because your family or culture told you those parts were unacceptable. For those of us healing from generational trauma, this means reclaiming pieces of our identities labeled as "wrong" or "too much."

Your shadow isn't your "bad" side—it's everything you learned to disown in order to survive within your family system. And here's the fucked-up truth: most of our shadows contain our greatest gifts. They've just been distorted by years of being forced underground.

BASIC SETUP (5 MINUTES)

Create Your Safe Space:

- Find somewhere private where you won't be interrupted.
- Light a candle or do whatever makes the space feel sacred to you.
- Have your journal and pen ready.
- Set a timer for 20-30 minutes max (don't overdo it).
- Keep water and tissues nearby because shit might come up.

Ground Yourself:

- Take 5 deep breaths.
- Set an intention: *I'm going to approach my shadow with curiosity and compassion.*
- Remind yourself: *I'm safe to explore these parts of myself.*

WEEK 1-2: FINDING YOUR SHADOW

Exercise 1: What Pisses You Off About Other People

Write down this question: *What qualities in other people irritate the fuck out of me?*

Then list 5-7 traits that really get under your skin:

- Too dramatic
- Weak/needy
- Show-offs
- Too emotional
- Selfish

Shadow Question:

How might I have these same qualities but learned to hide them?

Example: If dramatic people trigger you, ask yourself: *Where am I dramatic but don't allow myself to show it? When did I learn that being expressive was bad?*

This exercise works because we're often most triggered by traits we've buried in ourselves. The things that make us want to scream *"Don't be like that!"* are often the very things we were once told not to be.

Exercise 2: Family Shit You Swore You'd Never Do

Write about what parts of your family you vowed never to become.

Like how I watched my parents' trauma play out and vowed to be different, only to discover those same patterns living inside me—just in more sophisticated packaging.

- What traits did you reject in your parents?
- What behaviors did you judge in your siblings?
- What family patterns did you swear you'd break?

Shadow Question:

How do these rejected qualities show up in my life in hidden ways?

Maybe you swore you'd never be controlling like your mother, but you control by people-pleasing, manipulating, or withholding affection. Maybe you promised you'd never be angry like your father, so you became passive-aggressive or turned that anger inward.

WEEK 3-4: HAVING CONVERSATIONS WITH YOUR HIDDEN PARTS

Exercise 3: Talk to Your Disowned Self

Pick one rejected quality and write a dialogue with it. This might feel weird as hell at first, but stay with it.
   You: "I've been hiding you because . . ."
   Shadow: "I just wanted to . . ."
   You: "I was afraid that if I let you out . . ."
   Shadow: "What I really need is . . ."

Keep writing for 10-15 minutes, letting that shadow say whatever it wants. Don't edit or judge—just listen.

Example conversation with my hidden "sensitive" part:
   Me: "I've been hiding you because dad said sensitive boys get their asses kicked."
   Sensitivity: "I just wanted to feel things fully, to notice beauty, to care about people."
   Me: "I was afraid that if I let you out, everyone would see I'm weak."
   Sensitivity: "What I really need is permission to feel without having to defend it. I'm not weakness—I'm your capacity for empathy, intuition, and connection."

Exercise 4: Letter to Your Younger Self Who Learned to Hide

Write to yourself at the specific age you first learned to suppress this part of yourself:
   "Dear little one who learned to be quiet, tough, perfect, invisible . . . I see how hard you worked to keep us safe. I understand why you had to hide [specific quality]. The

adults around you couldn't handle your authentic expression, so you learned to make yourself smaller. You don't have to protect us that way anymore. It's safe now to . . ."

This isn't just therapeutic bullshit—this is you literally reparenting the parts of yourself that were wounded during your development.

WEEK 5-6: BRINGING YOUR SHADOW HOME

Exercise 5: Finding the Gifts in Your "Bad" Traits

For each shadow quality, explore:
- How might this trait actually serve me?
- What's the healthy way to express this?
- How can I integrate this consciously?

Example:
- **Rejected quality:** Being dramatic
- **Gift:** Emotional expressiveness and passion
- **Integration:** I can be dramatically joyful and authentically expressive

Example two:
- **Rejected quality:** Being selfish
- **Gift:** Knowing and honoring my own needs
- **Integration:** I can take care of myself without guilt or apology

Exercise 6: Give Yourself Permission

Write permission statements for your shadows. For example:
- I give myself permission to be emotional
- I allow my sensitivity to be a strength

- I can be both strong AND vulnerable
- My creativity and 'weirdness' are gifts
- I'm allowed to take up space
- I can be angry at injustice without being bad
- I can have needs without being needy

Say these out loud and feel how your body responds. Notice what feels scary or impossible—that's where the real work is.

ADVANCED PRACTICES (MONTH 2+)

The "Oh Shit, I Do That, Too" Process

When someone triggers you:
- **Pause:** *What am I seeing in them that bothers me?*
- **Own it:** *How do I do this same thing?*
- **Appreciate:** *What's the gift in this quality?*
- **Integrate:** *How can I express this in a healthy way?*

This process turns every triggering encounter into a mirror for your own shadow work.

Ancestral Shadow Work

Ask yourself: *What did my ancestors have to suppress just to survive?*
- What emotions weren't safe in my family line?
- What dreams got sacrificed for survival?
- What parts of my identity were repressed for acceptance?
- How can I honor these lost parts now?

For me, I realized my ancestors had to suppress:
- Artistic expression—it wasn't practical for survival

- Emotional vulnerability—it dangerous in violent environments
- Questioning authority—it could get you killed
- Individual desires—family survival came first

By reclaiming these parts of myself, I was healing not only my own wounds but also honoring the authentic selves my ancestors never got to express.

CULTURAL SHADOW WORK FOR LATINO AND HISPANIC HEALING

Exploring Cultural Shadows

Ask yourself:
- *What parts of my culture did I reject to fit into American society?*
- *How did I internalize messages about who I "should" be?*
- *What aspects of my heritage did I learn to hide?*
- *How can I reclaim the cultural parts of myself I abandoned?*

Machismo and Marianismo Shadow Work:

Ask yourself:
- How do rigid gender roles live inside me?
- What parts of my gender expression did I suppress?
- How can I honor both strength AND tenderness?
- *What would authentic masculinity or femininity look like for me?*

For Latino men especially, machismo taught us to suppress gentleness, creativity, emotional expression, and vulnerability—all the qualities that actually make us fully human. Reclaiming these isn't a betrayal of our culture; it's honoring the full spectrum of what our culture can be.

SAFETY GUIDELINES

Stop immediately if you experience:
- Overwhelming emotions that feel unmanageable
- Dissociation or feeling "spacey" and disconnected
- Intense shame spirals
- Suicidal or self-harm thoughts

Ground yourself with:
- 5-4-3-2-1 technique: Five things you see, four things you hear, three things you can touch, two you can smell, and one you can taste
- Cold water on your face and hands
- Call a trusted friend
- Write about feeling overwhelmed
- Do some breath work

INTEGRATION PRACTICES

Daily: Notice when you judge others and ask yourself: *How am I like this?*

Weekly: Review your shadow work journal for patterns

Monthly: Celebrate how you're integrating shadow aspects

Ongoing: Share your discoveries with trusted friends and therapists

FOR DIFFERENT COMMUNITIES

LGBTQ+ Folks: Your shadow often contains the parts of yourself that didn't fit heteronormative or cisnormative expectations. The "too gay," "too trans," "too queer" parts that you learned to hide—these aren't flaws; they're expressions of authentic diversity.

People of Color: Your shadow may include cultural expressions that were deemed "too much" for white spaces, emotions labeled "aggressive," or ways of being forced underground for survival in racist systems.

Abuse Survivors: Your shadow often contains your natural anger, your boundaries, your right to take up space—all the things that were beaten out of you (literally or figuratively) by people who couldn't handle your authentic power.

REMEMBER THIS SHIT

- Shadow work is about integration, not perfection.
- Your "negative" traits often contain your greatest gifts.
- Healing generational trauma means reclaiming what your ancestors had to hide.
- This work happens in layers.

CHAPTER 2

Breaking Generational Chains

The years following my abuelito's death became a master class in how untreated trauma turns children into walking time bombs, how grief without support becomes rage without direction, and how the absence of healthy models for processing pain creates perfect conditions for repeating every toxic pattern you swore you'd never recreate. I was twelve years old when the first real test of my new survival strategies arrived—delivered with the casual cruelty that only family members can achieve.

My father was incarcerated when I was twelve, sent away for crimes our family never discussed openly but that filled our house with a mixture of relief and shame no one knew how to process. You'd think his absence would have brought peace to our household, would have created space for healing from years of walking on eggshells around his volatile moods and explosive anger.

Instead, his imprisonment created a different kind of chaos—a power vacuum filled with my mother's attempts to hold everything together while drowning in her own unprocessed trauma, my brother's confused anger at being abandoned by the one parent he'd actually been able to connect with, and my own twisted relief at no longer having to monitor every gesture and vocal inflection to avoid triggering another episode of rage.

High school became my training ground for the performance of normalcy. I spent four years learning to hide the growing distance between who I was and who I needed to appear to be for basic social survival. I threw myself into drama class with the desperate intensity of someone who'd discovered that pretending to be other people was easier than figuring out how to be myself. The theater became my sanctuary—the one place where emotional expression was not just acceptable but required, where the sensitivity I'd learned to hide everywhere else was suddenly an asset.

I even had a girlfriend during this time—a sweet girl who deserved so much better than being used as camouflage by a confused kid trying to convince himself he could perform heterosexuality successfully if he just tried hard enough. That relationship ended like most of my attempts at conventional normalcy over the next two decades: badly, with hurt feelings and confusion on both sides about what had gone wrong.

The truth was simpler than either of us understood at the time: I was trying to love someone with equipment I didn't actually possess—attempting to generate authentic romantic feelings for a gender that, while I appreciated and respected deeply, simply didn't ignite the kind of passion and desire that made other guys my age act like complete idiots around girls. I was performing attraction based on cultural scripts rather than authentic response, and no performance, however dedicated, can sustain itself indefinitely without real feeling underneath.

After high school, I made my first real attempt at independence, enrolling in a pharmacy technician program with the kind of focused determination that trauma survivors often develop—the ability to laser-focus on practical goals as a way of avoiding the emotional complexity that feels too dangerous to navigate. I finished the course as quickly as possible, saved every penny I could, and moved to San Diego to live with my aunt—putting as much geographical distance as possible between myself and the family dynamics that felt like quicksand threatening to pull me under.

I thought I was escaping. I thought distance would somehow protect me from the patterns I'd inherited, as if toxic family dynamics were contagious diseases you could avoid through proper hygiene and careful boundaries. I was wrong, of course, but the wrongness wouldn't become apparent for several more years—during which I managed to recreate every dysfunction I was trying to escape, just with different people in different settings.

THE BETRAYAL THAT CHANGED EVERYTHING

At twenty, just as I was finally beginning to believe that maybe I could build a life separate from my family's chaos, my brother delivered a blow that would reshape my understanding of trust, loyalty, and the ways people who claim to love you can weaponize your truth against you. In a moment of what I thought was genuine connection, I had confided in him about my sexuality—not because I was ready to come out to the family, but because the weight of carrying that secret alone was becoming unbearable.

I was still figuring out what being gay meant in practical terms, still navigating the gap between attraction and identity, still learning that sexual orientation was about so much more than who you sleep with. It encompasses how you see the world, how you move through space, what kind of future you can imagine for yourself, what communities you might belong to, what forms of love and partnership might be available to you.

The conversation with my brother happened during one of those rare moments when our usual sibling antagonism had softened into something approaching genuine intimacy. We were both home for a weekend, both feeling the weight of family expectations and the impossibility of living up to ideals that seemed designed for someone else entirely. I thought I saw in him someone who might understand the particular burden of being different in a family that demanded conformity—someone who might offer support, or at least acceptance, for a truth I was tired of carrying alone.

I was catastrophically wrong.

The phone call that shattered everything came on a Saturday morning while I was passed out at a friend's house after a night of heavy partying—the kind of aggressive self-medication that had become my primary coping strategy for feelings I didn't have words for, or permission to experience. The buzzing of my phone cut through the haze of whatever substances I'd used to quiet my mind the night before, and my mother's voice came through the line like nothing I'd ever heard before.

It wasn't just crying, it was keening—a sound that seemed to come from somewhere beyond language, beyond the careful emotional control she usually maintained. For several terrifying minutes, I couldn't understand what she was saying through the sobs, couldn't piece together what catastrophe had prompted this complete breakdown of the composed facade she'd worn for as long as I could remember.

"*¿Cómo pudiste hacerme esto?*" she wailed, once she finally managed coherent words. *How could you do this to me?* The question was loaded with assumptions I was still too hungover and confused to fully process—that my sexuality was something I had chosen specifically to hurt her, that my truth was an act of violence against our family, that who I was existed primarily in relation to how it affected her, rather than as a fundamental aspect of my own identity.

It took several more minutes of careful questioning before I understood what had happened. My brother—ten years older, married, supposedly mature—had taken the private conversation we'd shared and weaponized it. Not because he thought it was time for honesty. Not because he believed the family deserved to know. But because he was angry about something completely unrelated—and wanted to inflict maximum damage.

The betrayal was so profound, so calculated, that it took my breath away. This wasn't an accidental revelation or a slip of the tongue during family drama—this was a deliberate decision to use my most vulnerable truth as ammunition in whatever petty war he was waging. The trust I'd extended to him, the vulnerability I'd offered in a moment of genuine connection, had been transformed into ammunition against both me and my mother.

"I trusted you," I wanted to scream at him, but by the time I understood what had happened, my rage had moved beyond words into something colder and more permanent. "The one time I fucking trusted you with the most important thing about myself, and you use it to hurt everyone."

But even as the betrayal carved itself into my understanding of how family could function, part of me felt something approaching relief. The secret that had been eating me alive was finally out, even if the circumstances were as far from ideal as possible. I was done hiding, done performing heterosexuality for an audience that would never fully accept the performance anyway. Whatever came next, at least it would be based on truth rather than on exhausting pretense. I didn't know yet that 'what came next' would be decades of self-destruction—but I also didn't know it would eventually lead to the kind of authentic life I couldn't even imagine from where I was standing.

MY MOTHER'S THEATRICAL RESPONSE

My mother's reaction was theatrical, even by her standards, which were already pretty high given her natural flair for drama and her belief that emotional expression required a certain level of performance to be taken seriously. The crying escalated into proclamations that I was going to "become a woman," that she had somehow failed as a mother, that our family was cursed or being punished for some unnamed transgression.

All I could do was look at her histrionics with a mixture of exhaustion and dark humor. *How uneducated can you be?* I thought, watching her transform my coming out into a telenovela, starring herself as the tragic mother whose son had chosen perversion over family loyalty. She made my sexuality about her suffering, her shame, her failure—leaving no space for my experience, my fear, my need for acceptance from the people who were supposed to love me unconditionally.

There was something particularly offensive about her assumption that being gay meant I wanted to be a woman, as if sexual orientation and gender identity were the same thing—as if loving men automatically meant rejecting masculinity entirely. The ignorance was breathtaking, but it was also revealing. It showed how completely our family lacked any real understanding of LGBTQ+ identities, how thoroughly we'd been isolated from communities that could have provided education, support, or even basic accurate information.

"I have to go," I told her when the dramatic monologue showed no signs of winding down. "I'm busy." The words came out harder than I'd intended, already carrying the emotional distance that would characterize our relationship for years to come. I wasn't ready to be her grief counselor, to manage her feelings about my identity, to comfort her for the loss of a son who had never actually existed anyway.

She took it exactly as I thought she would—as more evidence of my selfishness, my cruelty, my willingness to hurt the woman who had given birth to me and sacrificed everything for my well-being. But I was beyond caring about her comfort at that point. If she wanted to mourn the heterosexual son she'd imagined, she could do it without requiring me to participate in the funeral. I'd spent twenty-two years managing her feelings about my existence; I was fucking done.

FACING MY FATHER

The conversation with my father felt inevitable, like a storm that had been building on the horizon for years and was finally ready to make landfall. I drove to his house, my heart pounding against my ribs, practicing my speech in the car, trying to convince myself I was ready for whatever reaction would emerge from the man whose approval I'd spent my childhood desperately seeking, and whose rejection I'd spent my adolescence trying to prepare for.

I was twenty-one years old, which sounds like an adult when you say it out loud, but I felt incredibly young and unprepared for the magnitude of what was about to happen. I went there specifically to let him know that the secret was out, that the careful performance I'd maintained for years was over, and that whatever he had to say about my sexuality, he could fucking say it now and get it over with.

I walked into that house where I'd spent my childhood walking on eggshells, where his rage had been the weather that determined everyone else's mood, and where I'd learned that love was conditional and safety was temporary. But this time, it felt different. This time, I wasn't a scared little boy trying to avoid his anger—I was an adult telling him my truth, consequences be damned.

At this point, I was no longer living under his roof, no longer dependent on his approval for basic survival needs like food and shelter. I was paying my own bills, making my own decisions, building my own life with whatever tools I'd managed to develop despite his parenting. I felt like a man who could take whatever my dad was going to dish out, who had nothing left to lose because I'd already lost the most important thing—the illusion that his love for me was unconditional.

He looked at me with that familiar expression of disappointment, the same look I'd seen a thousand times when I'd failed to live up to his narrow vision of what a son should be. The disapproval that had once sent me scrambling to figure out what I'd done wrong and how I could fix it now felt almost anticlimactic, like the final scene in a movie I'd already figured out the ending to.

But this time, the disapproval felt final, absolute—like a judge delivering a verdict that couldn't be appealed or modified based on future behavior. There was no anger in his voice, no explosion of rage that might have suggested there was still emotional investment worth fighting for. Just cold assessment and the kind of clinical detachment that cut deeper than any shouting match could have.

"You are no longer my son. Please leave."

Eight words. That's all it took to sever a relationship that was supposed to last a lifetime, to erase twenty-one years of history as if they'd never happened, to reduce me from beloved child to stranger in the span of a single sentence. No emotion in his voice, no hesitation, no moment of consideration for what those words would do to someone who was still basically a child trying to figure out how to be an adult in a world that already felt hostile.

I wanted to say something back, to defend myself, to argue, to make him understand that I was still the same person I'd always been. But what do you say to someone who has just erased you from their life? What response is adequate when your own father tells you that your existence is so offensive to him that he'd rather have no son than have you?

So, I left. I walked out of that house knowing I'd never be welcome back, that the door was closing behind me forever. That I was officially an orphan, but by choice—his choice, not mine. The weight of his rejection should have crushed me, but instead it crystallized into something harder, colder—a rage that would keep me standing long after love would have let me fall.

THE REALITY OF DISOWNMENT

Disownment became my story after these occurrences, but here's what no one tells you about being rejected by your parents: at twenty-one, I was still a child in all the ways that matter for psychological development, and I didn't know what the fuck to do with that type of soul-crushing abandonment. Twenty-one sounds like an adult when you say it, but when your family throws you away like broken furniture that can't be fixed, you realize how much of being an adult depends on having some kind of safety net—a place to fall back on when life gets overwhelming.

Most kids who get rejected by their parents don't know what to do with that level of existential rejection. It's not like there's a guidebook for "So Your Family Just Decided You're Trash: A Practical Guide to Surviving Abandonment." The statistics around family rejection of LGBTQ+ youth are fucking heartbreaking, and they're not just numbers—they're real kids making life-or-death decisions about whether existence is worth the pain of being unwanted by the people who brought them into the world.

According to research from the Family Acceptance Project, between 26 and 50 percent of LGBTQ+ youth experience family rejection when they come out. That's not a small percentage of kids going through a difficult adjustment period—that's a massive epidemic of families choosing their prejudices over their children, picking their comfort zones over their kids' basic right to exist authentically.

And the outcomes are exactly what you'd expect when you throw children away for being who they are. LGBTQ+ youth who experience family rejection are eight times more likely to attempt suicide, six times more likely to experience severe depression, three times more likely to use illegal drugs, and three times more likely to engage in risky sexual behavior. These aren't moral failings or character weaknesses—these are predictable responses to trauma, to abandonment, to being told by the people who are supposed to love you unconditionally that your authentic self is unacceptable.

The homelessness rates are staggering and shameful. Up to 40 percent of homeless youth identify as LGBTQ+, even though we make up only about 10 percent of the general population. These kids aren't homeless because they chose adventure or independence—they're homeless because their families chose to throw them away rather than accept them as they are, because parents decided that their discomfort with their children's identities was more important than their children's safety and well-being.

I was one of the lucky ones. I had friends who caught me when I fell—chosen family who stepped in when biological family stepped out. But so many don't have that support and end up on the streets or in survival mode, doing whatever it takes to get by because the people who brought them into this world decided they were disposable.

The emotional impact goes far beyond practical concerns about housing and financial support. When your own parents decide you're not worth keeping around, it plants seeds of self-doubt that grow like weeds, choking out any possibility of feeling worthy of love for years to come. You start believing that maybe they were right—maybe there is something fundamentally wrong with you, maybe you really don't deserve the basic human experience of belonging somewhere.

The rejection fucks with your head in ways that don't show up immediately but compound over time like psychological interest. You walk around thinking you're fine, thinking you're independent and strong and don't need anyone, but underneath there's this constant ache—this voice that whispers maybe your father was right, maybe there really is something fundamentally broken about you that makes you impossible to love. His rejection becomes the lens through which you interpret every failed relationship, every disappointment, every moment someone doesn't choose you—not as their failure, but as confirmation of your defectiveness.

LEARNING TO FACE THE MUSIC ALONE

I needed to face the music alone, and alone I did, but no twenty-one-year-old should have to carry that kind of weight by themselves. The fact that I survived it—that any of us survive it—is a testament to human resilience that shouldn't have to be tested. Kids shouldn't have to be that strong. Love shouldn't be that conditional. Families shouldn't be able to throw away their children like broken furniture that can't be repaired.

Learning to face life alone meant figuring everything out from scratch—how to handle a medical emergency when you have no emergency contact who actually gives a shit about your well-being, how to navigate major life decisions without parental guidance, how to celebrate achievements when there's no one who is proud of you by default. It meant learning that chosen family can love you better than biological family ever did—but also accepting that chosen family can never entirely fill the void left by parental rejection.

The practical aspects were challenging but manageable—learning to budget when no one was going to bail you out of financial emergencies, figuring out how to maintain health insurance and navigate bureaucracy without family support, developing skills for adult life that others learned gradually, with safety nets in place. But the emotional aspects were devastating in ways I couldn't have anticipated.

It meant developing a relationship with loneliness that wasn't just about being alone but about being fundamentally unwanted by the people who were supposed to want you most. It meant learning to trust new people while carrying the knowledge that even "unconditional" love can have conditions, that even parents can decide you're not worth keeping around, that even the most basic relationships can be revoked without warning.

Holidays became exercises in creative avoidance—figuring out how to survive Christmas, birthdays, and family-oriented celebrations when you no longer had a family that wanted to celebrate with you. I learned to work extra shifts during holidays, to travel to places where family expectations couldn't follow me, to build new traditions that didn't require the participation of people who had written me out of their stories.

But facing the music alone also meant discovering strengths I didn't know I had, developing an independence that served me well, and learning that I could survive a rejection that should have destroyed me. It meant finding out that chosen family—the friends who become siblings, the lovers who become life partners, the mentors who become parental figures—can create bonds stronger than blood, and a love more reliable than biology.

Every holiday, I spent time with friends instead of family. Every achievement, I celebrated with people who had chosen to love me, rather than with those who were supposed to love me by default; every moment of joy I experienced in communities that welcomed my authentic self—all of it was proof that family isn't just about blood, but about who shows up, who stays, who loves you not despite who you are, but because of who you are.

The disownment became my story, but it didn't become my ending. It became the beginning of learning that sometimes being thrown away is the first step toward finding where you actually belong, that sometimes the greatest gift your family can give you is the freedom to discover who you are—without their limitations, their expectations, their narrow vision of what your life should look like. The family I built chose me every single day, and I chose them back—not out of obligation or guilt or shared DNA, but out of genuine love and mutual respect. That chosen family loved me better than my biological family ever could, not because they were better people, but because they were loving the real me instead of some fictional version they needed me to be.

MEETING MICHAEL: WHEN CHOSEN FAMILY BECOMES EVERYTHING

The year after I got outed, when I was still reeling from family rejection and trying to figure out how to build a life from scratch, I met Michael. He was thirty-two to my twenty-one, but the age difference felt less important than the recognition that passed between us—two gay men who had both survived family rejection and were learning to navigate a world that seemed designed to make our lives as difficult as possible.

Michael became my anchor in San Diego, my lighthouse in the storm of figuring out how to be gay in a world that often felt hostile to that existence. He was the first person who saw me fully—all my messy, confused, freshly-outed self—and didn't flinch, didn't try to fix me, didn't suggest I tone it down or make myself more acceptable. He just saw me and loved what he saw, which felt like a fucking miracle for someone who'd spent his entire life being told he was too much, too dramatic, too gay, too everything.

Michael had been out longer, had walked the path I was just starting on, and understood the particular challenges of being gay in ways my family never could and never would. When my mother's rejection felt like it was going to suffocate me, when her dramatic sobbing and accusations of betrayal made me feel like I'd committed some unforgivable sin, Michael reminded me that family isn't just blood—it's the people who choose to love you as you are, unconditionally, without requiring you to edit yourself for their comfort.

"We as gay men need to find our families through community," he told me during one of those long conversations we'd have over coffee or drinks—words that stuck with me like gospel because they felt like the first true thing anyone had ever said about what it meant to be queer in this world. He wasn't just talking theory; he was living proof that chosen family could be stronger, more loyal, more loving than the biological family that had decided I was disposable.

Michael became the gay big brother I'd never had but always needed, the mentor who understood exactly what I was going through because he'd walked similar terrain. He guided me through the gay scene in San Diego—introducing me to people, showing me the ropes, teaching me which bars were safe and which ones to avoid, which communities were welcoming, and which ones were just as judgmental as the straight world but with different criteria for exclusion.

He'd listen to me cry about my family's rejection without trying to minimize it or offering false comfort about how things would get better. He'd just hold space for my pain while reminding me that I wasn't alone—that there was a whole community of people who'd survived similar rejection and built beautiful lives despite it—that chosen family could love better than biological family ever had.

But what I didn't know then, and what Michael never let me see, was that he was fighting battles I couldn't even imagine. His HIV diagnosis had come years before I met him, back in the late '90s when treatment options were more limited and the stigma was even worse than what I would face years later when I received my own diagnosis. He carried the weight of that status like secret shame—even within our friendship, even though he was the one teaching me about community and acceptance and unconditional love.

The mental health struggles that came with navigating life as a positive gay man in the early 2000s—the isolation that came from feeling like damaged goods, the fear of disclosure that made dating feel like navigating a minefield, the constant management of medication, viral loads, and doctor's appointments—had been slowly eating away at his hope, his energy, his belief that things could get better.

He never talked about the depression that was consuming him from the inside out. Never mentioned the sleepless nights when he'd lie awake wondering if anyone would ever love him fully knowing his status. Never shared how exhausting it was to manage not just the physical aspects of HIV, but also the social, emotional, and psychological weight of being positive in a community that still whispered about HIV as if it were a moral failing rather than a medical condition.

I was so wrapped up in my own drama—my family's rejection, my own coming-out process, my financial struggles, my attempts to build a life from scratch—that I missed the signs. Or maybe there weren't obvious signs, because Michael had become an expert at hiding his pain—at being the strong one, the mentor, the anchor for people like me who were still figuring out how to survive in a world that didn't want us.

Looking back, I can see moments that might have been clues—times when his smile didn't quite reach his eyes, conversations that felt heavier than they should have, nights when he seemed more tired than someone his age should be. But at twenty-one, still reeling from my own trauma, I didn't have the emotional intelligence or life experience to recognize that someone could be drowning while appearing to keep everyone else afloat.

THE COMPLEXITY OF HIS SUFFERING

The early 2000s were a particularly brutal time to be HIV-positive and queer. The treatments that exist now were still in development, and the ones that were available came with side effects that could be almost as debilitating as the virus itself. The stigma was thick and poisonous—even within queer communities, there was often a sharp divide between HIV-positive and HIV-negative people, with those who were positive treated like walking warnings rather than whole human beings deserving of love and connection.Michael was navigating all of this while also trying to be a source of strength for younger guys like me who looked up to him, who needed his guidance and support to survive our own challenges. The pressure of being everyone's rock while his own foundation was crumbling must have been unbearable—like trying to be a lighthouse while your own structure is being eroded by storms you can't name or ask for help with.

The medication regimens were brutal back then—handfuls of pills at specific times, side effects that could include nausea, fatigue, mood changes, and physical symptoms that served as constant reminders of his status. The psychological impact of taking medication twice daily as a reminder that your body was fighting a virus that could kill you—that kind of constant awareness of mortality would eventually break anyone's spirit.

And then there was the dating scene, which was its own special kind of hell for HIV-positive men. The constant calculations about when and how to disclose; the fear of rejection that was often realized; the knowledge that some guys would run the moment they found out; the exhaustion of having to be grateful for the scraps of acceptance that came from men who treated dating someone with HIV like an act of charity rather than genuine attraction and connection—it all took a toll. Every rejection felt like confirmation that he was damaged goods, that his diagnosis had made him fundamentally unlovable. After a while, it seemed easier to just stop trying, to accept loneliness as the price of survival, to convince himself that he didn't need intimacy anyway. The isolation was compounded by the fact that mental health resources specifically designed for HIV-positive gay men were virtually nonexistent. Therapy was still stigmatized in many communities, and finding a therapist who understood both HIV and gay male culture was nearly impossible. The intersection of being gay, HIV-positive, and struggling with mental health created a perfect storm—one that made getting help feel impossible.

What made Michael's suffering even more tragic was how isolated he felt within the very community that was supposed to be his support system. The gay community in the early 2000s was still grappling with the trauma of the AIDS crisis, still processing the collective grief of losing an entire generation of elders, and still struggling to integrate HIV into our understanding of gay life and love.

There was pressure to be grateful for being alive when so many hadn't survived, pressure to stay positive (in every sense of the word) and not complain about side effects or stigma or the daily challenges of living with HIV. There was an unspoken expectation that surviving meant thriving—that making it through the worst of the crisis meant you should be happy just to be alive, regardless of the quality of that life.

Michael felt that pressure acutely. He'd lost friends, lovers, and mentors to AIDS in the '90s, and the survivor's guilt was crushing. Complaining about depression felt impossible when he was alive and they weren't. How could he admit to struggling when he'd been lucky enough to live through the worst of it? Asking for help seemed like an insult to everyone who'd needed more help and hadn't received it.

THE NIGHT EVERYTHING CHANGED

That last night, we had gone out to Rich's in Hillcrest to dance, hitting up Welfare Wednesday at Flicks next door because we could never turn down $2 cocktails—we were young and broke, and any excuse to have fun without going deeper into debt felt like a blessing. The night felt completely normal, routine even. Michael seemed like himself—laughing at my terrible dance moves, buying rounds when he could afford it, flirting with the cute bartender who always remembered his name and seemed genuinely glad to see him.

After the clubs closed, we picked up Mexican food from one of those 24-hour places that served as unofficial after-party spots for anyone too wired or drunk to go straight home. We shared Carne Asada Chips and stories about boys we were both interested in—the kind of conversation that had become ritual for us: Michael offering advice from his years of experience, me absorbing his wisdom like someone dying of thirst finally finding water.

I always sought his guidance about everything—dating, work, family drama, how to navigate the gay scene without losing myself in it or becoming someone I didn't recognize. He was the older gay brother I never had—the one who'd already made the mistakes I was about to make and could steer me away from the worst of them. That night was no different. We talked about guys, dreams, and plans for the upcoming weekend. Nothing felt heavy or final or like goodbye.

When we got back to my apartment, I assumed he'd crash on the couch like he always did when we'd been out late and he didn't want to drive across town to his place. It was routine, comfortable—the kind of easy intimacy that comes from chosen family, from people who've seen you at your worst and decided to stick around anyway. I went to bed thinking we'd have coffee in the morning, that he'd probably steal my last bagel like he always did, that we'd make plans for the weekend like we always did.

I woke up to Michael's lifeless body on my bedroom floor. The image is seared into my memory with the kind of clarity that trauma provides—every detail sharp and permanent, impossible to forget or blur with time. He was pale as snow, vomit coming from his mouth, his body positioned in a way that looked uncomfortable, unnatural, wrong. Next to him was a bottle of Lortab he'd grabbed from my cousin's bathroom the day before—something I'd barely noticed at the time but that now seemed significant in the most horrible way possible.

I rushed to his body and held his head in my arms like a mother holding a child, like I could somehow love him back to life through sheer force of will. I was in complete denial, my brain refusing to process what my eyes were seeing. This couldn't be real. This had to be a nightmare, a mistake, some kind of fucked-up joke that would resolve itself if I just refused to believe it, if I just held him tight enough and willed him back to consciousness.

The paramedics arrived within minutes of my frantic 911 call, but it was too late—had been too late for hours, probably since shortly after I'd gone to sleep. I remember them pulling me away from his lifeless body as I tried to shake him awake, as I begged a God I didn't believe in to please, please bring him back, as I screamed questions into a universe that had no fucking answers.

How had I not seen the signs? How had someone so central to my survival become so consumed by despair that death felt like his only option? How had we gone from sharing Carne Asada Chips and laughing about stupid shit to me holding his dead body in my arms? The questions came like a flood, each one more unanswerable than the last.

THE AFTERMATH OF INCOMPREHENSIBLE LOSS

The surrealism of that morning stayed with me for months—years—the way life could change so completely in the span of a few hours, the way someone could exist so fully one moment and not at all the next. Michael had been so alive just hours before—animated and engaged, giving me advice about dating like he had all the time in the world to keep being my guide through the complexities of gay life.

The speed of the transformation from presence to absence felt impossible to process. One moment we were sharing food, stories, and the easy intimacy of chosen family; the next, I was watching them zip his body into a bag and wheel him out of my apartment like he was just another casualty, another statistic, another gay man who couldn't handle the weight of being gay in a world determined to crush us.

The guilt was immediate and crushing. What had I missed? What signs had I ignored? What could I have said or done differently that might have changed the outcome? I replayed every conversation from the weeks leading up to his death, looking for clues I should have seen, warnings I should have heeded, moments when I might have intervened if I'd been less self-absorbed, more attentive—a better friend.

But the truth was that Michael had become an expert at hiding his pain, at being what everyone else needed him to be even when it was killing him. He'd spent years being the strong one, the mentor, the anchor—and admitting that he was drowning would have felt like failing everyone who depended on him. The very role that made him so valuable to people like me had become a prison that prevented him from seeking the help he desperately needed.

Michael's death didn't just take away my best friend—it shattered my understanding of how the world worked, how relationships functioned, how much you could trust your own perceptions of other people's well-being. If I could miss something this significant in someone I was so close to, how could I trust myself to read anyone else's emotional state? If someone who seemed so strong and wise and put together could be suffering this deeply, what did that say about everyone else who appeared to have their shit together?

The loss confirmed every fear I'd developed about getting close to people. Everyone I trusted eventually left—my father through rejection, the rest of my family through disownment, and now Michael through death. The pattern felt inescapable, like proof that I was cursed to lose everyone who mattered to me—that getting attached was just setting myself up for inevitable devastation.

The grief was unlike anything I'd experienced before—not just sadness, but a complete reorganization of reality that left me feeling unmoored and untethered, like I was floating in space without any fixed points of reference. Michael had been my North Star in navigating gay life, and without him, I felt completely lost—unable to distinguish between safe and dangerous, healthy and toxic, worth pursuing and worth avoiding.

A DIFFERENT KIND OF COMING OUT

His death also forced me into a different kind of coming out—explaining to straight friends, coworkers, and family members why I was so devastated by the loss of someone who wasn't technically family, why this friendship had meant more to me than some people's marriages meant to them. It meant educating people about chosen family, about how gay men create kinship networks that are often more intimate and supportive than biological families, about how losing someone from your chosen family can be more devastating than losing a blood relative who never really knew or accepted you.

Some people understood. Many didn't. The lack of social recognition for the depth of chosen family bonds added another layer of isolation to the grief—not just losing Michael, but feeling like the world didn't understand what I'd lost, why it mattered so much, why I couldn't just "get over it" and move on, as if it was just a friendship that had ended.

The gay community in San Diego rallied around me in ways my biological family never could. People who'd known Michael brought food, shared stories, sat with me during the worst of the grief. They understood that losing your chosen family elder—your guide through the complexities of gay life—was a particular kind of devastation that required its own rituals of mourning and support.

But even within that support, there was the unspoken understanding that Michael's death was part of a larger pattern—a statistical reality that too many of us wouldn't make it to old age, that suicide was one of the leading causes of death among gay men, especially those dealing with HIV, mental health issues, and the compound stresses of living as multiple minorities in a hostile world.

In the years that followed—as I struggled with my own HIV diagnosis, my own battles with depression, my own moments of wondering whether life was worth the effort it required—I would think about Michael's words: "We as gay men need to find our families through community." His death taught me that chosen family isn't just about finding people to love you—it's about learning to love them back completely, to pay attention to their struggles, to be present for their battles even when they don't ask for help.

I learned that being part of a community means more than just receiving support—it means offering it, even when you're struggling yourself. It means checking on people who seem strong because they might be the ones who need support the most. It means creating space for vulnerability in a world that often punishes gay men for showing weakness or need.

Michael's legacy became my education in how to be a better friend, a more attentive community member, and someone who could hold space for other people's pain without trying to fix or minimize it. His death taught me that sometimes the strongest people are the ones carrying the heaviest loads. That appearing to have your shit together doesn't mean you don't need support, love, or someone to remind you that your life has value beyond what you can offer others.

WORK AS AN ESCAPE

Instead of seeking help or finding someone to talk to—someone to help me process all the overwhelming shit that was happening to me—I just kept moving forward like some kind of emotional zombie. After my best friend died in my room, I went straight to work the next day, then straight to the bar that night. I started a cycle of self-harm from a twenty-one-year-old's perspective—not cutting or burning myself but destroying myself from the inside out through sheer refusal to feel anything that might require actual processing.

Work became my refuge—the one place where expectations were clear and performance was measurable, where I could lose myself in tasks that had nothing to do with death or grief or the image of Michael's lifeless body that played on repeat in my head whenever I had a quiet moment. I threw myself into the pharmacy routine with desperate intensity—memorizing drug interactions like my life depended on it, perfecting inventory systems that were already perfect, staying late to organize supplies that didn't need organizing.

Anything to avoid the silence where grief and abandonment waited for me like predators in the dark, ready to devour what little sanity I had left. The more mundane and mechanical the work, the better. Counting pills meant I wasn't counting the ways everyone I loved disappeared. Filing paperwork meant I wasn't filing away the memory of holding my best friend's dead body. Helping customers with their medications meant

I wasn't thinking about how no medication could've saved Michael from the depression that ate him alive.

I became the employee who never called in sick, never complained about overtime, never turned down extra shifts even when I was running on fumes and whatever drugs I could find to keep moving. Going home meant being alone with my thoughts, and being alone with my thoughts meant confronting the reality that I'd lost the one person who'd made me feel like I belonged somewhere—like I was worth keeping around.

Routine became my religion: clock in, focus on pills, prescriptions, and insurance claims; clock out. Rinse and repeat until the days blurred into an endless cycle of purposeful numbness. Each task completed was another small victory against the chaos in my head—another hour I'd managed to survive without falling apart completely.

But evenings were different. Evenings belonged to the bars in Hillcrest—to drinks that numbed the constant ache of loss that sat in my chest like a physical weight I couldn't set down. I'd walk into Rich's or Flicks—the same places Michael and I had gone just days before—and order drink after drink until the edges of everything got soft enough to tolerate, until the grief felt manageable instead of like quicksand trying to pull me under.

The alcohol gave me temporary relief from the hypervigilance that had become my default state—constantly scanning for signs that people were about to leave, hurt me, or use my vulnerability against me. When I was drunk enough, I could pretend that Michael's absence was temporary—that he was just running late, that he'd walk through the door any minute with that smile and some story about his day that would make everything feel normal again.

I drank with strangers who didn't know about Michael's suicide or my father's rejection or the way I felt like everyone I trusted eventually disappeared. These people had no context for my pain. I could pretend it didn't exist for a few hours—could be just another young gay guy at the bar instead of someone whose chosen-family elder had decided death was preferable to another day of living.

The drinking wasn't social—it was medicinal, strategic, necessary for survival. I'd sit at the bar with my back to the wall so I could see everyone coming and going, so I wouldn't be surprised by another disappearance. I'd drink until the voices in my head got quiet, until the grief felt manageable, until I could go home and pass out instead of lying awake replaying the morning I found Michael's body.

THE DANGEROUS PATTERN

What I didn't understand then was that I was establishing a pattern that would nearly kill me—using substances to avoid processing trauma, using busyness to avoid feeling grief, using strangers to avoid the vulnerability required for real connection. I was teaching myself that feelings were the enemy, that processing pain was optional, that the only way to survive loss was to pretend it hadn't happened.

The work-and-drink cycle became my new normal, my way of controlling when and how much I would feel. Days blurred into one another—pharmacy shifts where I functioned like a well-programmed robot, followed by nights when I drank myself into temporary numbness. I stopped eating regularly, stopped sleeping well, stopped doing anything that wasn't either work or drinking.

Friends invited me to things, but I'd make excuses, preferring the controlled environment of my job or the predictable numbness of alcohol to the unpredictability of genuine social connection. The possibility that someone else might get close enough to hurt me, leave me, or die on me, felt like a risk I couldn't afford to take again.

I convinced myself this was healing—that staying busy and drinking occasionally was just how people coped with loss. How adults handled death and disappointment. I told myself I was being strong and independent—handling things like a man instead of falling apart like some kind of weakling. The idea of therapy, grief counseling, or even talking to someone about what I was going through felt foreign and unnecessary—like something only people who couldn't handle their shit would need.

But my body was keeping score even when my mind was in denial. The exhaustion was bone-deep. The kind that sleep couldn't fix because it came from carrying emotional weight I refused to acknowledge. The anxiety was a constant, low-grade electrical current running through my nervous system that made everything feel urgent and dangerous. The depression was creeping in slowly, disguised as numbness—an absence of feeling rather than the presence of pain.

Morning anxiety morphed into something darker, more physical—hands shaking until the first drink, heart racing for no apparent reason, sweat-soaked sheets from nightmares I couldn't remember but could feel lurking at the edges of consciousness. My body was sending increasingly desperate messages that my mind refused to translate into actionable information.

The irony wasn't lost on me, at least in my more lucid moments. I'd left Long Beach partly to escape the constant pressure, the surface-level connections, the culture of appearance over substance. Yet here I was in San Diego, creating my own private version of the very things I'd tried to escape—performing wellness while falling apart, maintaining an external image that had nothing to do with internal reality, disconnecting from authentic experience through chemical assistance.

NUMBING THROUGH BODIES

The hookup culture in our community offers a different kind of numbness—one that's been sold to us as liberation but feels more like another prison with better marketing. Physical connection without emotional investment, pleasure without the terrifying risk of actually being seen, validation that disappears the moment you put your clothes back on. It's intimacy without intimacy, connection without actually connecting to anything real or lasting.

Most gay men I know have convinced themselves this is freedom—this ability to separate sex from emotion like we're some kind of evolved species that figured out how to have our cake and eat it too. But let's be real: it's just another form of hiding, another way to avoid the vulnerability that real intimacy requires. We're using bodies while keeping our hearts locked away in maximum security, telling ourselves we're liberated when really we're just protecting ourselves from the possibility of being hurt again.

The gay community practically worships this shit—especially in cities like San Diego where the weather is good and the bodies are better. Casual sex became a badge of honor, proof that we're living our "authentic" lives, free from the heteronormative constraints of monogamy and emotional attachment. Apps make it easier than ordering food—swipe, meet, hook up, delete. Rinse and repeat until the emptiness gets so loud you have to turn up the music to drown it out.

I had plenty of acquaintances pushing me hard in that direction, telling me I needed to "live a little" and "stop being so uptight" about casual encounters. "You're young, you're gay, you live in San Diego—what the fuck are you waiting for?"

They made it sound like I was wasting my youth by not collecting sexual experiences like Pokémon cards, like there was some gay quota I wasn't meeting, some level of promiscuity required to maintain my membership in the community.

But honestly, that whole scene never felt right to me, even when I was desperate for any kind of human connection that might fill the void Michael's death had left. I tried to get into it—God knows I tried—but something about the casual hookup culture felt fundamentally empty, like trying to satisfy genuine hunger with cotton candy: sweet for a second, then gone, leaving you even hollower than before.

Part of it was practical—I've always been particular about hygiene and stranger danger. The thought of being intimate with someone whose last STD test was a mystery, whose sexual history was a black box, whose idea of foreplay was "You clean?" on Grindr—it just didn't work for me. Call me old-fashioned, but I need to actually like someone before I let them into my personal space, before I trust them with my body and whatever emotional residue might come with physical intimacy.

But it was more than just being picky about partners. The whole culture felt performative, like we were all playing roles in some gay liberation fantasy that didn't actually liberate anyone. The guys who were most vocal about how "free" they were seemed to be the most trapped—addicted to validation from strangers, unable to be alone, constantly seeking the next hit of external approval to fill whatever void they were running from.

I would flirt at bars, make out on dance floors, maybe get a little handsy when the music was loud and the drinks were strong enough to quiet my overthinking. But when it came to actually going home with someone, something in me always pulled back. Not because I was ashamed of sex or afraid of pleasure, but because what I was really hungry for—real connection, genuine intimacy, someone who could see me and not run—couldn't be satisfied by anonymous encounters in dark rooms with people whose names I wouldn't remember in the morning.

I was starving for real food in a community that had convinced itself that junk food was a balanced diet. And while everyone around me was celebrating their freedom to consume empty calories, I was slowly starving—wondering if there was something wrong with me for wanting something more substantial, something that would actually nourish instead of just temporarily fill the void.

THE TOXIC PATTERN

There was a guy in my life during this period—let's call him the human embodiment of every red flag I'd learned to ignore, because I was so desperate for connection that I'd convinced myself any attention was better than none. We told ourselves it was nothing serious—just fun and casual, just two people who happened to keep finding their way back to each other like we were attached by some invisible fucking tether made of trauma and poor life choices.

But "casual" doesn't explain why we kept gravitating toward each other like magnets, even when logic screamed that we were terrible for each other, that this dynamic was toxic as hell and going nowhere good. "Nothing serious" doesn't explain the way my heart raced when he texted, or how I'd drop everything when he called, or how I'd convince myself that this time would be different—this time we'd figure it out, this time the dysfunction would magically transform into something healthy.

It always ended the same—screaming fights the moment we tried to make things real, to put a label on whatever toxic dance we were doing. He'd push for more intimacy, and I'd panic and pull away—because vulnerability felt like handing someone a loaded gun. I'd ask for commitment, and he'd disappear for weeks—because accountability felt like prison. We'd hurt each other with surgical precision, knowing exactly which buttons to push, because we'd mapped each other's wounds during those late-night conversations when our guards were down and we'd temporarily forgotten we were supposed to be protecting ourselves.

He became my toxic on-and-off boyfriend—though we never officially called him that, because labeling things would have required admitting we were in a pattern, that this wasn't just fun but compulsion. The guy I kept going back to like a fucking addict, even though I knew he was poison, even though every interaction left me feeling worse about myself, even though the drama was exhausting and the highs were never worth the inevitable lows.

Here's the fucked-up truth about loneliness: it makes you do things you'd never do if you were thinking clearly and accept treatment you'd never tolerate if you believed you deserved better. When the silence in your apartment gets so loud it feels like it's pressing against your eardrums—when your own thoughts become more unbearable than someone else's lies—any warm body starts to feel like salvation. Even when that body belongs to someone who's slowly destroying your capacity to trust, your sense of self-worth, your ability to believe you deserve better.

I'd lie awake at night after he'd leave, staring at the ceiling and wondering how the fuck I kept ending up here—feeling more alone after being with someone than I did when I was actually alone. But then he'd text, or I'd see him at the bar, and all that clarity would evaporate like smoke. The promise of not being alone—even temporarily, even toxically—felt better than the guarantee of solitude.

The lies started small, as they always do: "I'm not seeing anyone else." "You're the only one I care about." "I've never felt this way before." Classic lines that every player has memorized, but when you're desperate for connection, you want to believe them so badly you'll ignore the evidence piling up right in front of you like a mountain of red flags you've decided to call party decorations.

But lies have a way of breeding more lies, like bacteria in a petri dish. When I'd catch him in one, he'd tell three more to cover it up. When I'd call him out, he'd turn it around on me—I was being paranoid, jealous, crazy. I was imagining things, overreacting, ruining what we had with my insecurity. The gaslighting was so smooth, so practiced, that I started questioning my own reality—wondering if maybe I was the problem, if maybe my trauma was making me see threats that weren't actually there.

The betrayals started feeling inevitable, like a twisted form of foreplay that we both needed to feel alive. He'd hurt me, I'd hurt him back; he'd disappear, I'd chase him; he'd come back with apologies and promises, and we'd start the whole cycle over again. Each round left us both a little more damaged, a little less capable of real intimacy, a little more convinced that this toxic dance was the best either of us could hope for.

Talk about not having any goddamn self-worth. I was accepting crumbs and calling them a feast—tolerating behavior I wouldn't accept from a stranger, because at least it was something—at least it wasn't the crushing loneliness that felt like it might actually kill me if I had to endure it much longer.

THE DIAGNOSIS THAT CHANGED EVERYTHING

The guy I was dating on and off had been lying to me about everything—where he'd been, who he was with, what he was doing when he wasn't answering my calls. But the biggest lie—the one that would literally change the trajectory of my entire fucking life—was about his HIV status. And each time he lied, like a complete fucking idiot with the self-preservation instincts of a lemming walking off a cliff, I believed him.

Or maybe I convinced myself I believed him because the alternative—admitting I was involved with someone who could put my life at risk, someone who saw me as disposable enough to lie about something that serious—was too devastating to face. Maybe I needed to believe him because the truth would have forced me to confront how little I valued my own life, how desperate I was for connection, how willing I was to risk everything for the illusion of intimacy.

"I'm negative," he'd say when I'd ask, usually right before we'd have unprotected sex because I was young and stupid and thought that asking the question was the same as being responsible. "I get tested regularly." "You don't have to worry about me." Each lie was delivered with such convincing sincerity that I silenced the voice in my head that was screaming something wasn't right, that his story had holes big enough to drive trucks through.

Deep down, I knew. My gut knew. My intuition was practically beating down the door of my consciousness, trying to get my attention, sending up flares that I systematically ignored because I wanted the connection more than I wanted the safety. But I was so desperate for someone to choose me—so afraid of being alone again after losing Michael, so convinced that this dysfunctional relationship was the best I could hope for—that I ignored every red flag waving frantically in front of my face.

It all came crashing down on a Thursday morning in early 2003. I'd been feeling like absolute shit for about a week—exhausted in a way that sleep couldn't fix, achy like I was coming down with the flu that never quite arrived—just generally *off* in a way I couldn't put my finger on. My body felt like it was fighting something, but I figured it was just stress or too many late nights, or the beginning of whatever virus was going around the pharmacy where I worked.

I dragged myself to my doctor's office thinking I'd walk out with a Z-Pak prescription and be back to normal within a week. Just another minor health hiccup in an otherwise chaotic life. The last thing I expected was to have my entire future rewritten with a single finger prick—to have my life divided into "before" and "after" by a test that took thirty seconds to complete.

The test took maybe thirty seconds, but the results took both forever and no time at all. I watched the nurse's face change as she looked at the little device, her expression shifting from routine, to concerned, to carefully neutral. And I knew, even before she said the words, that my life had just been fundamentally altered in ways I couldn't yet comprehend.

"I need to have the doctor come in and talk to you," she said, and those ten words contained more weight than anything anyone had ever said to me. They held the weight of a future I'd never imagined, conversations I never wanted to have, decisions I never thought I'd need to make.

Working at an HIV specialty pharmacy probably saved me from complete psychological collapse at that moment. My immediate reaction was almost clinically detached, like I was watching this happen to someone else. Like I was a medical professional observing a case study rather than a patient receiving devastating news. "Okay, I'll start meds now. I know the protocols. I understand the treatment options. I know which drugs have the fewest side effects and which combinations work best for people my age."

I think I cried for maybe a whole minute—not because I was devastated, although I should have been—but because some part of me had been expecting this shoe to drop eventually. Like I'd been walking around with this low-level anxiety that something terrible was coming, and now that it had arrived, there was almost relief in knowing what the terrible thing was, in having the uncertainty resolved, even if it was my worst nightmare.

Then I went right back to work, because that's what you do when your world implodes but you still have bills to pay, when you're twenty-three years old and your survival instincts kick in harder than your grief. I told my supervisor I had a minor medical thing to deal with and would need to leave early for doctor's appointments sometimes. I didn't tell him I'd just joined a club I never wanted membership in—that I'd been handed a chronic condition that would define the rest of my life in ways I was only beginning to understand.

The clinical knowledge that had seemed like such a blessing in that doctor's office became a curse over the following days. I knew too much for comfort but not enough for peace of mind. I knew about viral loads, CD4 counts, drug resistance, and side effects. I knew about the difference between being HIV-positive and having AIDS. I knew about disclosure laws, and stigma, and the statistics about life expectancy—better than they used to be, but still not great.

What I didn't know was how to process the emotional reality of what had just happened to me. I didn't know how to grieve the future I'd imagined for myself, how to adjust to a new reality where every sexual encounter would require disclosure, where dating would become infinitely more complicated, where I'd joined a community I'd never wanted to be part of.

Most of all, I didn't know how to deal with the rage that was building inside me like a pressure cooker about to explode. Rage at Mr Red Flag for lying and using my trust as a weapon against me. Rage at myself for believing the lies—for being so desperate for connection that I'd ignored obvious warning signs. Rage at a world that had taught me so little about protecting myself that I'd walked into this situation with the sexual health knowledge of a middle schooler.

But rage was easier than grief, and denial was easier than acceptance, so I buried it all under the familiar routine of work and pretended that nothing fundamental had changed, even though everything had.

PROCESSING THE UNTHINKABLE

At twenty-three, after yet another failed attempt at what I'd hoped might become a real relationship, I got handed a diagnosis that would define the rest of my life. And my response? Straight back to work. Straight back to the routine. Straight back to pretending everything was manageable—as long as I stayed busy enough to avoid thinking about what had just happened, what it meant for my future, and what kind of life was possible with this new reality.

"If I start medication now, I'll be fine," I told myself, genuinely grateful for the clinical knowledge I'd gained from working in an HIV specialty pharmacy. I could rattle off drug names, side effects, resistance patterns—all the technical shit that made this feel less like a death sentence and more like a chronic condition to manage, like diabetes or high blood pressure—something that required attention but wouldn't necessarily define my entire existence.

Knowledge was power, right? Knowledge meant having control. Knowledge meant I didn't have to feel the full weight of what had just crashed down on my life like a meteor impact that would leave a crater where my old future used to be.

But knowledge couldn't touch the deeper wound: the realization that someone I'd trusted with my body had betrayed that trust in the most fundamental way possible. That I'd been so desperate for connection, so afraid of being alone after losing Michael, that I'd ignored red flags the size of fucking billboards. That my inherited understanding of love—chaotic, conditional, dangerous—had nearly killed me.

The HIV wasn't just a virus I contracted. It was physical proof of how little I valued myself, how willing I was to accept crumbs of affection from people who saw me as expendable. It was my body keeping score of every boundary I'd failed to set, every lie I'd chosen to believe, every time I'd settled for less than I deserved because I didn't think I deserved anything at all.

In the weeks that followed, I found myself caught between two realities. There was the practical reality—doctor's appointments, medication schedules, and learning to navigate a healthcare system that still treated HIV patients like modern lepers, like we were somehow morally responsible for our condition. And then there was the emotional reality I wasn't ready to face—the crushing weight of knowing that my trust had been weaponized against me, that my loneliness had been exploited by someone who claimed to care about me.

The betrayal felt even more profound because it came wrapped in intimacy disguised as connection. This wasn't a stranger who'd harmed me; this was someone who'd seen me naked, shared my bed, whispered things in the dark that made me believe I mattered to him. The violation wasn't just physical—it was spiritual and emotional—the kind of betrayal that makes you question everything you thought you knew about love, trust, and human decency.

I started having nightmares where I was drowning, gasping for air that wouldn't come, reaching for help that wasn't there. I'd wake up in cold sweats, my heart racing, my body remembering the terror my mind was trying to suppress through sheer force of will. But instead of processing what these dreams might be telling me, I'd get up, shower, and go to work like nothing had happened—like I was fine, like this was just another challenge to overcome through determination and appropriate medical management.

The isolation was the worst part, worse even than the fear about my health or the logistics of managing a chronic condition. Not the physical isolation—I could still have sex and go on dates, still find connection if I was willing to navigate the minefield of disclosure and stigma. It was the emotional isolation of carrying this secret, of feeling like damaged goods, of wondering whether anyone would ever love me fully, knowing this was part of the package I came with.

I joined online support groups for young people with HIV, but most of the conversations felt too heavy, too focused on the medical aspects, too removed from the specific intersection of trauma I was dealing with. I wasn't just a young person with HIV—I was a young, gay, Mexican man with HIV who'd been betrayed by someone he loved, whose family had already rejected him for being gay, and who was now dealing with another layer of stigma and shame on top of everything else.

The medication made me nauseous for the first few months, a daily reminder of what had been taken from me—what I'd allowed to be taken from me. Each dose was a small act of self-care and self-punishment rolled into one—keeping myself alive while being reminded of how I'd nearly killed myself through my own poor choices, my own desperate need for connection, my own inability to protect myself from people who didn't have my best interests at heart.

What haunted me most wasn't the virus itself but the story I told myself about how I'd gotten it. I wasn't some innocent victim who'd been unknowingly exposed. I was someone who'd ignored his instincts, who'd chosen connection over safety, who'd been so afraid of being alone that he'd accepted lies as love. The shame of that felt heavier than any physical symptoms—more debilitating than any side effects from medication.

But buried beneath the shame, the anger, and the disbelief was something else I wasn't ready to acknowledge yet: relief. Relief that the waiting was over, that the worst-case scenario I'd been unconsciously expecting had finally arrived. Relief that I no longer had to live in the anxiety of "what if." Relief that I could stop pretending I was invincible and start dealing with the reality of my own mortality, my own vulnerability, my own desperate need for healing that went far deeper than any virus.

The diagnosis forced me to confront truths I'd been avoiding for years: that I'd been living like someone already dead inside, taking reckless chances with my health and safety because some broken part of me believed I didn't deserve protection; that my relationship patterns weren't just bad luck but the predictable result of unhealed trauma and nonexistent self-worth; that I couldn't keep running from myself and expect to build anything real or lasting or healthy.

Years of therapy and healing work would pass before I could see the diagnosis as anything other than punishment for my poor choices. Eventually, I'd understand it wasn't divine retribution for being gay or the inevitable consequence of moral failure. It was the logical result of untreated trauma, unhealed attachment wounds, and a culture that had taught me nothing about protecting myself because it assumed people like me weren't worth protecting in the first place.

HEALING THE WOUNDS YOUR FAMILY NEVER COULD: YOUR PERSONAL REVOLUTION

After decades of family rejection, chosen-family loss, toxic relationships, and an HIV diagnosis that forced me to confront just how little I valued my own life, I had to learn something my family never taught me: how to break generational cycles instead of perpetuating them.

The trauma I carried wasn't just mine—it was inherited, passed down through bloodlines like some fucked-up family heirloom nobody wanted but everyone got.

This isn't just about "healing your inner child" or whatever New Age bullshit is trending on social media. This is about recognizing that the patterns destroying your life aren't personal failures—they're inherited survival strategies that served your ancestors but are killing you now. It's about understanding that your family's inability to accept your sexuality isn't separate from their inability to process their own trauma, heal their own wounds, or break their own cycles.

What I'm about to share isn't theoretical—it's the practical work I had to do to stop being a victim of my family's unhealed trauma. The work taught me I could honor my heritage while refusing its limitations. It broke cycles not just for me, but for future generations who won't have to carry the wounds I inherited.

SIMPLE AT-HOME GENERATIONAL TRAUMA HEALING PRACTICE

Important Note: This practice is designed to help you identify and begin healing generational patterns, but it's intense work that can bring up big emotions. Start slowly, be gentle with yourself, and have support available if you need it. This isn't about blaming your family—it's about understanding how their survival strategies became your limitations and consciously choosing something different.

UNDERSTANDING GENERATIONAL TRAUMA

Generational trauma is the emotional and psychological wounds that get passed down through families like some fucked-up inheritance nobody wanted. These aren't just family stories—they're actual changes in how your nervous system responds to stress, how your brain processes safety and danger, and how you understand love and relationships.

For LGBTQ+ people of color, we're often carrying multiple layers:

- **Historical trauma** (e.g., slavery, colonization, discrimination)
- **Cultural trauma** (e.g., immigration, poverty, systemic oppression)
- **Family trauma** (e.g., abuse, neglect, untreated mental health issues)
- **Personal trauma** (e.g., rejection, violence, discrimination for being LGBTQ+)

BASIC SETUP (10 MINUTES)

Create Your Sacred Space:

- Find a quiet space where you won't be interrupted
- Have your journal, colored pens or pencils, and tissues ready
- Light a candle or create some ritual that feels meaningful
- Set a timer for 30-45 minutes
- Have water and grounding objects nearby

Ground Yourself:

- Take 5 deep breaths
- Place both hands on your heart
- Say aloud, *"I am safe to explore my family patterns. I have the strength to heal what needs healing."*

WEEK 1-2: MAPPING YOUR FAMILY SYSTEM

Exercise 1: Family Tree of Trauma and Resilience

Draw your family tree going back as far as you know. For each person, note:

- What traumas did they experience? (e.g., war, poverty, abuse, discrimination, loss)
- What were their coping mechanisms? (e.g., alcohol, work, religion, silence, anger)
- What strengths did they have? (e.g., resilience, creativity, humor, love)
- What patterns can you see repeating?

Questions to explore:

- What traumas were never spoken about in your family?

- What emotions weren't allowed to be expressed?
- How did your family handle conflict, loss, or stress?
- What survival strategies did your ancestors develop?

Exercise 2: The Messages You Inherited

Finish these sentences about messages you received growing up:
- "In our family, men are supposed to . . ."
- "In our family, women are supposed to . . ."
- "Money is . . ."
- "Love means . . ."
- "To be safe, you must . . ."
- "People like us don't . . ."
- "The world is . . ."

Shadow Questions:

- Which of these messages still control your choices?
- Which ones have you been trying to rebel against?
- How do these beliefs show up in your relationships, work, and self-care?

WEEK 3-4: UNDERSTANDING CULTURAL TRAUMA

Exercise 3: Cultural Wounds and Gifts

For your specific cultural background, explore:
- What historical traumas affected your people?
- How do these show up in your family's behavior, beliefs, and fears?

- What cultural strengths and wisdom were passed down?
- Which cultural patterns serve you? Which harm you?

For Latino/Hispanic families, consider:
- Machismo/marianismo and rigid gender roles
- "La familia" loyalty vs. individual authenticity
- Immigration trauma and survivor's guilt
- Catholic guilt about sexuality and mental health
- Navigating between cultures and. the exhaustion that creates

Exercise 4: The Double Bind of Being LGBTQ+ and a POC

Write about:
- How does being LGBTQ+ conflict with your cultural identity?
- What messages did you receive about sexuality and gender expression?
- How did you learn to hide parts of yourself for safety?
- What was lost when you had to choose between culture and authenticity?
- How can you reclaim the gifts of your culture while rejecting its limitations?

WEEK 5-6: BREAKING THE CYCLES

Exercise 5: Identifying Patterns You Want to Break

List patterns you've inherited that you want to stop:
- **Emotional** (e.g., explosive anger, emotional shutdown, people-pleasing)

- **Relationship** (e.g., toxic masculinity, codependency, fear of intimacy)
- **Mental health** (e.g., ignoring problems, self-medication, avoiding help)
- **Communication** (e.g., silence, yelling, passive-aggression)

For each pattern, ask:
- How did this serve my ancestors' survival?
- How is it limiting me now?
- What would the healthy version of this pattern look like?
- How can I heal this in myself?

Exercise 6: Healing Conversations with Your Ancestors

Write letters to your ancestors (you don't have to send them—this is for your healing):
- **To ancestors who caused harm:** e.g., *"I understand you did the best you could with what you had. I see how your own trauma shaped your choices. I forgive you for the pain you caused, and I choose to heal what you couldn't."*
- **To ancestors who showed strength:** e.g., *"Thank you for surviving so I could be here. Thank you for the gifts you passed down—your resilience, your love, your determination. I honor your struggles and your victories."*
- **To your lineage:** e.g., *"I am breaking the cycles of pain that have been passed down. I am healing not just for myself, but for all of us. The trauma stops with me, and the healing begins with me."*

WEEK 7-8: CREATING NEW PATTERNS

Exercise 7: Designing Your Conscious Family Culture

If you were creating the family culture you wish you'd grown up in, what would it include?
- How would emotions be handled?
- How would conflicts be resolved?
- What would love look and feel like?
- How would differences be celebrated rather than corrected?
- What rituals and traditions would you create?

Exercise 8: Parenting Yourself with the Love You Needed

Write a letter to your younger self from the perspective of the healthy parent you wish you'd had: i.e. *"Dear sweet child, you are perfect exactly as you are. Your sensitivity is a gift. Your differences make you special. You deserve love that doesn't require you to be someone else. I will protect you, guide you, and never abandon you for being authentic."*

ADVANCED PRACTICES (MONTH 2+)

Ritual for Releasing Ancestral Wounds:
- Write the patterns you're releasing on pieces of paper
- Burn them safely while saying, *"I release what no longer serves our family line"*
- Plant something beautiful in the ashes

Creating an Ancestral Altar:

- Include photos of family members you want to honor
- Add items representing the gifts they gave you
- Spend time there regularly, talking to them about your healing journey

Body-Based Trauma Release:

- Notice where family trauma lives in your body (e.g., tight shoulders)

CHAPTER THREE

Tapping Into Healing

2020 hit all of us like a freight train loaded with anxiety, isolation, and the kind of existential dread that makes you question everything you thought you knew about how the world works. That visual still fucks with my head when I think about the beginning of that year. Six months before the world completely went to shit, my partner and I had decided we needed a fresh start and moved to Salt Lake City to escape the financial pressure cooker of San Diego, where we were burning through money just to maintain a basic existence.

We were excited about this new chapter—finally having our own place in a brand-new building with mountain views and the kind of space we'd never been able to afford in California. With twenty years in management under my belt and a successful career as a makeup artist and stylist, I took a more mainstream corporate job at Nordstrom downtown, while my partner chose property management, ready to retire from his long career as a professional ballet dancer.

Everything felt like it was finally falling into place—we had stable jobs, a beautiful apartment, a city that offered outdoor adventures we'd only dreamed about in crowded, expensive San Diego. We thought we'd figured out the formula for building a sustainable life together. That we'd learned from our previous financial struggles and relationship challenges.

Then March 2020 happened, and along with everyone else on the planet, we watched our carefully constructed plans disintegrate in real time. But for me, the pandemic didn't just disrupt external circumstances—it activated every dormant trauma response I'd spent decades trying to manage, triggered every abandonment wound I thought I'd healed, and sent my nervous system into a state of hypervigilance that made normal functioning feel impossible.

We were all there for the year 2020, so I don't need to explain the collective clusterfuck we all experienced. But what I do need to explain is how pandemic isolation, economic uncertainty, and the constant low-grade terror that characterized that year, combined with my personal history, created the perfect storm for a mental-health crisis that nearly killed me.

DISMISSING THE WARNING SIGNS

As the anxiety attacks started happening more frequently—increasing from occasional episodes to daily occurrences that left me gasping for air and convinced I was having heart attacks—I'd dismiss them as first-world problems, as weakness, as evidence that I was failing at the basic task of being an adult who could handle stress without falling apart.

Growing up Hispanic, mental health issues aren't just stigmatized—they're treated like character defects, like evidence that you're not strong enough to handle what life throws at you. Anxiety, depression, and panic attacks were all dismissed as *"pendejadas"*—*bullshit concerns for people who had too much time on their hands and not enough real problems to worry about.*

The cultural message I'd internalized was clear: real men don't have panic attacks—they handle their shit. Real men don't need therapy; they work harder. Real men don't take medication for their feelings; they drink beer and get over it. If anything, mental health struggles became a joke: *"take some Sprite and rub some Vicks on it; it'll all go away"*—as if complex psychological conditions could be cured with the same remedies used for minor physical ailments.

I was taught to bury feelings so deep they'd never see daylight again, to treat emotional expression as weakness, to view any form of vulnerability as an invitation for others to exploit me. "Don't be so dramatic" became the family response to any display of authentic emotion, and after I came out, this dismissal took on even more of a pointed edge. In Hispanic culture, coming out as gay automatically gets you labeled as a drama queen—as someone whose emotional responses can't be trusted because they're probably just for performance rather than genuine emotion.

When anxiety symptoms started showing up in my life with increasing frequency and intensity, I decided to ignore them completely. "Not valid," I'd tell myself when my heart would start racing for no apparent reason, when my palms got sweaty during routine conversations, and when I woke up in the middle of the night drenched in sweat, convinced something terrible was about to happen.

I had internalized the toxic belief that acknowledging mental health struggles was equivalent to admitting weakness, to giving up, to becoming one of those people who couldn't handle life without pharmaceutical assistance and therapeutic hand-holding. I was going to tough it out and prove that I was stronger than my circumstances and more resilient than my family history suggested.

But anxiety doesn't give a fuck about your cultural programming or your determination to be strong. It doesn't care if you've decided it's not valid or if you think you should be able to handle it on your own. Anxiety is your nervous system's way of telling you that something needs attention, and when you ignore it long enough, it starts speaking louder until you can't ignore it anymore.

I was afraid to have real conversations with my partner about what I was experiencing—partly because I didn't have language for it and partly because I was ashamed of not being the stable, capable man he'd fallen in love with—I chose drinking instead. The progression was so gradual I barely noticed it happening—or maybe I noticed but welcomed the softening of edges that alcohol provided, the blessed temporary relief from the tightness in my chest and the constant racing of my thoughts.

The first glass of wine at dinner became two, then three, then finishing the entire bottle became routine. On weekends, we'd start drinking earlier—mimosas with brunch that led to afternoon beers, then evening cocktails, creating an entire day structured around socially acceptable forms of self-medication.

I told myself this was normal, that everyone was drinking more during the pandemic—that this was just how people coped with unprecedented stress and uncertainty. Social media was full of jokes about "quarantinis" and wine-o-clock starting earlier each day, friends posting memes about needing alcohol to survive Zoom meetings and homeschooling and the general chaos of trying to maintain normal life under completely abnormal circumstances.

THE YEAR OF AVOIDANCE

For the next year, I decided I wasn't ready to feel or talk about any of the psychological chaos that was unfolding inside my head. The knocks on the door from these "silly symptoms" got louder and more insistent, but the alcohol muffled them enough to make them manageable—something I could ignore for another day, another week, another month.

When unemployment checks started arriving, it felt like permission to expand my numbness into a full-time occupation. No more morning alarm clocks forcing me into professional personas, no more workplace sobriety requirements, no more having to maintain the appearance of having my shit together for eight hours a day. I could drink whenever I wanted, sleep whenever I wanted, and avoid whatever I wanted without having to explain myself to supervisors or coworkers.

This wasn't my first relationship with alcohol as a coping mechanism—I'd used drinking to navigate difficult periods before, during other major life transitions when the emotional complexity felt too overwhelming to process sober. Like after coming out and facing family rejection, after Michael's suicide when grief felt like quicksand threatening to swallow me whole, and after receiving my HIV diagnosis when the future suddenly looked completely different than what I'd imagined.

But this time felt different because there was no clear timeline for when the crisis would end, no obvious light at the end of the tunnel, no return to normal that I could orient myself toward. Previous drinking phases had been temporary responses to acute stressors—I'd self-medicate for a few months while getting through the worst of whatever situation I was facing, then gradually return to moderation once the immediate crisis passed.

The pandemic stretched ahead like an endless desert with no visible oasis, each day bleeding into the next with no clear markers of progress or improvement. My drinking stretched along with it, evolving from occasional escape mechanism to daily requirement, from weekend indulgence to morning-to-night medication that I needed just to feel baseline normal.

My partner noticed, of course—how could he not notice the increasing frequency of our "happy hours," the way I'd become irritable and restless on days when we didn't drink, and the subtle changes in my personality that emerged after the third or fourth drink? He approached the subject carefully at first, with gentle suggestions about maybe taking a night off from alcohol, trying other ways to manage stress, or paying attention to how much we were both consuming daily.

"I'm fine" became my automatic defensive response, delivered with increasing hostility toward anyone who suggested that maybe I wasn't fine, that maybe my drinking had crossed the line from social activity to something more compulsive and concerning. I'd say, "Everyone's drinking more during quarantine. It's normal. We're coping with a global pandemic—what do you expect?"

And it was true that alcohol consumption had skyrocketed across the country, that we weren't unusual in drinking it as a primary strategy for managing pandemic stress. But the normalcy of it didn't make it any less destructive, and my defensive reactions to any mention of our drinking patterns should have been a red flag that something deeper was happening.

The alcohol gave me temporary relief from the hypervigilance that had become my default state—the constant scanning for threats, the inability to relax, the feeling that danger was always just around the corner, even when I was safe in my own apartment. When I was drunk enough, I could pretend that the anxiety was just temporary, that my relationship was stable, that I had some control over circumstances that felt completely chaotic and unpredictable.

WHEN DRINKING WASN'T ENOUGH

The cocaine started as an occasional weekend thing—just when drinking alone wasn't quite enough to keep the anxiety at bay, when alcohol was making me too sleepy to enjoy the temporary relief it provided. A friend of a friend knew someone in our new city—the transaction was simple, discreet, and completed in parking lots with masks that served the dual purpose of pandemic precaution and maintaining anonymity.

The familiar ritual of chopping lines on our living room table felt like reconnecting with an old acquaintance—not exactly a friend, but someone whose company I'd enjoyed during previous difficult periods in my life. The combination of alcohol and cocaine created a sweet spot where I could feel energized but not anxious, social but not vulnerable, present but not overwhelmed by the intensity of actually being present.

"It helps me stay engaged," I told my partner when he expressed concern about adding stimulants to our already problematic drinking routine—as if chemical stimulation while being emotionally numb were the same thing as actually engaging with life. As if the artificial energy and confidence that came from cocaine were equivalent to genuine vitality and authentic self-assurance.

He didn't buy my rationalization, but he also didn't know how to reach me across the growing divide that substances were creating between us. The very chemicals I was using to avoid difficult feelings and conversations were generating an even greater need for difficult conversations, creating a self-perpetuating cycle where each attempt to escape emotional complexity only generated more emotional complexity that required further escape.

Morning anxiety began morphing into something darker and more physical—hands shaking until the first drink of the day, heart racing for hours after waking up, sweat-soaked sheets from nightmares I couldn't remember but could feel lurking at the edges of consciousness like predators waiting for me to let my guard down.

My body was sending increasingly desperate signals that my mind refused to acknowledge or translate into action. The physical symptoms weren't random—they were communications from a nervous system that was overwhelmed, overstimulated, and operating in constant crisis mode because I kept feeding it substances designed to alter its natural functioning.

Looking back, the delusion is almost impressive. I genuinely believed that moving to Utah would somehow fix me—like the mountain air and Mormon influence would magically cure decades of unprocessed trauma. Instead, I'd just traded one form of avoidance for another, swapping California's party culture for isolated drinking in a place where I knew even fewer people who might notice I was falling apart..Sometimes, in those rare moments of honest self-reflection that typically happened during hangovers, when my defenses were down, I'd acknowledge what was happening and promise myself moderation, boundaries, a return to healthier coping strategies. These promises rarely lasted beyond the first wave of anxiety or the first triggering news story that sent me reaching for familiar forms of relief.

"It's just until things get back to normal," I'd tell myself, although "normal" was becoming an increasingly abstract concept. The pandemic stretched on, unemployment benefits continued, and my temporary solution was becoming permanent infrastructure. The escape routes I'd built were becoming the territory itself—no longer ways out of uncomfortable feelings but the primary landscape where I lived my daily life.

THE FALL OUT

Just as I was settling into what I told myself was a sustainable routine of work-from-home drinking and occasional recreational drug use, we lost our apartment and my car. The eviction notice arrived with clinical politeness—thirty days to vacate due to nonpayment of rent. The car repossession followed a week later, equally emotionless bureaucratic language about taking away what little independence and mobility I had left.

We didn't have enough money coming in to maintain our lifestyle, despite unemployment benefits and my partner's income from his new job. "Are you fucking kidding me?" became the mantra I lived by during those days—a constant stream of incredulous anger at the universe for orchestrating what felt like a cosmic joke at my expense. "Here we go again, what the fuck?" were the affirmations I spoke aloud to empty rooms, to a God I wasn't sure I believed in anymore.

The carefully constructed façade of our new life in Salt Lake City wasn't just cracking; it was collapsing entirely like a house of cards in a windstorm—revealing the hollow foundation beneath our fresh start. All our optimistic planning, the confidence we'd learned from previous financial mistakes, our belief that we could build stability through determination and smart choices—none of it had prepared us for the perfect storm of pandemic unemployment, mounting debt, and my escalating substance use.

We were fortunate enough that my best friend lived in the same city and offered us his spare room, an act of genuine kindness that my wounded pride transformed into another source of shame and self-recrimination. Even though we were genuinely grateful for his hospitality and understood that we had no other viable options, I felt worthless and useless, like a complete failure as a partner and provider.

"I can't even keep a roof over my man's head," I'd tell myself during the worst moments of self-loathing—the internal monologue becoming a poisonous mantra that reinforced every negative belief I'd ever held about my worth and competence. "What kind of shitty partner am I? What kind of man can't maintain basic financial stability?"

The move into my friend's spare room felt like the ultimate admission of defeat—concrete proof that I was incapable of adult responsibilities, that all my previous successes had been flukes or luck rather than genuine competence. Self-hatred became my full-time occupation. My internal dialogue was a constant stream of criticism that would have been unacceptable if directed at anyone else but felt justified when aimed at myself.

My partner didn't know the full extent of my self-loathing, but he could sense it in the way I'd avoid his eyes when discussions turned to our financial situation, in how I'd retreat into sullen silence whenever he tried to problem-solve our housing crisis, in the increasing frequency with which he'd find me staring at myself in mirrors with undisguised disgust.

I'd catch glimpses of myself and mutter "fat," "ugly," and "pathetic"—words meant only for my own ears but that occasionally escaped into the shared air between us. Each time he'd approach with concern etched around his eyes, I'd wave him off with a dismissive joke or change the subject, unwilling to let him witness the full depth of my self-directed cruelty.

"It's nothing," I'd say when he'd ask about the self-deprecating comments or the way I'd flinch when he complimented my appearance. "Just being dramatic." The irony of using the exact dismissive language my family had used about my sexuality to minimize my mental health struggles wasn't lost on me—I had become my own invalidator, my own silencer, continuing generational patterns of emotional suppression even when there was no external pressure to do so.

THE DARKEST HOUR

These were genuinely dark times, darker than any period I'd experienced since my early twenties, when family rejection and Michael's death had nearly broken me entirely. The spare room in my friend's house became both a refuge and a prison—a place we were grateful to have but a constant reminder of how far we'd fallen from our mountain-view apartment and our confident plans for building a stable life together.

My drinking accelerated beyond even the pandemic levels I'd normalized—now fueled not just by general anxiety about global circumstances but by acute shame about our personal failures, by the need to escape not just internal discomfort but an external reality that felt like a daily indictment of my inadequacy as a human being.

What I didn't realize at the time was that this darkness was only the beginning—the opening scene of a descent that would take me to places I couldn't have imagined. Like those horror movies where the protagonist thinks they've hit rock bottom, only to discover there's a deeper level of hell waiting to be explored, I was standing at the edge of an abyss that would challenge everything I thought I knew about my own resilience and capacity for survival.

The external losses—apartment, car, financial stability—were just visible symptoms of a more fundamental collapse happening inside me. The failure of all the coping mechanisms, personas, and avoidance strategies that had carried me through previous crises was becoming undeniable. The scaffolding of my identity as a competent, independent adult who could handle whatever life threw at him was being dismantled piece by piece.

Each piece revealed more of what lay beneath—the foundation I'd never properly examined because I'd been too busy building upward and outward, creating an impressive external structure on fundamentally unstable psychological ground. The confident, successful man my partner had fallen in love with was revealing himself to be a carefully constructed façade, covering decades of unprocessed trauma, unhealed attachment wounds, and a level of self-hatred that shocked even me.

My friend's spare room had a window facing east, and sometimes I'd wake before dawn, before my partner, before the previous night's alcohol had fully metabolized out of my system. In that strange liminal space between drunk and hungover, between night and morning, between sleeping and waking, I'd watch the light change over the Salt Lake Valley and feel something that might have been hope if I'd been able to recognize it.

There was a moment each day when the mountains would catch the first rays of sun while the valley remained in shadow—a perfect visual metaphor for the possibility that illumination might reach the highest points while darkness still held the depths. In those moments, a voice would sometimes break through the chemical haze, whispering that maybe this collapse was necessary, that perhaps everything needed to fall apart completely before something authentic could finally be built.

I'd push this voice away immediately, reach for my phone, and scroll mindlessly through social media until the moment passed and the day's familiar routines of avoidance could begin again. But the voice kept returning, suggesting that rock bottom might not be a destination but a foundation—that complete destruction might be the prerequisite for genuine reconstruction.

My partner watched me with increasing concern during this period, his patience stretching beyond what anyone should have to endure from someone they love. "We'll get through this," he'd say, meaning the external circumstances—the housing crisis, the financial pressure, the pandemic restrictions. But there was always a deeper question in his eyes, addressing the internal collapse he could sense but couldn't fully see: Will you get through this? Will *we*?

The darkness had indeed just begun, but darkness serves purposes beyond suffering that I wasn't yet able to recognize. Seeds germinate in darkness. Vision adjusts in darkness. Truth reveals itself in darkness, when all the distractions of light are temporarily removed. I wasn't ready to surrender to the painful necessity of this collapse—too busy fighting against what was happening instead of allowing it to complete itself.

But the demolition would continue, stripping away everything I thought defined me, until I'd finally stand naked before myself—no achievements to hide behind, no substances to numb the encounter, no personas to mediate the meeting between who I thought I was and who I actually was beneath all the performance and adaptation.

WHAT I WAS AVOIDING

What I avoided most during the pandemic wasn't just feeling difficult emotions—I avoided the fundamental reckoning with myself that had been decades in the making. Every drink, every line of cocaine, every hour spent scrolling mindlessly through social media was another postponement of the conversation I needed to have with the man in the mirror.

Therapy, in my mind, was for sissies and weak people who couldn't handle their problems through determination and appropriate life management. "Only white people go to therapy," my mother would say during our infrequent phone conversations, following the statement with one of her characteristic laughs that made it clear this wasn't just her personal opinion but an unquestionable cultural truth about how our family operated.

"I know," I'd agree, taking the path of least resistance that had become second nature in all family interactions—the automatic compliance that avoided conflict while reinforcing the very beliefs that were keeping me trapped in cycles of suffering. It was easier to agree than to challenge generational wisdom, easier to maintain family harmony than to advocate for my own mental health needs.

What I didn't realize at the time—already well into my thirties—was that I was living my entire life according to a set of limiting beliefs and inherited stories passed down through generations, none of which had ever been questioned or examined for their relevance to contemporary circumstances.

These weren't my original thoughts or personal convictions—they were cultural hand-me-downs that fit about as well as my cousin's outgrown church clothes I'd been forced to wear as a kid. The script for how to handle psychological distress had been written long before I was born—passed down through blood and language and unspoken expectations that real men handle their problems internally and privately.

In my family dynamic, psychological suffering wasn't just stigmatized—it was criminalized, treated as a moral failing that reflected poorly on your character, your upbringing, and your basic competence as a functional human being. Physical pain earned sympathy and appropriate medical attention; mental anguish earned contempt and suggestions that you needed to "get your shit together" through willpower and better life choices.

"Ponte las pilas," they'd say—*put in your batteries, get it together, stop being so dramatic about normal life challenges.* The metaphor was telling: emotional distress was seen as a mechanical problem that could be solved through proper maintenance and adequate energy, not a complex psychological condition requiring professional intervention and sustained attention.

This denial wasn't unique to my specific family but was woven into the fabric of Latino culture itself—especially for men, and even more so for gay men who had already violated one cardinal rule of acceptable masculinity and couldn't afford to break another by admitting to emotional vulnerability or psychological complexity.

The generations before me had survived poverty, migration, discrimination, and violence without the luxury of examining their inner lives or processing their emotional responses to trauma. Who was I to claim special treatment, to suggest that my comparatively privileged existence required professional mental health intervention that they'd never had access to and had somehow managed to survive without?

This cultural context created a perfect storm of resistance to seeking help. Therapy was seen not only as weakness but also as ingratitude—an implicit criticism of family members who'd endured far worse circumstances without requiring therapeutic support. Asking for professional help felt like betraying the people who'd sacrificed everything to give me opportunities they never had.

ANOTHER FRESH START

After unemployment benefits ran out and our financial situation became genuinely desperate, my partner and I both got jobs at the University of Utah Hospital. We deliberately chose separate departments, having learned from our previous experience of tying our professional fates together—working at the same company in California—led to the simultaneous collapse of our shared financial stability.

There was genuine excitement again—a renewed surge of optimism about our ability to rebuild stability through hard work and smart choices. The hospital badges hanging from lanyards around our necks felt like talismans of legitimacy: physical proof that we were essential workers, valued members of society, and legitimate participants in the healthcare system rather than unemployed drains on public resources.

The structure of hospital shifts provided exactly what my chaotic internal world needed—clear expectations, measurable outcomes, and tangible evidence of productivity and contribution that didn't depend on my emotional state or psychological stability. Here was purpose that existed outside my own head—meaning it didn't require introspection or self-examination; identity that was defined by function rather than feelings.

I threw myself into the work with the desperate energy of someone who'd finally found solid ground after months of feeling like I was drowning. Learning medical terminology, mastering computer systems, developing relationships with coworkers—all of it felt like evidence that I was still capable of normal adult functioning, that my substance use hadn't yet progressed to the point of interfering with my ability to hold down a job.

The hospital environment provided built-in justification for my stress levels and occasional physical symptoms. Working in healthcare during a pandemic was inherently stressful; everyone faced unusual levels of anxiety and exhaustion. My occasional shakiness, frequent breaks, and difficulty concentrating could all be attributed to the challenging work environment rather than seen as potential signs of escalating addiction.

For about three months, this new routine felt sustainable—even healthy. I was working, contributing, and maintaining a schedule that required sobriety during business hours. My drinking was limited to evenings and weekends, which felt like moderation compared to the all-day consumption that had characterized my unemployment period.

But stability has always made me nervous, and success has always felt temporary. As the initial excitement of the new job began to wear off and the work became routine rather than novel, familiar patterns of self-sabotage began to assert themselves with the reliability of seasonal weather changes.

Until it wasn't sustainable anymore. Again, *"Are you fucking kidding me?"* became the soundtrack of my life— the constant background noise of disbelief and anger at my own inability to maintain forward momentum when opportunities presented themselves.

THE SELF-SABOTAGE CYCLE

The pattern emerged with terrifying predictability, following a script I'd unconsciously memorized through decades of repetition. Three months into any new job, just as stability began to feel possible and confidence started to build, the self-sabotage cycle would activate with the precision of a Swiss timepiece, as if some internal alarm was programmed to sound whenever things got too comfortable.

First came the tardiness—five minutes here and there that gradually expanded to fifteen, then thirty, then calling in with fabricated illnesses that became increasingly elaborate and less believable. Then came conflicts with supervisors over increasingly minor issues that my fragile ego transformed into matters of principle and personal dignity rather than ordinary workplace dynamics that could be resolved through communication and compromise.

Self-sabotage is real, and let me tell you, I developed that particular skill into a fine art form over the years. I was an expert saboteur—so practiced at derailing my own progress that I probably could have gotten certification to teach it. The University of Fucking Yourself Over had no more dedicated student, no more consistent practitioner of the delicate craft of destroying opportunities before they could threaten the comfortable familiarity of chaos and crisis.

The worst part wasn't even the external consequences—the written warnings, the concerned conversations with HR representatives who genuinely wanted to help me succeed, the disappointed looks from my partner, who had witnessed this exact cycle multiple times before and already knew how it would end. The worst part was the voice in my head giving constant commentary throughout the cycle: "See? This is who you really are. This is all you're capable of. This is what you deserve."

That voice didn't originate with me—it was an amalgamation of every person who had ever predicted I would fail or fall short of expectations—internalized so completely that I couldn't distinguish it from my own thoughts. It spoke in my father's dismissive tone, echoed my mother's dramatic sighs of disappointment, and carried my extended family's coded language about my "lifestyle choices" and their supposed impact on my stability and reliability.

The voice also contained fragments of elementary school teachers' notes about my "attention problems," high school counselors' lowered expectations for my academic potential, and the subtle messaging from healthcare providers who treated my HIV status as evidence of poor judgment rather than a medical condition requiring appropriate care and management.

Each episode of self-sabotage felt simultaneously voluntary and involuntary—I could see myself making choices that would lead to negative consequences, yet I felt powerless to choose differently, as if I were watching someone else drive my life toward a cliff while I sat in the passenger seat, screaming warnings that went unheeded.

The hospital job lasted four months—one month longer than my usual three-month cycle, which I initially interpreted as progress before recognizing it was just a slight variation in timing rather than fundamental change in pattern. The termination wasn't dramatic or contentious, just a quiet meeting where my supervisor expressed genuine regret about letting me go and acknowledged that I had skills and potential that weren't being utilized effectively.

"You have so much potential," she said—a phrase I'd heard throughout my life that had evolved from encouragement to the cruelest possible epitaph for my professional aspirations. *Potential* meant the gap between what might have been and what actually was. *Potential* meant perpetual disappointment—a lifetime of falling short of possibilities that everyone could see but I couldn't seem to access.

My partner didn't express anger or frustration when I told him about the termination. That would have been easier to handle than the quiet resignation that settled over his features like a familiar mask—the slow nod of acknowledgment that we were trapped in a pattern neither of us knew how to break, that my employment history was becoming a series of failed experiments rather than genuine career development.

He had managed to secure a permanent position in hospital administration, a rare stroke of good fortune in our otherwise unraveling professional lives. At least one of us was capable of maintaining forward momentum, of building something sustainable rather than repeatedly destroying whatever progress we had managed to achieve. At least one of us could be trusted with responsibility and opportunity.

THE SUGGESTION

"Maybe you should talk to someone," he suggested one evening as we sat in my friend's living room, his voice carefully neutral, the suggestion wrapped in the safest possible language that wouldn't trigger my defensive reactions or activate my shame about needing help. Not "therapy," not "professional intervention," not any terminology that might evoke my cultural resistance to mental health treatment.

"Talk to who?" I snapped, playing dumb—though I knew exactly what he meant and why he was suggesting it. The defensive response was automatic, programmed through years of family conditioning that treated any suggestion of psychological support as an insult to my strength, competence, and basic adequacy as a functioning adult.

"The hospital has resources," he continued patiently, having clearly thought through this conversation before initiating it. "People you can speak with. Employee assistance programs. It's confidential, and it's covered by your insurance." The practical details were intended to address the logistical barriers I might raise—cost, privacy, accessibility—but they couldn't touch the deeper resistance that had nothing to do with practicalities.

"I'm not crazy," I said automatically—the default response programmed into me since childhood, the reflexive conflation of mental health care with serious mental illness that kept generations of my family suffering in silence rather than seeking appropriate professional support. In my understanding, therapy was for people who heard voices or couldn't distinguish reality from delusion, not for people dealing with ordinary life stress and emotional challenges.

"I didn't say you were," he replied, and I could hear the weariness in his voice that cut through my defenses more effectively than anger or frustration could have. "But something has to change. We can't keep doing this cycle over and over again. I can't keep watching you destroy every opportunity you get."

The "we" hung in the air between us—acknowledgment that my patterns weren't just destroying my own life but eroding the foundation of our relationship, our shared future, and whatever remained of our partnership after months of crisis and my escalating substance use. For the first time, I heard the unspoken ultimatum beneath his gentle suggestion: *Get help—or lose me, too.*

This wasn't just about employment or financial stability anymore. This was about whether our relationship could survive my refusal to address whatever psychological issues were driving my self-destructive patterns, whether he could continue to love someone who seemed determined to destroy himself and everything good in his life.

The conversation marked a turning point, though I wasn't ready to acknowledge it at the time. Someone who loved me was telling me—with remarkable patience and kindness—that my current approach to life wasn't working, and that professional help might be necessary. The suggestion came not from a place of judgment or criticism but from genuine concern for my well-being and our future together.

But even faced with this evidence that my patterns were affecting more than just myself, even hearing the exhaustion in my partner's voice and recognizing the sweet assertiveness. , I wasn't ready to admit that I needed help. The cultural programming was too strong, the shame too deep, and the fear of being seen as weak or broken too overwhelming to overcome through logical arguments about the benefits of therapeutic intervention.

SABOTAGING LOVE

There were so many warning signs that my mental health was deteriorating rapidly, but the noise in my head was louder than any physical symptoms or external feedback I was receiving. The constant self-sabotaging, the limiting beliefs inherited from generations of family trauma, and the cultural conditioning that treated emotional vulnerability as character weakness, it was all drowning out the increasingly desperate signals my body and my relationships were sending.

My world continued crumbling in real time, and with it was going my relationship with the real true love of my life, the one person who had seen something valuable in me even when I couldn't see it myself. The self-sabotage didn't just apply to my professional life; it was actively poisoning my personal relationships through patterns I couldn't even recognize, let alone interrupt.

Every anniversary, I would ask my partner the same toxic question that revealed how deeply I believed I was fundamentally unlovable: "Are you tired of me yet? If I were you, I'd run." I'd deliver this with what I thought was humor, but it was really a carefully placed landmine designed to test his commitment, to push him away before he could leave me on his own timeline and initiative.

He would dismiss these questions with humor and patience that I didn't deserve, deflecting my attempts to sabotage our relationship while refusing to engage with the underlying beliefs that drove such toxic testing. Looking back now, with the clarity that comes from years of therapy and healing work, I can see how fucked up this pattern was, how destructive and unfair it was to both of us.

Who does that? Well, this guy right here. Who tests love until it breaks? Who plants seeds of doubt and insecurity in otherwise healthy relationships? Who turns anniversaries into opportunities for self-fulfilling prophecies about abandonment? Someone whose attachment system was so damaged by early trauma that genuine love felt impossible to trust—someone whose nervous system had been trained to expect rejection and betrayal as inevitable outcomes of emotional intimacy.

He saw something in me at the beginning of our relationship and continued to see it even seven years later, something that remained invisible to me until my perception changed through intensive therapeutic work. But given all the evidence of my deteriorating mental health and escalating self-destruction, I was still in complete denial about my need for professional help.

"Therapy is for *pendejos*," I'd mutter when he'd gently suggest I might benefit from talking to someone about the anxiety, the job instability, and the drinking that was becoming increasingly difficult to ignore or rationalize. The Spanish insult felt particularly appropriate. Therapy wasn't just for fools, but for a specific kind of fool who exposed their weakness voluntarily, who invited scrutiny of the very aspects of themselves that should be most fiercely protected from outside examination.

I wasn't going to be that kind of pendejo. I was the kind who destroyed good things before they could be taken away, who controlled the narrative of my own unworthiness rather than allowing others to discover and name it for themselves. I was going to handle my problems through willpower, work ethic, and whatever chemical assistance was necessary to maintain the appearance of functional adulthood.

"I'll be fine . . . I always am" became my automatic response to any expression of concern about my mental health, job stability, drinking, or the way I was treating our relationship like it was temporary and conditional rather than the committed partnership we'd both agreed to build together.

The phrase "I'll be fine" had lost all meaning except as a conversation-ender, a wall I could build between his perception of my struggle and my own experience of barely holding on. Fine didn't mean good or healthy or happy or stable. Fine meant surviving, continuing to move forward despite the increasing weight of unprocessed emotion and unhealed trauma, and maintaining basic life functions while my internal world became increasingly chaotic and unmanageable.

And technically, I was always "fine" by this definition. I had survived my father's rage and my family's rejection of my sexuality. I'd survived Michael's suicide and my HIV diagnosis. I'd survived multiple relocations, job losses, financial collapses, and relationship challenges that would have broken people with more stability and better coping mechanisms.

If survival alone was the measure of "fine," then yes, I always was fine. But survival and thriving exist in completely different dimensions, and while I'd become expert at the former, the latter remained foreign territory that I couldn't even imagine, let alone navigate.

The most insidious aspect of this dynamic was how my testing and sabotage were actually creating the very rejection I claimed to fear. By constantly asking if he was tired of me, by treating our relationship like it was temporary, and by refusing to fully invest in building something stable together, I was making it increasingly difficult for him to stay committed to someone who seemed determined to prove that he was not worth staying committed to.

My behavior was becoming a self-fulfilling prophecy, creating the abandonment I'd spent my entire life expecting and preparing for. Instead of learning to trust that someone might actually love me consistently and unconditionally, I was working overtime to give him reasons to leave, to prove that my original assessment of my own unworthiness was accurate.

WHEN THE HEART TAKES OVER

As my self-destructive cycles kicked into high gear and the psychological pressure became unbearable, my body began staging an intervention that my mind couldn't ignore or rationalize. The constant anxiety, the unprocessed trauma, the escalating substance use, and the crushing weight of untreated depression were taking a toll that went far beyond what I could manage through denial and determination.

The world playing in my head became like those childhood circuses I'd shared with my abuelito, but it had twisted into something much darker and more sinister than the magical experiences of my youth. The clowns were no longer colorful and full of glitter and happiness; my traumatized mind had transformed them into demons dressed as clowns, grotesque parodies of joy that reflected my internal state back to me in the most disturbing way possible.

The noise grew louder and louder, my drinking and drug use became heavier, and the coping mechanisms that had once provided relief were now barely keeping me functional. I was medicating increasingly severe symptoms with increasingly dangerous combinations of substances, chasing temporary peace while creating conditions that made peace impossible to achieve.

That's when my heart started screaming at me—literally, physically, through palpitations and chest pain that could no longer be ignored or attributed to anxiety or stress or normal responses to difficult circumstances.

I'd be sitting on my friend's couch, scrolling mindlessly through social media in an attempt to quiet my racing thoughts, when my heart would suddenly start hammering against my ribs as if it were trying to escape from my chest. The first time it happened, I was convinced I was having a heart attack, with pain radiating down my left arm, shortness of breath, and dizziness that made the room tilt and spin in ways suggesting a serious medical emergency rather than psychological crisis.

My best friend, who worked as a nurse at one of the local hospitals, took one look at my symptoms and threw me into a cold shower, both of us terrified that I was experiencing cardiac arrest at thirty-seven years old. The shock of ice-cold water against my overheated skin provided temporary relief, but the underlying condition that was causing these episodes remained unaddressed and was actually getting worse with each passing week.

My heart continued its rebellion against the toxic lifestyle I'd been maintaining, insisting on being heard above the noise of my psychological defenses and chemical numbing strategies. I'd wake up gasping for air, panic attacks in full swing that felt indistinguishable from heart attacks, jumping into cold showers to shock my nervous system back to some semblance of normal functioning.

The icy water would provide momentary relief by overwhelming my sensory system with one intense sensation that temporarily overrode the electrical storm of anxiety and panic coursing through my body. But the relief was always short-lived—the panic would resume within minutes of stepping out of the shower, leaving me shivering and still fundamentally fucked up, just with the added discomfort of being soaking wet and freezing cold.

PILLS INSTEAD OF HELP

At this point, my relationship with pharmaceuticals had expanded far beyond my HIV medication to include anxiety drugs, depression medication, ADHD treatment, and anything else a doctor would prescribe to address the symptoms I was experiencing. Any pill that promised to drown out the noise in my head, I'd accept without question, grateful for scientific interventions that didn't require emotional vulnerability or therapeutic processing.

The irony wasn't lost on me, at least during my more self-aware moments, that I, who had dismissed therapy as weakness and cultural betrayal, had no hesitation about pharmaceutical solutions to psychological problems. Pills were concrete, medical, lacking the stigma of talking about feelings or admitting to emotional complexity that couldn't be managed through willpower and determination.

My medicine cabinet became a chemical arsenal against my own consciousness, a collection of compounds designed to alter, suppress, or redirect the internal experience I couldn't tolerate. I followed dosage instructions with religious precision while simultaneously undermining their effectiveness with alcohol and recreational drugs, a contradiction my mind somehow managed to justify through increasingly twisted logic.

The medications were supposed to help me function normally, but I was using them as yet another layer of numbing on top of the alcohol and cocaine that were already compromising my system's ability to regulate itself naturally. Instead of creating stability, I was creating a complex chemical dependency that required constant management and adjustment to maintain even basic equilibrium.

I was on a one-way train to self-destruction, momentum building with each poor decision, each avoided emotion, each denied truth about the severity of my condition. The train had left the station so long ago that I couldn't remember boarding it—couldn't recall a time when this trajectory toward complete collapse was not my accepted reality.

Sometimes I caught glimpses of alternate routes—-moments of genuine connection with my partner that reminded me what love felt like, brief periods of sobriety that brought unexpected clarity about my situation, and rare instances of creative fulfillment that temporarily silenced the critical voices in my head. But these instances were only scenery passing through the window of a vehicle I couldn't figure out how to stop or redirect.

The combination of prescription medications, alcohol, and illegal substances created a perfect storm of chemical chaos that made rational decision-making nearly impossible. Each substance altered the affect of others, creating unpredictable interactions that left me feeling either completely numb or overwhelmingly anxious, with very little middle ground where normal human emotions and responses were accessible.

My body was trying to adapt to constantly changing chemical conditions while simultaneously processing the psychological trauma I was refusing to address through appropriate therapeutic channels. The result was a system in complete overload, sending increasingly desperate distress signals that I kept interpreting as evidence that I needed more medication—rather than an entirely different approach to healing.

DREAMS OF NOT WAKING UP

As the panic attacks grew more frequent and the heart palpitations became a daily occurrence I could no longer dismiss as stress or caffeine sensitivity, I began having recurring dreams that felt more like peaceful visions than the nightmares that had plagued me for months. In these dreams, I simply didn't wake up in the morning—not dramatically, not violently—but quietly, gently, like slipping into a deeper sleep that never required returning to consciousness.

These weren't typical anxiety dreams or the kind of death-focused nightmares that usually accompany severe depression and suicidal ideation. They carried a strange serenity, an alluring quietness that felt like the ultimate relief from the constant noise that had taken over my waking hours. In the dream space where I didn't wake up, all the struggle finally ended—the financial pressure, the job instability, the relationship tensions, the family rejection, the internal war between who I was and who I thought I should be.

Most significantly, in these dreams the noise finally stopped. The constant critical commentary that ran through my head from the moment I opened my eyes until I lost consciousness each night—all of it simply ceased. The exhausting effort of maintaining various personas for different audiences, the hypervigilance required to navigate a world that felt fundamentally hostile to my existence, the performance of wellness while drowning internally—all of it was revealed as optional rather than mandatory, something I could simply choose to stop doing.

The idea of peaceful non-existence was becoming increasingly appealing—not because I wanted to die, but because the alternative—living with such relentless inner chaos and outer instability—felt unsustainable. "No one will miss a failure like me," I'd think during those hazy moments between sleep and waking, when the death-dream still clung to me like morning mist and returning to consciousness felt more like punishment than opportunity.

The thought wasn't dramatic or self-pitying, but a matter-of-fact assessment of what I perceived as reality. I'd failed at maintaining employment, failed at building financial stability, failed at being the kind of partner my boyfriend deserved, failed at meeting my family's expectations, failed at managing my mental health without professional help. The evidence felt overwhelming: the world would function just fine without me.

What I didn't realize then—couldn't, given the chemical haze and psychological distortion I was under—was that these dreams and thoughts weren't accurate assessments of my worth or realistic predictions of how others would respond to my absence. They were symptoms of severe depression, signs of a nervous system so overwhelmed that death began to feel like a reasonable solution to problems that actually had other solutions I couldn't see.

My body was staging an intervention when my mind couldn't—producing physical symptoms too severe to ignore or rationalize as normal stress. The heart palpitations, the panic attacks, the dreams of non-existence—these weren't separate issues, but different expressions of the same desperate message: this path leads to real death, not just metaphorical, and immediate course correction is required for survival.

But I interpreted these signals as further evidence of my fundamental brokenness rather than as my system's attempt to save itself. Instead of recognizing the physical symptoms as messages from a self still fighting for life—despite my conscious mind's growing resignation—I took them as proof that I was defective at the most basic biological level—that even my own body was failing me when I needed it most.

I FINALLY LISTENED

My heart was screaming at me louder every day through physical symptoms too severe to dismiss as anxiety, stress, or normal responses to life's challenges. I lived in constant fear that the next panic attack might actually be a heart attack—that the chest pain and shortness of breath signaled a genuine cardiac emergency rather than psychological crisis.

Death felt closer than I'd ever imagined possible, and honestly, after multiple attempts at trying to end my own life during my darkest periods, I never thought I'd make it to forty. That milestone seemed foreign to men like me, like longevity was a privilege reserved for those who'd faced different circumstances and made better choices along the way.

The men in my family, in my culture, weren't designed for old age. We burned bright and fast, disappearing in flashes of self-destruction that were romanticized as passion or intensity rather than seen as the tragic waste of human potential they were. Forty felt like an impossible aspiration, fifty seemed pure fantasy, and anything beyond that wasn't even worth considering.

Then one day, the love of my life approached me and delivered what felt like both an ultimatum and a lifeline, depending on how I chose to respond to it.

"You need to get help," he said, his voice steady but his eyes betraying the cost of this confrontation—the emotional toll of watching someone you love systematically destroy themselves while refusing to acknowledge it. "I can't do this anymore, and I feel like you might die."

Those words hit me harder than any heart palpitation or panic attack had managed to do. This wasn't a medical professional explaining the potential consequences of my lifestyle choices or family members expressing generic concern about my well-being. This was the person who knew me most intimately, who had witnessed my daily deterioration for months, telling me plainly that he believed I was in mortal danger.

Backhanded, loud, and direct, like the dramatic confrontations in the telenovelas I grew up watching—when the protagonist finally faces the truth they've been avoiding for fifteen episodes, when denial is impossible because someone who loves them refuses to enable it any longer.

When those words came from my partner—the same one I had tested anniversary after anniversary with questions about whether he was tired of me yet—they pierced defenses that had withstood every other form of intervention or persuasion. This wasn't a stranger making clinical observations about my condition; it was someone who had chosen to love me despite my best efforts to prove I wasn't worth loving.

SEVEN YEARS OF PATIENCE

Seven years. Seven years of his patience, his hope, his stubborn belief in some version of me I couldn't see or access, but that he insisted was real and worth fighting for. Seven years of watching me self-destruct in cycles, picking up the pieces when I let him, loving someone who couldn't love himself and seemed determined to prove that love was impossible to sustain.

Seven years of him being the stable one while I created chaos, employed while I sabotaged every job opportunity, optimistic while I sank deeper into depression and addiction. Seven years of making excuses for my behavior to friends and family, covering for my absences and failures, maintaining hope when I had abandoned it entirely.

There was a finality in his voice that had never been there before, a boundary that felt qualitatively different from previous expressions of concern or frustration. This wasn't a negotiation or a plea or an attempt to change my behavior through emotional manipulation. It was a statement of fact: get professional help or lose the most important relationship in your life.

The ultimatum was delivered with love, not anger, but it was an ultimatum, nonetheless. He wasn't threatening to leave as a way to control my choices; he was simply acknowledging that he couldn't keep participating in my self-destruction, that watching me die slowly was more than he could bear, and that his own mental health required boundaries around what he would and wouldn't witness.

That was my wake-up call—not the heart palpitations or the panic attacks or the dreams of not waking up, but the realization that my refusal to seek help was about to cost me the one person who had consistently shown me what unconditional love looked like, even when I couldn't return it.

Time to man up and do something about it—or he's gone. The thought of losing him—the one constant in my increasingly unstable life, the one person who had seen me at my absolute worst and somehow still found something worth staying for—created terror more immediate and motivating than any of the physical symptoms I'd been experiencing.

So that's what I did. I got help. Not because I suddenly believed I deserved it or because the cultural programming about therapy being for weak people had magically disappeared, but because losing him felt like a fate worse than the temporary discomfort of admitting I needed professional intervention.

FINDING HELP

There are so many resources available for queer people that we shouldn't take for granted, especially in cities like Salt Lake City where LGBTQ+ organizations have worked for decades to create support systems for people exactly like me. I picked up my laptop and started searching for help with the same desperate intensity I'd once applied to finding dealers or drinking partners.

The Utah LGBTQ+ Center directed me to several local resources, and through what felt like divine intervention—or the universe finally deciding to throw me a bone—I found him: the therapist who would guide me not just away from self-destruction, but toward something resembling authentic healing and sustainable recovery.

Finding someone who was also queer felt essential—not just preferred, but necessary for the kind of work I suspected

I'd need to do. My life up to that point hadn't just been difficult—it was specifically complicated by the intersection of being gay, Latino, HIV-positive, and burdened with family rejection, cultural shame, and the unique trauma of existing at multiple points of marginalization simultaneously.

I couldn't bear the thought of having to explain gay culture to someone who would see my experiences through an outsider's lens—of having to define the dynamics of chosen family, unpack the role of HIV stigma in relationships, explain how substance use functions differently in queer communities, or describe the complexity of coming out in traditional Latino families. I needed someone who wouldn't need footnotes or explanations for the life I'd lived.

More than that, I needed someone who could hear the full, unvarnished truth without flinching—without that subtle widening of eyes that betrays unfamiliarity or judgment. Someone who wouldn't pathologize my sexuality or reduce my struggles to clichés about dramatic gay men or troubled people of color. Someone who understood that my problems weren't because I was gay, but because of how the world had treated me for being gay.

And he didn't disappoint. I remember sitting in his office during our first session, hesitant as hell despite my desperate need for help, listing every medication I was taking like a confession to a priest who might grant absolution or deliver judgment depending on my level of honesty.

I rattled them off like a pharmaceutical inventory—HIV antiretrovirals that I'd been taking for over a decade, anxiety medications that barely touched the edge of my panic, sleep aids that provided a few hours of unconsciousness before the nightmares resumed, depression pills that hadn't made any noticeable impact on my mood, ADHD treatment that was supposed to help with focus but mostly just made me feel more agitated.

Each medication felt like evidence of some perceived failing, some part of me that needed chemical correction just to function at a baseline level that other people seemed to achieve naturally. I expected the familiar medical dismissal I'd encountered before—that slight professional glaze of distance suggesting my problems were routine and manageable rather than complex and urgent.

Instead, he nodded with recognition that felt personal rather than clinical—like he'd worked with people carrying similar pharmaceutical loads and understood the desperation that drives someone to accept multiple chemical solutions rather than confronting the underlying causes.

I also told him about my heart issues—how I'd seen multiple doctors, done all the tests, and been told my heart was physically healthy in every cardiac evaluation. The chest pain and palpitations seemed to be anxiety-related rather than signs of actual heart disease. I expected him to minimize these symptoms or dismiss them as "just" psychological, as if psychological pain were somehow less real or urgent than physical suffering.

Instead, he asked thoughtful questions—when the symptoms were worst, what triggered them, how long they'd been happening, and what I'd tried to manage them. He treated my body's distress as legitimate data, rather than inconvenient side effects of emotional problems that should be ignored or suppressed.

THE PROZAC QUESTION

When I told him my doctor was pushing Prozac for my heart palpitations, he didn't jump to endorse it or shut it down. I thought I knew about psychiatric meds from working in pharmacy, but what I really knew was the stigma—the cultural bullshit that said taking pills meant you were weak, broken, unable to handle life like a real man.

"Look," I said, the words feeling like I was handing him a loaded gun, "I'll bring my guard down and trust you. If you think I should take it, I will. But I need your actual opinion about whether I truly need medication right now."

That admission was fucking enormous. Saying I'd consider psychiatric drugs, that I'd trust someone else's judgment about my brain, that maybe I couldn't white-knuckle my way through this alone anymore.

For someone raised to suffer in silence, to handle internal struggles without involving outside help, this wasn't just medical consultation—it was a betrayal of everything I'd been taught about manhood and strength.

His response floored me. No immediate prescription pad, no dismissive wave-off. He wanted to understand my experience—not just the symptoms I reported, but what they meant to me, how they fit into the story I'd built about myself.

"What do you think your heart is trying to tell you?" he asked.

No one had ever suggested my symptoms might mean something beyond malfunction—that my panic might be communication rather than dysfunction to suppress, that my body's rebellion against the lifestyle I'd been living might actually be intelligent rather than arbitrary misfiring.

That question cracked something open—the possibility that my body was trying to save me, not betray me; that my symptoms were information, not inconvenience; that healing might require listening to what my system was screaming rather than silencing it with medication.

THE FIRST CRACK

That first session cracked something in me—not dramatically, but enough to create a hairline fracture in the fortress I'd built around my inner life. I left with questions I hadn't allowed myself to consider: What if my heart palpitations weren't anxiety but a nervous system pushed beyond capacity, demanding attention? What if my insomnia wasn't depression but my psyche refusing to rest until certain truths were acknowledged? What if my job instability wasn't self-sabotage but unconscious wisdom protecting me from environments misaligned with who I truly was?

Transformation wasn't immediate. I still fought the process, minimized symptoms, and reached for familiar numbing instead of facing the unfamiliar terrain of genuine vulnerability. But something had shifted—a door had opened that couldn't fully close, a perspective quietly challenging the certainties I'd built my life around.

The weeks that followed brought more sessions, more questions, more reluctant revelations about the depth of pain I'd been carrying and the elaborate strategies I'd developed to avoid feeling it. The journey wasn't linear but spiraling, like an archaeological excavation revealing new layers of truth with each careful brushstroke.

My therapist didn't push or rush but remained steadily present, offering neither rescue nor judgment—something rarer: genuine witness to whatever I was experiencing.

What began as crisis intervention gradually evolved into something more profound. Between discussions of panic attacks and medication options, a deeper conversation emerged: Who am I beneath all the adaptations?

What pain have I been running from? What might life look like if it weren't governed by fear and shame?

DISCOVERING EMDR

About a month in, my therapist introduced something called EMDR—Eye Movement Desensitization and Reprocessing. When he first explained it, I thought it sounded like the biggest load of new-age bullshit I'd ever heard.

"You're going to have me follow your finger with my eyes and that's supposed to fix decades of trauma? What's next, crystal healing and sage burning?" I asked.

But I was desperate enough to try anything that didn't involve more pills or explaining to my family why I needed professional help.

"I know it sounds weird," he said, completely unfazed. "But there's solid science behind it. Your brain has a natural way of processing traumatic memories, but sometimes that system gets stuck. The eye movements help activate both sides of your brain so it can finish processing things that got frozen in time."

He explained that trauma memories are stored differently than regular ones—that they can feel like they're happening in the present even when they're decades old, and that my nervous system might be reacting to current situations as if they were life-threatening because of unprocessed experiences from my past.

"You've had panic attacks that feel like heart attacks, but every medical test shows your heart is fine. Your body is having a real response to something—just not what's happening right now. It's what happened back then that never got fully processed."

The idea that my physical symptoms weren't random malfunctions but intelligent responses to unresolved trauma was revolutionary. My anxiety and panic weren't defects—they were protective mechanisms still running in the background like computer programs that couldn't be shut down.

THE FIRST SESSION

The first time we actually did EMDR, I was skeptical as hell but curious enough to follow instructions. He had me think about a specific memory—not the worst trauma, but something manageable that still caused distress. I chose my father screaming at me when I was eight, calling me weak and pathetic for crying when he'd hit me.

"Rate how disturbing this feels on a scale of one to ten," he said. Seven, I told him. The memory felt electric, charged with the same shame and terror I'd experienced as a child, like it was happening right then instead of thirty years ago.

He held up his finger about eighteen inches from my face. "Just follow my finger with your eyes. Don't try to make anything happen."

I followed his finger moving slowly left to right while holding the memory in my mind. At first, I felt ridiculous—like some weird hypnosis bullshit that couldn't possibly help. But after thirty seconds, something shifted.

The memory was still there, but different—less immediate, less overwhelming. My father's furious face started to feel more like a photograph than live-action replay. The sensations in my body—tight chest, racing heart, urge to run—began to settle.

"What are you noticing?"

"It feels . . . less intense. Like it's further away somehow."

We did several more rounds, and with each one the memory continued to shift. New images surfaced—memories of my abuelito holding me after my father had been particularly cruel, moments when I'd felt protected and loved despite the chaos. The child in the memory started to feel less alone, less defenseless.

By the end, when he asked me to rate the disturbance level, it had dropped from seven to three. The memory was still sad, still unfortunate, but it no longer felt like a live wire in my nervous system—something that *had* happened to me, not something *still* happening to me.

"How is that possible?" I asked, genuinely amazed. "Thirty minutes ago, thinking about that memory made me want to hide under my desk. Now it just feels like a sad story about my childhood."

THE DEEPER WORK

Over the following months, we used EMDR to process layers of trauma I'd been carrying since childhood., the constant fear of my father's rage, the shame and rejection when I came out, the devastating loss of my abuelito, years of being told I was broken and wrong and too much.

Each session revealed how these experiences had been living in my body, fueling the chronic anxiety and hypervigilance that had been my constant companions for decades. The heart palpitations weren't random—they were my nervous system screaming *danger*, because it had learned that being different, being vulnerable, being authentically myself was unsafe.

What amazed me most was how physical the healing process was. I'd expected therapy to be all talking and analyzing, but EMDR involved my whole body. During sessions, I'd feel sensations moving through me—warmth, tingling, sometimes trembling as my nervous system released tension it had been holding for years.

"Trauma lives in the body," my therapist explained. "You can't think your way out of it. You have to feel your way through it."

Bilateral stimulation wasn't just helping my brain process memories—it was helping my body discharge trapped energy that had been keeping me in constant fight-or-flight mode. For the first time in my adult life, I started understanding what actual relaxation felt like, not just chemical numbness disguised as peace.

My biggest breakthrough came when we targeted the core belief driving all my self-sabotage: I am not worthy of love. It wasn't just some negative thought I could logic my way out of—it was a cellular conviction, programmed through years of rejection and conditional acceptance that had shaped how I moved through the world.

EMDR helped me trace this belief back to where it started and actually feel the kid who'd internalized the message that he was fundamentally flawed. But I also accessed resources I'd forgotten existed—memories of my abuelito's unconditional love, moments when I'd felt truly seen and valued, glimpses of my own strength and resilience that trauma had buried so deep I'd stopped believing they were real.

Processing bad memories was only half the work—integrating the good ones mattered just as much, letting healing experiences carry equal weight in my nervous system instead of always defaulting to the trauma. My brain started developing new neural pathways that could hold complexity: I could acknowledge trauma while also recognizing my inherent worth, feel pain while accessing my capacity for joy.

HOW EMDR CHANGED EVERYTHING

Healing trauma isn't about forgetting what happened or pretending it didn't affect you. It's about changing your relationship to those experiences, so they become part of your story rather than the whole story—informing your wisdom rather than dictating your choices.

The memories were still there—I could recall every detail of my father's rage, my family's rejection, the losses that had shaped my early life—but they no longer had an electrical charge that sent me into panic or self-destruction. They felt like past experiences that had happened to me rather than current experiences happening to me.

My nervous system began to recalibrate. The constant hypervigilance that had been my default for decades started to relax. I could be in relationships without constantly testing them for signs of impending abandonment. I could take risks without assuming they'd inevitably lead to failure.

The heart palpitations that had been terrorizing me for months began to subside. My body was no longer screaming warnings about dangers that existed only in traumatized memories. I could feel my chest expand with full breaths for the first time in years.

Most importantly, I began reclaiming parts of myself buried beneath protective armor. The creativity shut down by shame began to resurface. Sensitivity, once pathologized as weakness, revealed itself as a gift. The emotional expressiveness labeled as "too much" became a source of connection rather than isolation.

My relationship began to heal when I stopped projecting trauma onto present-moment reality. I could receive love without immediately questioning it. I could share authentic feelings without fearing they'd be too much to handle.

The self-sabotage cycles that had been destroying every opportunity began to break down. I started recognizing early warning signs—familiar thoughts and sensations that preceded destructive choices—and I had tools to interrupt the pattern before it gained momentum.

THE REAL WORK BEGINS

After months of EMDR sessions, my therapist taught me gentle practices I could do at home. He was clear that the heavy lifting needed professional supervision—the complex trauma I'd been carrying required trained guidance to process safely—but there were techniques that could help me manage daily stress between sessions.

"What I'm going to teach you isn't a replacement for our work together. Think of it as maintenance, like brushing your teeth. These practices will help you stay regulated day-to-day, but when big stuff comes up, you bring it here."

The at-home techniques were gentle versions of the bilateral stimulation we used in sessions—simple eye movements, tapping exercises, and breathing practices that helped my nervous system stay balanced when old triggers arose.

But the real gift wasn't just the techniques themselves; it was understanding that healing was possible, that trauma responses weren't permanent traits of my personality but learned patterns that could be unlearned. For the first time in my life, I had hope that I could be different, that I could break the generational cycles passed down through my family.

The work was far from over. There would be setbacks, moments when old patterns resurfaced, times when I'd still reach for familiar coping mechanisms instead of facing difficult feelings directly. But now I had a foundation: tools that actually worked, and, most importantly, a relationship with a therapist who understood not just the clinical aspects of trauma but the cultural and spiritual dimensions of healing.

LEARNING TO TEND MY OWN WOUNDS

After several months of professional EMDR sessions, I started feeling like I'd learned a foreign language—the language of my own nervous system. I could recognize when old trauma was being activated, feel the difference between past pain and present reality, and sense when my body was trying to tell me something important.

But I was also becoming dependent on those weekly sessions in ways that felt familiar and uncomfortable. Every time stress built up during the week, I'd think, "I'll deal with this on Thursday in therapy." Every time an old trigger was activated, I'd white-knuckle it until my next appointment. I was outsourcing my emotional regulation to someone else, which felt too much like the old patterns of looking for external salvation that had gotten me into trouble before.

My therapist noticed this dependency developing before I did.

"You're getting really good at this work," he said during one session. "How would you feel about learning some techniques you could use at home between our sessions?"

My first reaction was panic. The idea of doing this work without professional supervision felt like being asked to perform surgery on myself with a butter knife. What if I accessed something too big to handle? What if I opened a door I couldn't close? What if I fucked up and made everything worse?

There was also something appealing about the possibility of not being completely helpless between sessions—of having some tools I could reach for when old patterns resurfaced. The dependent part of me wanted to stay protected in the therapeutic container forever, but the part that was healing wanted autonomy, some capacity to tend my own wounds when they inevitably reopened.

"I'm scared I'll do it wrong," I admitted.

"That's exactly why we're going to start small," he said. "What I'm going to teach you isn't the deep trauma processing we do here—think of it more like emotional first aid. Simple techniques for managing daily stress and staying regulated when old stuff tries to hijack your system."

He explained that I wouldn't be learning full EMDR sessions but gentler, EMDR-inspired practices to help me process smaller stresses before they accumulated into overwhelming anxiety. Like the difference between treating a paper cut and performing major surgery—both valuable but requiring very different levels of training and support.

"The goal isn't to replace our work together," he clarified. "It's to give you some tools for the spaces between sessions, to help you stay connected to this healing process even when you're not in this room."

That resonated with something deep in me—the part that had always needed to feel capable of taking care of myself, even while accepting help from others. Growing up in a chaotic household had taught me early that my survival often depended on my ability to self-soothe and self-regulate when the adults around me were too overwhelmed to provide stability.

But I'd swung too far toward complete self-reliance, convinced that needing help was weakness and that I should be able to handle everything alone. Learning to accept professional support had been revolutionary, but now I needed to find a middle ground—accepting help while also developing genuine self-care skills.

"What would this look like?" I asked.

"Simple bilateral stimulation techniques you can use for daily stress management," he said. "Eye movements, tapping exercises, breathing practices that can help your nervous system stay balanced when triggers try to activate. Nothing dramatic, nothing that accesses major trauma—just tools for emotional maintenance."

The word "maintenance" helped. I could think of it like learning to change my own oil instead of taking my car to the mechanic for every minor issue—still bringing the big problems to the professionals but developing competence for basic upkeep.

Over the next few sessions, he taught me these gentler techniques, repeatedly emphasizing the importance of staying within my window of tolerance, stopping immediately if anything felt too intense, and understanding these practices as supplements to professional work rather than replacements.

"Your nervous system is already learning to trust the healing process," he said. "These practices will help you stay connected to that trust even when you're not in therapy."

What I didn't expect was how empowering it felt to have these tools—not because they made me completely self-sufficient, as I still needed and valued my professional sessions, but because they gave me some agency in my own healing process. Instead of feeling like a passive recipient of therapeutic intervention, I became an active participant in my own recovery.

The first time I used the techniques at home during a stressful moment and felt my nervous system actually calm down, I almost cried with relief. It wasn't that the technique was magic—it was that I had successfully taken care of myself when I might otherwise have spiraled into old patterns of panic or self-destruction.

I was learning that healing wasn't something that happened only in a therapist's office—it was something I could participate in, cultivate, and maintain in my daily life. The professional sessions provided the foundation and guidance, but these at-home practices helped me build a sustainable relationship with my own nervous system.

But my therapist's warnings about safety and limitations stayed with me. These weren't parlor tricks or quick fixes—they were tools that required respect, boundaries, and a clear understanding of when professional help was necessary. Like any powerful medicine, they required thoughtfulness and careful use.

"Think of yourself as learning to be a really good friend to your nervous system," he said. "You're not trying to be its therapist—you're just learning how to offer it comfort and support when it's having a hard time."

That metaphor stuck with me. I wasn't trying to replace professional care with DIY healing—I was learning how to be a compassionate companion to myself between sessions, offering my system the kind of gentle attention and care I was learning to receive from others.

The techniques he taught me were deceptively simple, but that simplicity made them accessible for daily use. No complex protocols or elaborate setups—just gentle ways of working with my body's natural healing capacity when stress threatened to overwhelm me.

"Remember," he said as I prepared to try these practices on my own, "the goal isn't to fix everything or process major trauma at home. It's to stay connected to your healing and maintain the progress we're making here. When big stuff comes up—and it will—you bring it back to this room."

I left that session with a sense of cautious excitement, carrying these new tools like treasures. Not because they would solve all my problems, but because they represented a different relationship with my own capacity for healing—one that honored both my need for professional support and my growing ability to care for myself with wisdom and compassion.

For the first time since beginning therapy, I felt like I was becoming not just a recipient of healing but a participant, learning to tend my own wounds with the same gentleness and patience my therapist had shown me. It was time to discover what these simple practices could teach me about befriending my own nervous system.

SIMPLE AT-HOME EMDR PRACTICE

CRITICAL WARNING: True EMDR therapy should only be practiced under the supervision of a certified facilitator—I can't stress this enough. What I'm sharing here are gentler, EMDR-inspired techniques that can safely introduce you to this powerful modality without you losing your shit or triggering a crisis. These practices will give you a taste of the transformative potential while staying in a safe zone for solo practice.

UNDERSTANDING EMDR

EMDR stands for Eye Movement Desensitization and Reprocessing. It's a therapy that uses bilateral stimulation—usually eye movements—to help your brain process traumatic memories and reduce their emotional charge. Think of it as helping your brain digest experiences that got stuck in your system.

Important Prerequisites Before You Begin:

- You must be in good physical and mental health
- No history of severe mental illness, seizures, or cardiovascular issues
- Not pregnant or taking medications that affect consciousness
- Have a completely private space where you won't be interrupted
- Someone available by phone if you need support
- Clear understanding that if anything feels overwhelming, you STOP immediately

Basic EMDR-Inspired Practice (10-15 minutes maximum)

Setup:

- Lie down or sit comfortably with good back support
- Have water, tissues, and a journal nearby
- Set a timer so you're not watching the clock
- Tell a trusted person when you're doing this practice

The Simple Eye Movement Technique:

1. Think of a mildly distressing memory or current stress (NOT major trauma)
2. Rate how disturbing it feels from 1-10 (start with 3-5 level issues)
3. Hold your finger about 12 inches from your face
4. Follow your finger slowly left to right with your eyes while thinking about the issue
5. Do this for 30 seconds, then pause and notice what comes up
6. Repeat 4-6 times, checking in with yourself between sets

Alternative Bilateral Stimulation Methods:

- **Butterfly Hug:** Cross arms over chest, alternately tap shoulders
- **Knee Tapping:** Sit and alternately tap left and right knees
- **Audio Bilateral:** Listen to music that moves between left and right ears

What May Happen:

- Images, feelings, or thoughts shift or change
- You feel temporary increases in emotion
- Physical sensations arise (tingling, warmth, tension release)
- Insights or new perspectives emerge
- Sometimes nothing dramatic happens—that's also normal

PROCESSING CURRENT STRESS (WEEK 1-2)

Daily Stress EMDR:

- Use this for work stress, relationship tensions, daily anxiety
- Follow the basic technique above
- Focus on one specific stressful situation at a time
- Notice how the stress feels in your body before and after

Example Issues to Start With:

- Anxiety about upcoming events
- Irritation with specific people
- Work-related stress
- Minor conflicts or misunderstandings
- General worry or restlessness

EMOTIONAL REGULATION PRACTICE (WEEK 3-4)

For Overwhelming Emotions:

1. When you feel intense emotion, don't try to stop it
2. Use bilateral stimulation while feeling the emotion
3. Let the feeling move through you rather than fighting it

4. Notice how the intensity changes with the eye movements
5. Continue until the emotion feels more manageable

Body-Based EMDR:

1. Focus on physical sensations (tight chest, clenched jaw, etc.)
2. Use bilateral stimulation while breathing into these areas
3. Let your body release tension naturally
4. Don't force anything, just observe and allow

CHILDHOOD WOUND HEALING (MONTH 2+)

ONLY attempt this if you're stable and have support available

Gentle Childhood Memory Work:

1. Start with mildly difficult childhood memories (NOT severe trauma)
2. Use the basic EMDR technique while thinking about the memory
3. Send love and protection to your younger self
4. Imagine adult you comforting child you
5. Stop if anything feels too intense

Inner Child Dialogue:

1. After bilateral stimulation, write in your journal as your child self
2. Then respond as your adult self
3. Keep this conversation going for 10-15 minutes
4. End with affirmations of love and protection

ADVANCED INTEGRATION (MONTH 3+)

Family Pattern Processing:

1. Think about repeating family patterns you want to change
2. Use bilateral stimulation while holding the pattern in awareness
3. Ask yourself: "What does this pattern serve? What would I prefer instead?"
4. Let insights emerge naturally without forcing them

Future Visioning:

1. Use EMDR while imagining your healed future self
2. See yourself healthy, happy, and whole
3. Let this positive vision integrate through bilateral stimulation
4. Notice resistance and work with it gently

SAFETY GUIDELINES

STOP if You Experience:

- Severe emotional overwhelm that doesn't subside
- Dissociation or feeling disconnected from reality
- Flashbacks to traumatic events
- Panic attacks or physical distress
- Feeling unsafe or out of control

Grounding Techniques When Needed:

- 5-4-3-2-1: Name 5 things you see, 4 you hear, 3 you touch, 2 you smell, 1 you taste
- Cold water on face and hands

- Deep breathing with longer exhales
- Physical movement (e.g. walk, stretch, shake)
- Call your support person

Integration After Each Session:

- Write about your experience for 5-10 minutes
- Drink water and eat something nourishing
- Be gentle with yourself for the rest of the day
- Avoid major decisions for a few hours
- Practice extra self-care

Building Your Practice:

- Week 1-2: Daily stress only, 5-10 minutes max
- Week 3-4: Add emotional regulation, 10-15 minutes max
- Month 2+: Gentle childhood work with professional backup
- Month 3+: Pattern work and integration

When This Points to Professional EMDR:

If you find this work helpful but need to go deeper, or if significant trauma material arises, seek out a certified EMDR therapist. Professional EMDR can safely process:

- Childhood abuse or neglect
- Sexual trauma
- Accidents or medical trauma
- Complex PTSD
- Severe anxiety or depression
- Addiction recovery

Remember:

- This is a gateway to professional work, not a replacement
- Start small and build slowly
- Honor your nervous system's capacity
- Healing happens in layers over time
- You deserve professional support for the deeper work

The Goal:

These practices should help you:
- Manage daily stress more effectively
- Develop emotional regulation skills
- Reduce the charge on difficult memories
- Build confidence in your ability to process feelings
- Prepare you for deeper therapeutic work when you're ready

This isn't about becoming your own therapist—it's about developing tools for emotional self-regulation while building trust in the healing process. When you're ready for deeper work, find a qualified EMDR therapist who understands your cultural background and can guide you safely through processing major trauma.

Your nervous system is wise and wants to heal. These gentle practices can help you start working with it instead of against it.

CHAPTER 4

Writing Myself Back to Me

Shadow work and EMDR were crucial to getting my healing journey off the ground. But when journaling entered the picture? Holy shit—it brought a completely different perspective to everything. It awakened a side of me that had been buried alive for years—years of repressing not just my identity, but every feeling I was too scared to explore.

Journaling became my ride-or-die companion at that point in the healing process. I would literally write about any fucking thing that came up—the bizarre dream from the night before, the way my chest seized up when I heard my father's voice on the phone, the memory that got triggered by some random stranger's cologne that smelled exactly like my abuelito's workshop. No filter, no editing, no concern for grammar or making any goddamn sense. Just raw, unprocessed thoughts flowing from my mind to paper without the usual censorship my internal critic loved to impose.

But this wasn't just therapeutic word vomit—it was an archaeological excavation of my own soul. Each page I filled revealed another layer of myself that had been buried under decades of "shoulds" and "cants " and "what will people fucking think?" The shadow work had shown me what I'd rejected about myself; EMDR had processed the trauma that created those rejections but journaling—journaling was where I actively began reclaiming those lost pieces of who I really was.

REDISCOVERING MY BURIED CREATIVITY

Slowly, writing daily, I started realizing something that knocked me on my ass: I had completely lost sight of the creativity that used to live inside me. I was all about theater throughout school—I was that theater kid, taking art classes, living for that shit. The stage had been my playground, makeup and costumes my transformation tools, and scripts and characters my escape route into possibilities way beyond the suffocating confines of my daily life.

I was even accepted to The Art Institute after high school. I remember clutching that acceptance letter in my trembling hands like it was a golden ticket to freedom—a life where I could finally be who I truly was, instead of who everyone expected me to be.

There's this one memory that captures the pure joy I felt about performing: I was in our high school's production of *Fiddler on the Roof*. During rehearsals, I'd lose myself completely in the work—learning the music, finding the character, becoming part of something bigger than my own small, suffocating world. For those few weeks, I wasn't Peter trying to be acceptable—I was someone else entirely, part of a story that mattered, contributing something that people actually wanted to see.

The night of the performance, I watched from backstage as the audience responded to our show. Real emotion, genuine connection. People seeing something beautiful in what we were offering instead of something that needed to be fixed or hidden. That feeling—of being witnessed and celebrated for expressing something true—was better than any drug I'd ever try. *Fiddler* would be my last production. I held onto that memory for years, like proof that I'd once been capable of creating something meaningful.

But right after graduation, reality hit like a fucking steamroller. My family made it clear that art school was impractical, that creativity was a hobby not a career, that I needed to get serious about real life and stop chasing fantasies. So, I did what I was told—I abandoned the one thing that had ever made me feel fully alive and spent the next twenty years trying to convince myself it didn't matter.

DREAMS CRUSHED BY FEAR

"Not enough money," my parents said when I showed them The Art Institute acceptance letter. But I could see what was really underneath that practical bullshit—pure fear that their son's artistic inclinations were just another confirmation of what they already suspected about my sexuality—another step away from the rigid masculine ideal they desperately needed me to embody.

My father didn't even try to hide his disgust. "Stop being artistic; it's not lucrative," he said—his go-to response whenever I mentioned anything creative. But it wasn't really about money: it was about control, about forcing me into a box that would make him feel safer about having a son who moved through the world differently than other boys.

My mother was subtler but equally effective. She'd sigh whenever I talked about theater or art, asking pointed questions about how I planned to "support a family" with such "hobbies." She'd mention cousins who had "grown out of" their creative phases and found "real careers." Every conversation became a slow erosion of possibility—a steady drip of messages that creativity was self-indulgent, impractical, and ultimately worthless.

What I hadn't realized until I started writing daily was how completely I had internalized their terror. It wasn't just that I'd given up on creative pursuits—I had developed a visceral aversion to them, a knee-jerk dismissal of anything that felt too expressive, too emotional, too authentically me. The boy who had once loved disappearing into characters and costumes had learned to see artistic expression as weakness, creativity as self-indulgent bullshit, imagination as a luxury he couldn't afford.

So, I adopted their broke-ass state of mind—their scarcity mentality that equated creativity with financial irresponsibility and artistic expression with selfish luxury. Over the years, I had internalized this toxic message so completely that I had forgotten I ever wanted anything beyond basic stability and security—the narrow path of acceptability that led to management positions, steady paychecks, and relationships that looked "normal" from the outside.

I became someone who dismissed artists as flaky, who rolled his eyes at "emotional" movies, who couldn't understand why anyone would waste time on "frivolous" pursuits when there were bills to pay and responsibilities to handle. I turned into my father without even realizing it—practical to the point of spiritual death, so focused on survival that I'd forgotten what it meant to actually live.

THE CRACK THAT LET LIGHT IN

But journaling cracked something wide fucking open. The act of putting pen to paper without any agenda, without any audience, without concern for productivity or purpose—it awakened something that had been dormant for decades. My handwriting, usually precise and controlled, became loose and flowing. Words poured out in configurations I'd never attempted; metaphors emerged without planning; entire pages filled with streams of consciousness that revealed truths I didn't even know I knew.

It was in those pages that I first admitted something I'd been afraid to acknowledge: I missed performing. Not the validation or applause—fuck that external bullshit—but the pure joy of inhabiting different possibilities, of exploring aspects of human experience that felt completely forbidden in my daily life. I wrote about costume shops and theater makeup, about the electric thrill of opening nights and the sacred quiet of empty stages. Emotions I hadn't allowed myself to feel for decades came spilling onto the page—grief for the artist I'd abandoned, rage at the family messages that had made creativity feel dangerous, deep longing for the expressive freedom I'd lost.

One morning, I found myself writing about colors—not practical shit like "the walls need painting," but actual fascination with how light moved through my apartment at different times of day: how the morning sun turned my coffee cup into something that belonged in a still life painting, how the blue hour just before darkness had its own particular quality of melancholy that made me want to write poetry.

I'd been living in that apartment for three years and had never fucking noticed any of this. I'd been so focused on functionality—does the coffee get me awake, do the walls keep out the weather—that I'd completely numbed myself to beauty, to the aesthetic dimension of experience that had once been my natural language.

Writing about these observations felt like remembering how to breathe after years of suffocating. The creative kid who'd been buried under layers of "practical" choices and "responsible" decisions—he was still in there, waiting patiently for permission to exist again. And by putting pen to paper every morning, I was finally giving him that permission.

FINDING MY WAY BACK HOME

Journaling didn't just give me a place to vent; it gave me a creative outlet that would eventually lead me to write this damn book. The connection wasn't immediately obvious—those early journal entries were hardly literary masterpieces, more like emergency pressure releases for psychological steam that had nowhere else to go. But something profound was happening beneath the surface: some essential part of myself was stirring back to life after being pronounced dead years ago.

I started noticing things differently. The way my partner moved through our kitchen in the morning had a rhythm to it that reminded me of choreography. Conversations with friends contained dramatic moments that would have made great scenes in plays. Even my therapy sessions had narrative arcs—setups, conflicts, resolutions—that my old theater brain recognized as good storytelling.

The world had always been full of stories and beauty and creative potential. I had just trained myself not to see it, convinced myself that noticing such things was impractical, self-indulgent, and a waste of mental energy that should be focused on more important shit. But my journal was teaching me that there was nothing more important than staying connected to what made me feel alive, what sparked my curiosity, what reminded me that existence could be more than just survival.

Writing became my way back to myself—not the self I thought I should be, not the self that would make everyone else comfortable, but the self I'd always been underneath all the performance and adaptation. The self who had stories to tell, truths to explore, and a voice that deserved to be heard.

And let me tell you: once that creative floodgate opened, there was no fucking way I was ever going to close it again.

THE BEAUTY OF WRITING LIKE SHIT

The beauty isn't in the quality of what gets written, but in the permission to write badly, to contradict yourself within the same sentence, to explore thoughts without needing to defend them or make them coherent for anyone else. My journal became the one space where I could be completely unfiltered, where the masks I wore for family, friends, partners, and employers could be set aside entirely.

In those pages, the angry part of me could rage without consequences. The grief-stricken child could sob without being told to "get over it." The creative dreamer could imagine possibilities without being reminded of practical limitations. The confused seeker could ask questions without needing immediate answers. All the fragmented aspects of myself could coexist on paper in ways they couldn't coexist in my daily life.

Most surprisingly, the creative part of me began emerging with a vengeance. After years of forcing myself into purely practical thinking, my journal became a playground for imagination. I wrote fictional scenarios, created characters who were bold enough to live authentically, and crafted dialogue for conversations I wished I could have with my family. Without realizing it, I was returning to the storytelling and character creation that had once been my greatest joy.

MORNING PAGES: MY DAILY RITUAL

The format was simple but revolutionary: stream of consciousness writing for twenty minutes every morning, ideally before the day's demands could colonize my mental space. Sometimes I wrote about dreams, sometimes about memories that surfaced during therapy, sometimes about present frustrations or future anxieties. Often I wrote about nothing at all, letting my hand move across paper until something interesting emerged from the apparent randomness.

I later discovered that Julia Cameron calls this practice "morning pages" in her book *The Artist's Way*, though I stumbled into it through therapeutic necessity rather than artistic aspiration. Three pages of longhand, stream-of-consciousness writing, first thing every morning. No editing, no censoring, no concern for quality or relevance. Just purging the mental debris that accumulates overnight, clearing space for whatever wants to emerge.

What emerged surprised me. Buried beneath decades of practical thinking and acceptable opinions were landscapes of imagination I'd forgotten existed. Metaphors began appearing in my writing—not forced literary devices but organic ways my mind made meaning from experience. The workshop became more than just a memory of my grandfather's space; it became a symbol for transformation, for seeing potential in damaged things, for the patient craft of restoration.

My HIV diagnosis, which I had carried for years as a badge of shame, began appearing in my journal entries as something more complex—not just disease but teacher, not just limitation but invitation to examine what really mattered, not just personal failure but a window into compassion for all the ways humans seek connection and sometimes find pain instead.

The panic attacks that had terrorized me for months began revealing their messages. Page after page of describing the sensations—racing heart, shortened breath, overwhelming sense of impending doom—gradually shifted my relationship to these experiences from victim to observer, from helpless sufferer to curious investigator of my own internal landscape.

DIFFERENT WAYS OF WRITING THAT SAVED MY LIFE

As my practice deepened, I discovered that different types of writing served different aspects of my healing. What started as simple morning pages evolved into a tool kit of techniques, each one offering a different doorway into self-understanding and emotional processing.

Stream of Consciousness Writing became my foundation—the raw, unfiltered download of whatever was moving through my consciousness. I'd set a timer for fifteen to twenty minutes and wrote continuously, not lifting my pen from the paper, not pausing to think or edit or make things sound good. The only rule was to keep writing, even if all I could write was "I don't know what to write" over and over until something else emerged.

This technique taught me that beneath the surface chatter of my conscious mind was a deeper well of wisdom, creativity, and truth that could only be accessed when I stopped trying to control what came out. Some of my most profound insights emerged from sessions that started with complete mental blankness, where I had to trust that something meaningful would eventually surface if I just kept my hand moving.

Dialogue with Myself happened when I encountered conflicting feelings or internal arguments. Instead of trying to resolve internal conflicts through thinking, I created conversations between different parts of my psyche.

"You can't trust anyone," the scared part would write.

"But isolation is killing us," the lonely part would respond.

"What if we tried trusting carefully, in small steps?" the wise part would suggest.

These dialogues revealed that my internal conflicts weren't problems to solve but different aspects of myself trying to be heard and understood. Instead of one voice drowning out the others, I could create space for all parts of my experience to contribute to my understanding.

Character Creation for Self-Understanding drew on my theater background. I started creating fictional characters who could embody the shit I was too scared to look at directly. I wrote stories about a gay Mexican man dealing with family rejection, but because it was "fiction," I could explore all the raw, painful territory I couldn't touch autobiographically.

These characters became vehicles for processing emotions and experiences I couldn't yet claim as my own. Through their stories, I could explore what courage looked like, what healing might feel like, what authentic relationships could become without all the baggage and fear I carried in real life.

Letters I Never Sent became crucial for processing relationships and expressing emotions that had never found their voice. I wrote letters to everyone who had hurt me, disappointed me, or failed to see me clearly—but I never sent them. The purpose wasn't communication but emotional release and clarity.

I wrote screaming, profanity-filled letters to my father about the abuse, tender letters to my abuelito expressing gratitude and ongoing love, and confused letters to God asking why everything had to be so fucking hard. I wrote letters to ex-boyfriends, to family members who had rejected me, to teachers who had dismissed my creativity, to therapists who hadn't understood my cultural background.

The power wasn't in crafting perfect messages but in finally giving voice to everything I'd been holding inside. Many of these letters dissolved old resentments simply through the act of expression, while others revealed ongoing needs that required attention in my current relationships.

MAKING PEACE WITH MY 20S

With these writing tools, I was ready to tackle the hardest material—making peace with my twenties, that decade of self-destruction that I'd spent years trying to forget or minimize. I had touched on my HIV diagnosis before, but I hadn't talked about the shit that led to that point in my life: a series of domino effects that started when my father went to prison when I was twelve.

Instead of feeling sad about his incarceration, I felt relieved—no more insults, no more getting knocked around for being flamboyant, no more walking on eggshells around his rage. High school was rough, but it is for everyone. I focused on drama and art and even had a girlfriend to keep people from asking too many questions. That situation ended badly, like all my relationships would for years afterward.

After high school, I got myself through a pharmacy tech vocational program, finished the course as fast as possible, saved all my money, and moved to San Diego with my aunt—as far as I could get from my family, or so I thought.

Just when I thought I was free, the spiral began. Years later, through painful honesty in my journal, I discovered it wasn't "bad luck" but a set of limiting beliefs and lack of self-worth that led me down a dark path of self-destruction and self-loathing.

THE BETRAYAL-LOOKING BACK

At twenty, my brother outed me to my mother in the most brutal way possible. Something I'd told him in confidence; he weaponized and made about himself. My mother's reaction was so severe she nearly had a breakdown. At that time, I wasn't surprised—how could I trust anyone in my family? The ones who should have protected me kept turning their backs on me.

Writing about this betrayal years later allowed me to process it in ways I never could have at twenty. I filled pages with the specific pain of having my truth stolen from me—about the way this violation of trust shaped my ability to be vulnerable with others for years afterward.

I wrote unsent letters to my brother, expressing the rage and hurt I'd never been able to voice directly:

You fucking coward. You took something that belonged to me—my story, my timing, my choice of when and how to tell my truth—and you made it about your discomfort. You couldn't handle carrying my secret, so you threw it back at me like a grenade—not caring who got hurt in the explosion.

Do you know what it's like to have your coming-out story stolen from you? To have someone else control the narrative of your own life? You robbed me of the chance to prepare, to choose my words, to control the timing. You turned my truth into a weapon against me.

I also wrote about understanding his motivation—how he'd probably been carrying the burden of my secret, and how his own internalized homophobia might have made my truth feel threatening to him. This understanding didn't excuse his actions, but it helped me separate his limitations from my worth.

FACING MY FATHER- LOOKING BACK

Writing about this confrontation later, I could explore it from multiple angles—the scared child who still wanted his father's approval, the angry young man who was tired of hiding, the adult who could see the limitations of both perspectives.

I wrote about walking into that house where I'd spent my childhood walking on eggshells, where his rage had been the weather that determined everyone else's mood, where I'd learned that love was conditional and safety was temporary. But this time felt different. In my journal, I wrote about those words thousands of times, approaching them from every angle, trying to understand their impact, their meaning, their lasting effect on my sense of self.

I wrote about the immediate shock, the delayed grief, the way those words would echo in my head during moments of self-doubt for years afterward. But I also wrote about the unexpected relief—finally knowing exactly where I stood, no longer having to wonder if acceptance was possible.

I could process the complexity of being rejected by someone whose approval I'd spent twenty-one years trying to earn. I could feel both the devastation and the liberation, the loss and the freedom that came with his rejection.

THE REALITY OF DISOWNMENT-LOOKING BACK

Years later, I could see my twenties for what they really were. The "bad luck" story I'd been telling myself was such bullshit, but it was easier than facing the truth that would have destroyed me if I'd understood it then: I had been living like someone who was already dead inside, taking reckless chances with my health and safety because some broken part of me believed I didn't deserve protection.

Writing about this period required tremendous self-compassion. I had to learn to approach my younger self with the same kindness I'd offer a friend going through similar trauma, rather than the harsh judgment I'd been carrying for decades.

I wrote letters to my twenty-something self, acknowledging the impossible situation he'd been placed in:

You weren't just unlucky. You were a walking suicide mission disguised as a young man trying to figure out his life. Every dangerous choice, every toxic relationship, every moment you ignored your instincts—it was all part of an unconscious death wish you didn't even know you had.

I could finally see the pattern that had been invisible at the time—how family rejection had convinced me I was fundamentally unworthy of protection, and how that belief had led to increasingly dangerous choices, confirming my unworthiness in a self-perpetuating cycle.

LOSING MICHAEL

The year after I got outed, my best friend Michael, who was thirty-two at the time, took his own life in my room in the middle of the night. Writing about this loss later allowed me to process it in ways I never could have at twenty-one, when I was too overwhelmed by my own survival to fully grieve what I had lost.

I wrote about Michael's role in my life—how he'd been my introduction to the gay community, my guide through the complexities of being queer in a hostile world, my living example that love from people who choose to show up can run deeper than any blood relation.Michael had been beautiful in a way that made people stop and stare—tall, lean, with cheekbones that belonged in fashion magazines and a smile that could light up entire rooms. But more than his physical beauty, he had this quality of genuine warmth that made everyone feel like they were the most interesting person in the world when he was talking to them.

He'd taken me under his wing when I first moved to San Diego, showing me which bars were safe, which guys to avoid, how to navigate the complex social dynamics of gay life in the early 2000s. He taught me about HIV prevention, the importance of regular testing, and how to demand respect in relationships even when the world was telling us we didn't deserve it.

But Michael was also carrying wounds I was too young and self-absorbed to fully understand: the way he'd sometimes disappear for days without explanation, the pills I'd see him taking that weren't just his HIV medication, the men he'd bring home who seemed to drain the light out of him rather than adding to it.

His death taught me about the particular vulnerabilities of gay men, especially HIV-positive gay men in the early 2000s, when stigma was still thick and treatment options were more limited. His suicide confirmed my worst fears about being gay—that we were destined for tragedy, that real love and acceptance were fairy tales meant for other people.

I could process the guilt I'd carried about missing the signs, about being too wrapped up in my own drama to see his pain. I wrote about how his death had shaped my understanding of community responsibility—about how we had to take care of each other because no one else would.

THE DIAGNOSIS THAT CHANGED EVERYTHING-LOOKING BACK

Writing about my HIV diagnosis years later allowed me to understand it not as divine punishment for being gay or the consequence of moral failure, but as what happens when someone who believes they're fundamentally worthless stops protecting themselves.

I wrote pages about the specific betrayal—how someone I'd trusted with my body had lied about something that could literally kill me. But I also wrote about my own participation in that betrayal: how my desperation for connection had led me to ignore red flags that were visible from space.

The guy was beautiful in a dangerous way—the kind of beautiful that makes you stupid, that makes you believe whatever they tell you because you want so badly for someone that gorgeous to want you back. He told me he was negative, told me he'd been tested recently, told me exactly what I needed to hear to let my guard down.

I found out later he'd been positive for years, had infected at least three other guys with the same lies, the same performance of innocence and safety. But I also had to own my part in it—how desperately I'd wanted to believe him, how my hunger for connection had overridden every safety protocol Michael had taught me.

I could explore how growing up believing I was fundamentally flawed had created a worldview where I didn't deserve protection, where my life wasn't valuable enough to safeguard carefully. The diagnosis forced me to confront my own mortality while also teaching me to value my life in ways I'd never learned to do before.

I wrote about the particular shame of being a young gay man with HIV in the early 2000s, when stigma was still thick and treatment options were more limited. But I also wrote about how the diagnosis had become a teacher, forcing me to develop a relationship with my body based on care rather than punishment, with my future based on hope rather than despair.

LETTERS OF HEALING

Journaling gave me the outlet I desperately fucking needed. I was able to write letters to my 9-year-old self and apologize for abandoning that little boy, letters to my teenage self to make peace with how I'd let things destroy me from the inside out. Writing letters and asking for forgiveness from every version of myself at every age—not just asking for forgiveness but also accepting and owning those experiences and finally, finally allowing myself to let that shit go.

The first letter I wrote was to the boy sitting on the edge of my abuelito's bed—the one who lost his safe space at nine years old and never learned how to create another fucking one. I could see him so clearly in my mind: small hands folded in his lap, eyes way too serious for his age, already learning to carry weight that didn't belong to him.

Dear Petey,

I'm sorry I left you behind like that. I'm sorry that when the world demanded I become someone harder, someone who felt less, someone more "acceptable," I abandoned you completely instead of finding a way to keep you safe while still growing up.

You deserved protection, not rejection. You deserved to have your sensitivity honored, not treated like some kind of fucking liability. I see now how you tried to get my attention for decades—through the creative dreams I kept dismissing as "impractical bullshit," through the tears I wouldn't let fall because "real men don't cry," through the gentleness I kept rejecting as weakness.

You were never the problem. The world that couldn't handle your authenticity was the problem. I'm here now, I'm listening now. It's safe to come home.

Writing those words released something I hadn't expected—not just grief for that lost child, but profound relief that he was finally being acknowledged, finally being invited back into my life after decades of exile.

THE HARDEST LETTER TO WRITE

The letter to my teenage self was harder to write because that version of me made choices I'd spent years judging the fuck out of:

Dear sixteen-year-old me,

I'm sorry I've been so goddamn ashamed of you. I'm sorry I've spent decades criticizing your desperate attempts to fit in, your girlfriend phase, your pathetic efforts to be "normal" enough to avoid rejection.

You were doing the best you could with no roadmap, no examples of how to be authentically gay in a Mexican Catholic family that would rather pretend you didn't exist than deal with your truth. You weren't weak for trying to conform—you were strategic as hell. You weren't dishonest for dating girls—you were trying to survive in a world that wanted to destroy you for being different.

I forgive you for the performance. I forgive you for the lies you told yourself and others. I forgive you for not being brave enough to come out sooner. You weren't ready, and that's perfectly fucking okay. You kept us alive until we could be ready.

That letter broke something wide open in my chest—years of brutal self-criticism, of wishing I'd been braver sooner, of judging my younger self for choices made under impossible circumstances.

THE MOST NECESSARY LETTER

The letter to my twenty-something self was perhaps the most necessary and the most painful to write:

Dear wounded twenty-something Peter,

I fucking see you. I see how much you're hurting, how lost you feel, how desperate you are for any kind of connection and acceptance. I see how Michael's death shattered your faith in the possibility of lasting love. I see how your family's rejection convinced you that you were fundamentally unlovable.

I'm not going to tell you that the destructive choices were okay—they weren't. But I understand why you made them. I understand that you were medicating pain you had no other tools to process. I understand that you were seeking connection in the only ways that felt available to someone who believed he was worthless.

The HIV diagnosis that feels like the end of everything? It's not. It's going to become a lesson, a path to deeper compassion, a way of understanding that health is something precious that requires daily attention. The shame you're carrying about your sexuality? It's going to transform into pride, into advocacy, into the foundation for helping other people break free from similar shame.

I forgive you for the self-destruction. I forgive you for the isolation. I forgive you for not knowing how to ask for help. Thank you for keeping us alive. Thank you for not giving up completely, even when everything seemed hopeless.

You matter. Your life has value. The love you're seeking exists, and you're worthy of receiving it exactly as you are.

A WEEKLY PRACTICE OF COMING HOME

Writing these letters became a weekly practice, each one addressing a different age, a different wound, a different aspect of my development that I'd learned to reject or judge harshly. I wrote to the child who was "too sensitive," to the teenager who was "too dramatic," to the young adult who was "too lost," to the man who was "too broken."

But the letters weren't just about forgiveness—they were also about integration, about inviting these rejected aspects of myself back into my current life.

I wrote to the creative child and asked what he wanted to create now:

Dear creative nine-year-old, What do you want to make now that we're finally safe? What stories are you dying to tell? What colors want to come through your hands? I'm ready to listen. I'm ready to create space for your imagination without needing it to be profitable or practical or acceptable to anyone else.

I wrote to the teenage performer and asked how he might want to express himself authentically:

Dear dramatic teenager, How do you want to take up space now? What emotions have you been suppressing that you want to express? What parts of life deserve more passion, more intensity, more authentic response? I'm ready to stop apologizing for feeling things deeply.

I wrote to the wounded young adult and asked what wisdom he'd gained from his struggles:

Dear wounded twenty-something, What did you learn about resilience that I need to remember? What survival skills developed during those dark years might serve us differently now? How can we honor the strength it took to keep going when everything seemed fucking hopeless?

"I forgive you, I thank you, and I invite you home" became the closing line of every letter. Forgiveness for the pain caused and received. Gratitude for the lessons learned and the strength developed. Invitation for these aspects to return from exile and contribute to the wholeness I was learning to embody.

UNDERSTANDING MY FAMILY'S FEAR

One of the most important insights that emerged from this letter-writing practice was understanding that my family's rejection of my creativity wasn't just about practicality or even homophobia—it was about their own relationship with dreams deferred and the harsh realities of survival.

My father wasn't a creative person in the traditional sense, but he had his own relationship with craft and skill. He was a brilliant mechanic, could diagnose car problems by sound alone, and could take apart an engine and rebuild it better than it was before. His hands were always stained with grease, but they moved with the precision of a surgeon when he worked. There was artistry in what he did, even if he'd never call it that.

But in his world, that kind of hands-on skill was survival, not self-expression. Cars broke down, and people needed them fixed to get to work, to feed their families. His talent with engines wasn't about passion or fulfillment—it was about necessity, about being useful in ways that couldn't be questioned or dismissed as frivolous.

My mother had loved to draw before marriage and children consumed all her time and energy. I discovered this when I was going through old boxes after she died, finding sketchbooks filled with portraits and landscapes that showed real talent, real vision. But she'd never mentioned this artistic side of herself to any of her children, as if acknowledging it would somehow undermine her commitment to the practical business of raising a family.

When they looked at my theater aspirations, my art classes, my acceptance letter to The Art Institute, they saw danger. Not because creativity itself was evil, but because they'd learned that pursuing anything that wasn't immediately practical was a luxury that led to hunger, to instability, to the kind of vulnerability they'd spent their lives trying to escape.

Their rejection of my artistic inclinations wasn't just about my future—it was about protecting me from what they saw as inevitable disappointment. In their experience, dreams were dangerous things that distracted you from the serious business of survival. My father could fix cars because people would always need cars fixed. My mother could cook and clean and manage a household because families would always need those services. But who needed actors? Who needed artists? And what happened to dreamers when the dreams didn't pay the bills?

Understanding this allowed me to feel compassion for their limitations while refusing to inherit them. I could honor their survival strategies while choosing differently for myself, could appreciate the harsh lessons they'd learned while developing my own approach to balancing security and creative expression.

This revelation came from writing a letter to my father that I never intended to send:

Dear Dad,

I understand now why my creativity felt so threatening to you. It wasn't because you hated art—it was because you'd learned that anything that didn't directly contribute to survival was dangerous—it was a luxury that could destroy a family if you weren't careful.

You taught me to work with my hands, to take pride in fixing broken things, to see value in useful skills. I get it now—that was your form of creativity, your way of making something better than it was before. But I'm going to take those lessons and apply them differently.

I'm going to find a way to honor both the practical wisdom you gave me and the creative spirit you couldn't afford to encourage. I'm going to prove that creativity and responsibility aren't opposites, that you can make art and still pay the bills, that dreams don't have to lead to poverty if you're smart about how you pursue them.

I forgive you for crushing my artistic dreams because I understand now that you were protecting me from what you saw as inevitable disappointment. But I also forgive myself for refusing to inherit your limitations.

COMING FULL CIRCLE

In writing myself back to wholeness, I discovered that the outlet I needed wasn't just expression but integration, not just release but reclamation. The nine-year-old who lost his abuelito, the teenager who hid his sexuality, the young adult who survived unthinkable trauma—they weren't chapters I needed to close but voices I needed to include in the choir of who I was becoming.

This practice of writing became more than therapeutic release—it became a technology for transformation, a daily ritual of returning to myself with curiosity rather than judgment. What had started as resistance to keeping a "diary" evolved into one of the most powerful healing tools in my arsenal.

The beauty of journaling isn't in crafting beautiful prose but in creating sacred space for authentic encounter with yourself. In those twenty minutes each morning—before the world can flood your thoughts with its demands and expectations—you can exist fully on the page: contradicting yourself, exploring half-formed ideas, feeling whatever wants to be felt without needing to fix or explain or justify any of it to anyone. My therapist noticed the shift before I did. "You seem more like yourself," he said one session, "like who you were when we first met—but more grounded, more whole."

He was right. Journaling didn't just excavate an authentic self buried beneath years of adaptation and performance—it created a space where all aspects of my identity could coexist. Not a new self, but an integrated one: the practical adult I'd become and the creative dreamer I'd always been.

The page became my sanctuary where integration was finally possible—where all aspects of my experience could coexist without judgment, where the wounded boy and the healing man could finally have the conversation they'd been waiting decades to have.

That spark would eventually grow into this book—into the courage to share not just struggle but strategy, not just wounds but wisdom earned through slow, patient transformation. The boy who had once dreamed of stages and costumes and stories that might transform audiences was finding his voice again—not through performance, but through authenticity; not by escaping himself, but by finally coming home to who he'd always been beneath the masks.

Writing myself back to me wasn't a destination but a daily practice—twenty minutes each morning when I could set aside the roles I played for others and simply be in conversation with my authentic self. On those pages, the creative child I'd been and the healed adult I was becoming could finally meet, could finally recognize each other, could finally collaborate on creating a life that honored both survival and expression, both safety and authenticity.

The beauty of journaling isn't in becoming a writer—though that might happen—but in becoming intimate with your own mind, in developing curiosity about your inner world, in creating sacred space for whatever wants to emerge when external pressures fall away. In those pages, between the lines of stream of consciousness rambling, healing happens one word at a time. And sometimes, if you're very lucky, you write yourself all the way back home.

SIMPLE AT-HOME JOURNALING PRACTICE

Important Note: This practice is designed to be gentle and accessible, but let's be real—sometimes shit gets intense. If heavy emotions come up, pause and use grounding techniques. Remember: healing happens at your own damn pace—not anyone else's timeline.

GETTING STARTED: YOUR SACRED SPACE

Create Your Writing Sanctuary:

- Find a quiet corner where you won't be interrupted for 20-30 minutes (tell people to fuck off if necessary)
- Use a physical notebook and pen—handwriting activates different brain pathways than typing, and there's something powerful about the physical act itself

- Choose a notebook that feels special—this is your healing container, so make it count
- Set up a consistent time to write (mornings work best, before the world's bullshit takes over your headspace)
- Have tissues and water nearby— this work can get messy

Supplies You'll Need:

- A dedicated journal (not used for grocery lists or work notes—this is sacred space)
- A pen that flows smoothly (nothing worse than fighting with a shitty pen when you're trying to process trauma)
- A timer or clock
- Tissues for emotional releases
- Optional: candle or soft music for ambiance— whatever makes you feel safe

THE BASIC PRACTICE: STREAM OF CONSCIOUSNESS

Daily Foundation (20 minutes minimum)

The "Brain Dump" Method:

- Set your timer for 20 minutes
- Put pen to paper and don't stop writing until time is fucking up
- Write whatever comes to mind—no editing, no censoring, no making it pretty
- If you can't think of anything, write "I can't think of anything" until something else emerges

- Don't worry about grammar, spelling, or making sense to anyone else
- Let your hand move across the page without thinking ahead—just let it flow

Sample Starting Prompts:

- "Right now I'm feeling..."
- "What's really on my mind is..."
- "If I could say anything without consequences, I would say..."
- "The dream I had last night was..."
- "My body is telling me..."

WEEK 1-2: BUILDING THE HABIT

Daily Practice Structure:

Morning Pages (Julia Cameron Method):

- Write 3 pages of stream of consciousness first thing in the morning
- No agenda, no purpose, just clearing the mental debris
- Think of it as emptying the dishwasher of your mind—all that accumulated crap needs to go somewhere
- Don't read what you wrote for at least a week (trust the process)

Evening Check-ins (10 minutes):

- "Today I noticed..."
- "What triggered me today was..."
- "Something I'm grateful for is..."
- "Tomorrow I want to remember..."

WEEK 3-4: DEEPER EXPLORATION

Specific Healing Prompts:

For Cultural or Family Healing:

- "The family messages I carry about being a man are..."
- "What I wish I could tell my family about who I really am is..."
- "The cultural expectations that no longer serve me are..."
- "How I want to honor my heritage while being authentic is by..."

For Self-Forgiveness:

- "I forgive myself for..."
- "The younger version of me that needs compassion is..."
- "If I could talk to my [age]-year-old self, I would say..."
- "The mistakes I made were trying to meet [this] need..."

For Trauma Processing:

- "When I think about [difficult memory], my body feels..."
- "The story I tell myself about what happened is..."
- "What that experience taught me about survival was..."
- "How I've grown since then has been by..."

ADVANCED PRACTICES (MONTH 2+)

Letter-Writing Technique:

Write letters to different aspects of yourself or others—this is where the real magic happens.

To Your Younger Self:

- "Dear 9-year-old me, I want you to know..."
- "Dear teenager who was so fucking scared, I see you..."
- "Dear young adult making survival choices, I understand..."

To Family Members (never to be sent—this is for YOU):

- "Dear Mom, what I never got to tell you..."
- "Dear Dad, what I needed from you was..."
- "Dear Brother, when you outed me, it affected me..."

To Your Future Self:

- "Dear healed version of me, I'm working toward..."
- "Dear wise, elder self, what do I need to know?"

Dialogue Journaling:

Create conversations between different sides of yourself:

You: "I'm scared to be vulnerable in my relationship."
Wise Self: "What are you really afraid will happen?"
You: "That he'll see I'm broken and leave."

Inner Child: "That's what always happened before."
You: "But what's different now?"

Continue for 10-15 minutes, letting each "voice" respond naturally. Don't overthink it—just let the conversation flow.

SPECIALIZED TECHNIQUES

Somatic Journaling (Body-Based):

- Start by scanning your body from head to toe
- Write about physical sensations without trying to fix them
- "My chest feels tight when I think about . . ."
- "The tension in my shoulders is telling me . . ."
- "When I breathe deeply, I notice . . ."

Dream Work:

- Keep your journal by your bedside for immediate dream recording
- Write dreams in present tense: e.g., "I am walking through . . ."
- Don't interpret the dreams immediately—just record the raw material
- Look for patterns over time

Gratitude with Depth:

Move beyond simple gratitude lists to something more meaningful:
- "I'm grateful for [struggle] because it taught me . . ."
- "The person who challenged me most gave me the gift of . . ."

- "Even my worst day contained this small moment of grace..."

PROCESSING GUIDELINES

When Difficult Emotions Arise

Stay Present and:

- Keep writing through tears, anger, or whatever comes up
- Describe what you're feeling: e.g., "I'm crying now because..."
- Don't stop to analyze—just express the raw truth

Grounding Techniques:

- If overwhelmed, put your feet flat on the floor and breathe
- Look around the room and name five things you can see
- Write: "I am safe in this moment"

Integration:

- After intense sessions, do something nurturing for yourself
- Take a walk, have tea, listen to calming music
- Don't make major life decisions immediately after deep processing

What NOT to Do:

- Edit while writing (perfectionism is the enemy of healing)
- Worry about spelling or grammar

- Plan what you'll write ahead of time
- Judge what emerges—it's all valid
- Share without careful consideration of your safety
- Use this as a substitute for professional therapy when you need real support

Making It Sustainable

Building Consistency:

- Start with just ten minutes if twenty feels overwhelming—something is better than nothing
- Keeping the same time and place creates routine and signals to your brain that this matters
- Link journaling to an existing habit: e.g., "After I have coffee, I journal"
- Track days completed without judging missed days—life happens; be gentle with yourself)

When Resistance Arises:

- Write about the resistance: e.g., "I don't want to journal today because..."
- Remember that resistance often means you're approaching something important
- Lower the bar: e.g., "I'll just write one page today"
- Use prompts when you feel stuck

Monthly Review:

- Read previous entries for patterns and growth
- Notice recurring themes or triggers
- Celebrate insights and progress (this shit is hard work)

- Adjust your practice based on what's actually working

INTEGRATION WITH OTHER HEALING PRACTICES

Before Therapy Sessions:

- Journal about what you want to discuss
- Process immediate reactions after sessions
- Track insights between appointments

Combined with Meditation:

- Meditate for five minutes, then journal what arose
- Use journaling to process meditation experiences
- Write about spiritual insights or questions

Supporting Other Healing Work:

- Journal before and after EMDR sessions
- Process shadow work discoveries
- Track how different healing modalities affect you

SAFETY AND SELF-CARE

Protecting Your Privacy:

- Keep your journal in a secure location
- Consider destroying pages that feel too vulnerable to keep
- Use initials or code words for sensitive content
- Trust your instincts about what to write versus what to keep private

When to Seek Additional Support:

- If suicidal thoughts arise consistently
- If traumatic memories become overwhelming
- If you're stuck in rumination without relief
- If isolation increases despite journaling

REMEMBER:

- Progress over perfection—some days will flow, while others will feel like pulling teeth
- Healing isn't linear—expect waves and cycles, ups and downs
- Your story matters—what you're experiencing is valid and worthy of attention
- Integration takes time—be patient with the fucking process
- You're not alone—your struggles are shared by many others on similar journeys

THE REAL GOAL

The goal isn't to become some fancy writer or produce beautiful prose; it's to become intimate with your own experience, to develop genuine compassion for your journey, and to create sacred space for whatever wants to emerge when external pressures are temporarily set aside.

Your journal is a sanctuary where all parts of you are welcome—the wounded and the wise, the confused and the clear, the past and the emerging future. In those pages, healing happens one honest, messy, imperfect word at a time.

This isn't just writing; it's coming home to yourself, one page at a time.

CHAPTER 5

Searching for Faith

I always struggled with faith like it was my full-time fucking job. I grew up Catholic, explored Jehovah's Witness, Christianity, non-denominational Christianity, Buddhism—you name it, I've tried it. But here's the thing: I never stopped believing in something greater than myself. I was just lost somewhere between organized religion and actual faith, searching for a spiritual home where I could exist as I truly am instead of who everyone thought I should be.

Growing up first-generation Mexican American means carrying your family's belief systems like inherited luggage—heavy, essential, but not always fitting the life you're trying to build. We're all trying to create something new in a new place while honoring what came before, translating not just language but entire ways of understanding the sacred. The navigation required is constant, and when you add being queer to the mix, it becomes a spiritual obstacle course in which every tradition seems to demand that you check essential parts of yourself at the door.

The Catholic conditioning ran deep as hell. As a child, I was taught that Catholicism was the only way and that everything else was complete bullshit. But as I got older, the cognitive dissonance became overwhelming. How was I supposed to trust a God who seemed to require so much suffering for so little intervention? Sunday mornings meant putting on our best clothes and our best fake-ass faces, walking into church as if we were the happy Mexican family everyone expected, while our home fell apart behind closed doors.

When my prayers for my father to stop drinking and my mother to stop crying seemed to evaporate before they reached the ceiling, my faith didn't disappear—it evolved. If the Catholic God wasn't answering prayers or protecting innocent children, maybe there was another version of divinity that made more fucking sense. Maybe the problem wasn't with God but with human interpretations that seemed far too small to contain the vastness I felt when I looked at the stars or experienced genuine love.

I wasn't rejecting the sacred—I was searching for it. And that search would take me through every tradition I could find, not because I was spiritually confused, but because I was spiritually hungry. I knew there was something greater out there; I just needed to find where I belonged within it.

THE CATHOLIC FOUNDATION THAT CRACKED

The first crack in my Catholic foundation appeared when I was about eight, sitting in catechism class while Sister Margaret explained that people who weren't Catholic wouldn't go to heaven. Even as a kid, this struck me as fundamentally fucked up. My abuelito, the kindest man I'd ever known, wasn't a regular churchgoer.

He was more spiritual than religious, finding God in his workshop, in nature, in acts of service to his family and community.

The idea that this gentle soul would be condemned to eternal punishment because he hadn't jumped through the right religious hoops felt like cosmic injustice. When I raised my hand to ask about this, Sister Margaret's response was swift and dismissive: "We don't question God's plan, Peter. We trust in His wisdom."

But I was questioning it. Not God—God felt real and loving and vast in ways that made my chest expand with wonder. I was questioning the humans who claimed to speak for God, who seemed to know remarkably specific details about divine preferences that coincidentally aligned with their own prejudices and power structures.

The second crack came during confirmation classes, when I was thirteen. Father Rodriguez explained that homosexuality was a sin against God's natural order, that people with "same-sex attraction" could be forgiven if they remained celibate and never acted on their desires. I sat in that pew, feeling like he was describing some abstract theological concept—not realizing he was essentially sentencing me to a lifetime of spiritual exile.

At thirteen, I didn't have the words for what I was feeling, but my body knew. The way I responded to other boys versus girls, the dreams that came unbidden, the stirring feelings that felt as natural as breathing—all of it was apparently an offense to the very God who had supposedly created me with these inclinations. The logical inconsistency was staggering but pointing it out wasn't an option in a tradition that valued obedience over inquiry.

The final crack in my Catholic foundation came when my father went to prison. I prayed harder than I'd ever prayed for anything, bargaining with God like a desperate child: "If you bring him back changed, if you make him stop drinking, if you fix our family, I'll be good forever." But my father came back unchanged, maybe worse. The drinking continued, the rage intensified, and our family dysfunction reached new levels of chaos.

Where was God in all of this? Where was the divine intervention I'd been promised if I just had enough faith? The standard Catholic responses—God's plan, mysterious ways, suffering as spiritual growth—felt like cruel jokes when applied to a child trying to survive domestic violence while maintaining belief in a loving creator.

SPIRITUAL WANDERING BEGINS

My first exploration beyond Catholicism came through my ex-girlfriend whose family were Jehovah's Witnesses. At seventeen, still deeply closeted and desperate to be "normal," I threw myself into their biblical study with the intensity of someone trying to pray away feelings he could not yet name. The precision of their biblical interpretation appealed to the part of me that needed logical frameworks, clear answers, and definitive interpretations of spiritual truth.

For a few months, I attended Kingdom Hall meetings, participated in Bible studies, and even went door-to-door witnessing. The sense of purpose felt intoxicating after years of spiritual emptiness, and the community aspect provided a belonging I'd never experienced in Catholic churches. There was something powerful about being part of a group that took its faith seriously enough to structure its entire live around it.

But the more I learned, the more familiar the exclusivity became. Once again, I was being told that this was the only true path to salvation, that questioning leadership was tantamount to questioning God himself. The same authoritarian structure that had driven me from Catholicism was present here—just with different uniforms and meeting locations.

When I stopped attending meetings because I couldn't reconcile their teachings with the feelings I was starting to acknowledge about my sexuality, my ex-girlfriend and I broke up entirely. The conditional love I'd experienced—warm and welcoming as long as I conformed completely—revealed itself as no love at all. It was my first lesson in how spiritual communities could offer belonging with one hand while demanding total submission with the other.

THE PROTESTANT EXPERIMENT

Christianity came next, through various denominations that promised a more personal relationship with Jesus, less institutional control, and greater emphasis on grace rather than rules. The personal relationship aspect appealed to me—the idea that spirituality could be individual rather than institutional, that I could have direct access to the divine without relying on human intermediaries who seemed consistently disappointed in my existence.

I tried Methodist churches that felt warm but ultimately empty, Baptist congregations with great music but terrible theology about people like me, and non-denominational communities that claimed to be more progressive but usually just meant they had better marketing. Some communities were more welcoming than others, but ultimately, they all arrived at the same fucking conclusion about people like me: "God loves you exactly as you are, but He loves you too much to leave you that way."

For a brief period, I convinced myself this might actually work. Maybe I could pray away the gay. Maybe if I surrendered completely to God's will, He would rewire my attractions to align with biblical teachings. I attended prayer meetings where well-meaning straight people laid hands on me and begged God to "heal" my same-sex attraction, as if my capacity for love were a disease requiring divine intervention.

The failure of this approach was devastating in ways I hadn't anticipated. If God wouldn't change me despite my desperate prayers, despite my willingness to surrender everything, what did that say about my worth, my purpose, my right to exist authentically? Either God didn't care enough to help me, or I wasn't worthy of divine intervention, or—most terrifyingly—maybe there was no God at all.

The prayer sessions became psychological torture. I'd leave feeling more broken than when I arrived, convinced that my inability to change was evidence of insufficient faith rather than recognition that there was nothing wrong with me that needed changing in the first place.

EASTERN EXPLORATIONS

I tapped into Buddhism here and there—if Madonna practiced it, then maybe I should too, right? I didn't take it seriously at first. I was just trying to fit in somewhere, anywhere, gravitating toward whatever spiritual practice seemed sophisticated enough to make me feel evolved while secretly hoping it would provide the peace that Christianity had failed to deliver.

Buddhism offered a completely different framework for understanding suffering. Instead of sin requiring redemption, there was attachment creating pain. Instead of divine judgment, there were karmic consequences. Instead of salvation through faith, there was liberation through understanding. For someone raised on Catholic guilt and Protestant shame, this felt like breathing clean air after years in a smoky room.

I attended meditation sessions at local temples, read books about mindfulness and compassion, tried to apply Buddhist principles to my daily life. The emphasis on personal responsibility rather than divine intervention appealed to the part of me that was tired of waiting for external salvation. If I could understand the nature of suffering, maybe I could transcend it through my own efforts.

But Buddhism, at least as I understood it then, seemed to require a detachment from desire that felt impossible for someone whose primary spiritual wound was being told his desires were wrong. The goal of eliminating attachment seemed to include eliminating my capacity for romantic love, which felt like another form of spiritual violence—just more sophisticated than Christian condemnation.

I also struggled with the cultural context. Most of the Buddhist teachers I encountered were either Asian masters speaking through translators or white Americans who had adopted Eastern practices without acknowledging the colonial implications of spiritual appropriation. As a Mexican American, I was sensitive to how the wisdom of marginalized cultures could be extracted and repackaged for privileged consumption while the original practitioners remained invisible.

OCCULT AND ALTERNATIVE PATHS

When Buddhism didn't provide the quick fix I was unconsciously seeking, I wandered into even more esoteric territory. I studied the occult and witchcraft for a while, drawn to spiritual systems that seemed to celebrate rather than suppress human desire, that worked with natural forces rather than demanded submission to divine authority, and that offered personal power rather than salvation through surrender.

The occult felt rebellious in ways that appealed to my lifelong pattern of rejecting whatever authority figures told me I should accept. If Christianity condemned me and Buddhism wanted me to dissolve my ego, maybe I needed a spiritual path that encouraged me to claim my power and to work with forces mainstream religions considered dangerous or forbidden.

I collected crystals, studied tarot cards, and learned energy work and spellcasting. I attended gatherings where people discussed manifesting their desires, connecting with goddess energy, and reclaiming spiritual practices that predated patriarchal religions. For a brief period, it felt empowering to engage with spirituality on my own terms, to explore traditions that didn't police my sexuality or require my conformity.

But the occult community had its own problems—spiritual materialism disguised as enlightenment, cultural appropriation of indigenous practices, and often the same personality disorders that plagued religious communities, just with different costumes and vocabulary. Many practitioners seemed more interested in feeling special than in genuine spiritual development, more focused on accumulating esoteric knowledge than on developing wisdom or compassion.

I also discovered that rebellion for its own sake wasn't spirituality; it was just reaction. Defining myself in opposition to Christianity didn't create authentic spiritual connection any more than trying to conform to Christian standards had. I was still letting external authorities determine my spiritual direction, just in reverse.

WHAT I WAS REALLY SEEKING

What I was really doing during all those years was wandering through a spiritual shopping mall, trying on different belief systems like clothes to see which might make me look and feel more acceptable to myself and others. Buddhism felt sophisticated and non-judgmental. Christianity felt familiar, even when it was painful. Each tradition offered something, but none seemed designed for someone like me—someone who couldn't separate his sexuality from his spirituality, who needed both transcendence and belonging, who wanted to honor his ancestors while living authentically.

I was carrying around multiple forms of spiritual trauma—the Catholic guilt about sexuality, the Protestant emphasis on personal transformation that never seemed to work, the Buddhist insistence that attachment was the root of suffering, the occult promise that I could create my own reality if I just had enough personal power. None of these systems spoke to one another, and none of them addressed the specific intersection of trauma I carried as a gay Mexican American rejected by his family for being authentic.

The spiritual seeking became another form of self-improvement, another way to try to become acceptable rather than learning to accept myself as I was. I chased validation from spiritual authorities, trying to find a tradition that would tell me I was okay exactly as I was, not realizing that no external system could grant me the self-acceptance I was desperately seeking.

What I didn't understand yet was that my spiritual homelessness wasn't a bug—it was a feature. Being rejected by mainstream religious traditions was forcing me to develop a more personal, authentic relationship with the divine than I could have achieved by simply inheriting someone else's beliefs. The wandering wasn't evidence of spiritual failure but of hunger, not proof that I was unsuited for sacred relationship but proof that I was determined to find it on terms that honored, rather than denied, my authentic nature.

THE GUILT THAT FOLLOWED ME EVERYWHERE

The guilt for living a "homosexual lifestyle" followed me through every spiritual exploration like a persistent demon assigned to me at birth, programmed into my DNA alongside the inherited trauma of generations who'd never had the luxury of questioning religious authority. Even in Buddhism, where sexuality wasn't explicitly condemned, the emphasis on desire as the root of suffering made me wonder if my attractions were just another craving to overcome, another attachment keeping me from enlightenment. Even in pagan traditions that celebrated sexuality as sacred, I carried decades of internalized shame—religious messages telling me my love was inherently disordered and fundamentally wrong, an offense to the natural order.

This wasn't just personal guilt—this was generational programming, layers upon layers of inherited shame about sexuality, spirituality, and authenticity, passed down through bloodlines like some kind of spiritual poison. My great-grandparents had probably carried guilt about questioning the Church; my grandparents had carried guilt about surviving when others didn't; my parents had carried guilt about leaving Mexico and potentially abandoning their cultural identity. And now I was carrying guilt about being gay on top of all that inherited shame—like the final weight that would either crush me completely or force me to finally break the fucking cycle.

The Catholic guilt wasn't just about sexuality—it was woven into every aspect of how my family understood suffering, sacrifice, and what it meant to be a good person. We'd been taught that suffering was holy, that questioning authority was dangerous, that our desires were probably sinful and needed to be suppressed for the good of our souls. Generation after generation had learned to distrust their own instincts, their own needs, their own truth, in favor of what priests and parents and cultural authorities told them was right.

Talk about getting completely fucked up by systemic beliefs and religion as a first-generation Mexican American. I was caught between multiple worlds—the traditional Catholicism of my family, so deeply embedded in Mexican identity it felt impossible to separate; the progressive spirituality of California culture that promised acceptance but often felt shallow and culturally disconnected; the ancient wisdom traditions I was trying to understand through books written by people who'd never experienced my particular intersection of marginalization; the occult practices that promised personal empowerment but couldn't touch the deep wounds carved by centuries of cultural conditioning.

Each tradition had something to offer, but none were designed for someone like me—someone whose sexuality and spirituality were inseparable, both essential parts of who I was; someone who needed both transcendence and belonging, because isolation felt like death; someone who wanted to honor his ancestors while living authentically, knowing that betraying either felt like spiritual suicide.

THE IMPOSSIBLE CHOICE

The systemic beliefs ran deeper than I realized—roots of a poisonous tree extending far beyond what I could see above ground. Even after consciously rejecting Catholic doctrine, its framework still lived in my nervous system: the idea that spiritual growth required the sacrifice of earthly desires, that authenticity was somehow less important than conformity to divine will, that my attraction to men was a problem to solve rather than a gift to celebrate, that questioning religious authority was not just dangerous but potentially deadly.

This wasn't just individual conditioning—it was generational trauma playing out in real time. My ancestors had survived conquest and colonization, the violent imposition of Christianity over indigenous spiritual practices that had sustained them for centuries. They'd learned that challenging religious authority could literally get you killed, that assimilation meant survival, that keeping your head down and your mouth shut was often the difference between life and death.

The Catholic Church hadn't just given my family spiritual guidance—it had been their lifeline during immigration, their community center, their source of identity and belonging in a foreign country that treated them like outsiders. Rejecting Catholicism wasn't just rejecting a set of beliefs; it was rejecting the institution that had helped my grandparents survive poverty, discrimination, and displacement when no one else could.

As a first-generation Mexican American, I was navigating not just personal spiritual confusion but cultural displacement that went back generations. My parents had brought their faith from Mexico as part of their identity—their connection to homeland and heritage, their way of preserving cultural continuity in a country that demanded assimilation. Their Catholicism wasn't just religion—it was resistance, community, and a way of staying connected to ancestors and traditions that American culture was trying to erase.

Rejecting Catholicism felt like rejecting them—my culture and my ancestors who had found meaning and community through these traditions for generations. These were people who had suffered and died to preserve these beliefs, passing them down to ungrateful descendants like me who had the luxury of questioning what they'd never been allowed to question.

But staying within Catholicism meant rejecting myself—participating in my own spiritual exile, accepting that I would only ever be welcome conditionally, only partially, only if I agreed to see my authentic self as fundamentally flawed. It meant continuing the cycle of self-rejection passed down through generations who'd learned to see their desires, questions, and authentic selves as problems to be solved rather than gifts to be celebrated.

The choice felt impossible—honor my heritage or honor my truth, maintain family connection or preserve personal integrity, carry forward the spiritual traditions that had sustained my ancestors or break free from the limitations those same traditions imposed. Either choice felt like a betrayal of something essential, like cutting off a limb to save the body.

SALT LAKE CITY–FINDING UNIVERSAL TRUTH

Moving to Salt Lake City added another layer of complexity to my already fucked-up spiritual journey. Here was a city literally built on religious conviction, where the dominant culture was shaped by LDS beliefs that felt even more restrictive than the Catholicism I'd grown up with. The beautiful temples and well-maintained neighborhoods spoke to the power of collective faith, but beneath that beauty ran an undercurrent of exclusion that was suffocating for anyone who didn't fit the prescribed mold. It was in Salt Lake City that I first encountered the stories of gay men who had left the Mormon Church, and their experiences illuminated aspects of my own journey I hadn't fully understood. These were men raised with even more intensive religious indoctrination than I had—men who had served missions, married women in temple ceremonies, and tried desperately to live according to divine commandments that demanded complete denial of their authentic selves.

"I thought if I just had enough faith, if I prayed hard enough, if I served faithfully enough, God would change me," one man told me during a chance conversation at a coffee shop in the Avenues. "I thought my attractions to men were a test, something to overcome through righteousness. It took me forty fucking years to realize that maybe the test wasn't whether I could stop being gay, but whether I could learn to love myself the way God apparently already did."

His story resonated with something deep in me. We'd both grown up believing that our sexuality was evidence of spiritual failure, that authentic love was somehow less important than religious compliance, that we needed fixing rather than acceptance. Yet we'd also both discovered that God—or the divine, or whatever sacred force governs the universe—seemed way fucking bigger than the interpretations offered by human institutions.

These conversations—in coffee shops and support groups throughout Salt Lake—became my informal theological education. I met former Mormons who had lost everything—families, communities, economic networks—when they chose authenticity over acceptance. I heard stories of men living double lives for decades, serving in church leadership while secretly meeting other men in bathrooms and hotel rooms, the psychological torture of trying to stay faithful to institutions that demanded they hate themselves.

But I also met men who had found peace—who had created new spiritual practices that honored both their sexuality and their hunger for transcendence. Some had joined affirming Christian denominations; others had developed personal spiritual practices that borrowed from multiple traditions. A few had moved toward secular humanism, maintaining what they described as a "spiritual sensibility" or a "connection to something greater."

What we all shared was the recognition that spirituality and religion were not the same fucking thing—that faith could exist independently of institutional approval, and that divine love might be far more expansive than human interpretations suggested. We'd all learned to distinguish between God and religion, between authentic spiritual experience and theological interpretation, between divine truth and human prejudice masquerading as divine will.

THE MORMON MIRROR

Living in Salt Lake City felt like looking into a funhouse mirror of my own spiritual journey. The Mormons I met wrestled with the same fundamental conflicts I was—the tension between religious obedience and personal authenticity, the question of whether institutions claiming divine authority could be fundamentally wrong about something as basic as human sexuality, and the challenge of maintaining spiritual connection while rejecting spiritual violence.

But the Mormon experience was intensified in ways that made my Catholic upbringing look casual. The LDS Church wasn't just a Sunday morning commitment—it was a total life system: community, economics, social structure, family networks, and cultural identity all wrapped into religious affiliation. Leaving the church didn't just mean changing religious beliefs; it meant losing everything that defined home, belonging, and identity.

I attended several support group meetings for former Mormons—not because I was ex-LDS, but because their struggles illuminated my own. The phrases they used to describe their experience—"losing your entire world," "being cast out from everything you've ever known," "having to rebuild your identity from scratch"—could have come from my own mouth, describing what happened when my family rejected me for being gay.

"The hardest part," one man shared during a particularly intense meeting, "wasn't losing my faith in the church. It was learning to trust my own spiritual experience again after being told for forty years that my feelings, my instincts, my direct experience of the divine couldn't be trusted if they contradicted what the authorities taught."

This struck me like lightning. I realized I'd been carrying the same wound—the systematic destruction of trust in my own spiritual instincts, the learned inability to distinguish authentic divine connection from religious programming, the fear that any spiritual experience outside approved channels was somehow dangerous or deceptive.

LEARNING TO TRUST MY OWN SPIRITUAL INSTINCTS

These conversations with spiritual refugees from various traditions taught me something crucial: the problem wasn't that I was spiritually deficient or incapable of faith. The problem was that I'd been looking for a spiritual home in institutions designed to exclude people like me, seeking acceptance from systems built on the foundation of my rejection.

Slowly, through this community of fellow seekers and misfits, I began to develop what I'd never been encouraged to: trust in my own spiritual experience. Not the grandiose spiritual ego that claims special revelation or superior understanding, but the quiet confidence that my direct experience with the sacred was as valid as anyone else's, that my questions were as valuable as anyone's certainties, and that my spiritual journey was as legitimate as any path blessed by institutional authority.

I started paying attention to moments when I felt genuinely connected to something greater than myself—not during religious services or prescribed spiritual practices, but in spontaneous experiences that seemed to arise from life itself: the transcendence of music that moved me to tears, the sense of divine presence I felt in natural settings where the beauty was so overwhelming it felt like communion, the spiritual connection I experienced during moments of authentic intimacy with my partner, when love felt too vast to be contained by individual bodies.

These experiences didn't fit into the categories provided by any religious tradition I'd explored, yet they felt more real, more nourishing, more genuinely sacred than anything I'd experienced in churches, temples, or meditation halls. Gradually, I began to trust that maybe these spontaneous moments of connection were more reliable indicators of spiritual truth than any doctrine or teaching I'd inherited.

I also began noticing how different spiritual practices affected my well-being, not just my ideas about spirituality. Prayer focused on gratitude and wonder left me feeling expanded and connected, while prayer focused on confession and unworthiness made me feel contracted and separated. Meditation emphasizing compassion and acceptance created peace, whereas meditation that emphasized detachment and transcendence often left me feeling emotionally disconnected from life.

This pragmatic approach to spirituality—paying attention to what actually served my flourishing, rather that what I thought should work based on spiritual theory—became my compass for navigating the confusing landscape of spiritual options available in a pluralistic culture.

BUILDING MY OWN BRIDGE TO THE DIVINE

I spent most of my twenties and thirties desperately seeking faith like some kind of spiritual refugee, wandering from tradition to tradition with my heart in my hands, begging someone, anyone, to tell me I was worthy of divine love. Looking back now, I see that I was just a tainted gay man looking for love, belonging, acceptance, and purpose—the basic shit that every human being needs to survive, yet felt impossibly out of reach for someone like me.

The journey to faith was not an easy one, but it was one that needed to be fucking taken, even when it felt like I was walking through a spiritual desert with no map, no compass, and no guarantee that there was an oasis waiting for me anywhere. I always had some kind of relationship with God—even when I was pissed at Him, even when I wasn't sure He existed, even when every religious authority told me He didn't want me. I always made it a point to talk to Him in my own way, usually through tears, sometimes through rage, always with the desperate honesty of someone who had nothing left to lose.

These conversations weren't the polite, formal prayers I'd been taught as a child—those scripted requests felt like talking to a distant authority figure who might grant your wishes if you asked nicely enough.

These were raw, honest, sometimes angry-as-hell dialogues that happened in my car during long drives when the silence got too loud; in my apartment during sleepless nights when the loneliness felt like it might actually kill me; in moments of profound isolation when institutional religion had failed me, but the need for divine connection remained stronger than ever.

"I don't understand your fucking plan," I'd say aloud to the empty air, not sure if anyone was listening but needing to speak the words anyway, needing to get them off my chest before they suffocated me. "If you made me this way, why does every religion say you hate how you made me? If you love me unconditionally like everyone claims, why does loving another man feel like the most natural thing in the world, but also the most condemned thing I could possibly do?"

I figured at that point that I just needed to build my own relationship with Him and let it be that, regardless of what anyone else thought about it. Fuck the priests, fuck the pastors, fuck the spiritual authorities who'd spent my entire life telling me I was an abomination. If God was real, He could handle my questions, my anger, and my refusal to pretend I was someone I wasn't just to gain His approval.

These conversations gradually evolved from angry confrontations to genuine dialogue. I started listening as much as talking, paying attention to responses that came not through dramatic revelations, but through subtle shifts in my understanding—synchronicities that felt too meaningful to dismiss, moments of clarity that arose during the raw honesty of unfiltered prayer.

What I discovered through this process was a God who felt nothing like the demanding deity of my childhood religion and everything like the unconditional love I'd glimpsed in my abuelito's workshop—creative, accepting, transformative, seeing beauty in what others might consider broken. This God didn't need me to be different; this God needed me to be authentically myself, completely and without apology.

I learned that faith wasn't about believing the right things or performing the right rituals, but about trusting the relationship itself—trusting that whatever force had created me had done so intentionally, lovingly, without the mistakes or oversights that religious teachings suggested. My sexuality wasn't a cosmic error requiring correction, but an expression of the infinite creativity that underlies all existence.

FINDING TEACHERS WHO GOT IT

The discovery of Osho's writings came at exactly the right time in my healing journey, though I wouldn't have been ready for his radical approach to spirituality during my earlier seeking phases. Here was a teacher who talked about enlightenment without requiring sexual suppression, who discussed divine love while celebrating human sexuality, and who taught transcendence through embracing rather than rejecting the fullness of human experience.

"The only way out is in," Osho wrote, and something in me recognized this as the missing piece I'd been searching for through all those years of external spiritual shopping. Instead of requiring me to conform to predetermined ideas about holiness, his teachings invited me to dive deeper into my authentic experience—to find the sacred not by rejecting my humanity, but by fully fucking inhabiting it.

Reading Osho felt like having conversations with a spiritual teacher who actually understood that sexuality and spirituality weren't opposing forces, but complementary aspects of human wholeness. His writings about love—not just romantic love, but the divine love that underlies all existence—spoke directly to the part of me that had been told my capacity for love was somehow flawed or misdirected.

"Love is not a relationship. Love is a state of being; it has nothing to do with anybody else," he wrote, and I began to understand that the divine love I'd been desperately seeking through religious institutions had always been available within me—not as a reward for good behavior, but as my fundamental nature.

I devoured his books on meditation, on consciousness, on the integration of spirituality and psychology. His approach felt revolutionary after years of religious teachings that seemed designed to make humans feel ashamed of their humanness. Instead of seeing spiritual development as the gradual elimination of human desires and experiences, Osho taught that awakening happened through full acceptance and conscious exploration of whatever arose.

This wasn't spiritual bypassing or indulgence disguised as enlightenment. Osho's teachings required tremendous honesty, courage, and commitment to truth. But the truth he pointed toward included, rather than excluded, the full spectrum of human experience—including sexuality, anger, grief, joy, and all the messy complexity that other spiritual traditions seemed determined to transcend or transform.

THE AUTOBIOGRAPHY THAT CHANGED EVERYTHING

Autobiography of a Yogi opened up entirely new possibilities for understanding the spiritual journey. Paramahansa Yogananda's stories of direct divine experience, of miracles that transcended religious boundaries, and of enlightened beings who had discovered the unity underlying all religious traditions—all of it resonated with something deep in my spiritual DNA that had always known there was more to existence than what conventional religion offered.

What struck me most about Yogananda's teachings was how they honored both Eastern and Western spiritual traditions, finding common ground where I'd previously seen only conflict. His integration of Christ consciousness with yogic principles, his emphasis on direct experience over dogmatic belief, and his teachings about the underlying unity of all spiritual paths—all of it provided a framework for understanding my own eclectic spiritual journey not as confused wandering, but as necessary exploration.

Yogananda wrote about meeting saints and sages from various traditions who recognized each other's realization despite vastly different cultural and religious backgrounds. This gave me permission to honor the wisdom I'd found in different traditions without needing to choose one as exclusively true. I could appreciate the contemplative depth of Catholic mysticism while rejecting Catholic sexual ethics. I could value Buddhist teachings on compassion while disagreeing with certain interpretations of detachment. I could find inspiration in occult practices of personal empowerment while avoiding their tendency toward spiritual materialism.

The autobiography also introduced me to the concept of a guru-disciple relationship based on love and conscious evolution rather than submission and obedience. Yogananda's relationship with his teacher wasn't about giving up his autonomy but about receiving guidance for developing his unique spiritual potential. This felt radically different from the religious authority structures I'd experienced, which seemed designed to maintain hierarchy rather than foster genuine spiritual development.

BECOMING A READER

Not much of a reader in my younger years, I suddenly couldn't get enough of these spiritual texts. My late thirties marked the beginning of what would become a lifelong love affair with books, with ideas, with the endless possibilities for understanding consciousness and existence that I'd never explored during my practical, survival-focused twenties.

Reading became a sacred practice in itself—not just intellectual consumption, but communion with wisdom traditions that had been preserved across centuries specifically for seekers like me. I'd sit with these books the way I'd once sat in my abuelito's workshop, absorbing not just information but transformation, not just concepts but actual shifts in consciousness that occurred through engaging with enlightened perspectives.

I read everything I could find about non-dual spirituality, transpersonal psychology, mystical Christianity, Sufism, and various forms of yoga philosophy. I discovered that there was an entire underground network of spiritual teachings that honored both transcendence and embodiment, and that saw sexuality and spirituality as potentially complementary rather than necessarily conflicting.

Authors like Ram Dass, Pema Chödrön, Thomas Merton, Rumi, and contemporary teachers like Eckhart Tolle and Adyashanti offered perspectives that felt refreshingly honest about the challenges of spiritual development, without the moralizing judgment that had characterized my religious upbringing. These teachers acknowledged that awakening happened through life experience rather than despite it—that spiritual growth often involved embracing, rather than transcending, the full spectrum of human experience.

Reading also connected me to a global community of seekers who had found spiritual fulfillment outside traditional religious structures. Through books, I discovered that my spiritual homelessness wasn't a personal failing, but a common experience among people who valued authenticity over acceptance, truth over comfort, direct experience over inherited beliefs.

REAL MEDITATION, NOT THE BULLSHIT KIND

These teachings taught me the beauty of meditation and the worlds you can unlock when you sit in silence. This wasn't the meditation I'd dabbled with during my Buddhist phase—formal, rule-bound, focused on achieving specific states or outcomes. This was meditation as an intimate relationship with existence itself, as direct communion with the divine presence that both pervaded and transcended individual consciousness.

The first time I experienced what Osho called "witnessing consciousness"—that space of pure awareness that observes thoughts and emotions without being identified with them—I understood what he meant about finding the divine within. This wasn't the angry, judgmental God of my childhood religion, but the peaceful, all-encompassing awareness that was my deepest nature, that had always been present beneath the noise of conditioning and seeking.

I started with simple awareness practices—just sitting quietly and noticing whatever arose in my experience without trying to change or fix anything. This was radically different from prayer, which had always involved talking to God, requesting something, or trying to align my will with divine will. This was more like resting in the presence of the divine, discovering that awareness itself was sacred, that consciousness was not something I had but something I was.

As my practice deepened, I began to understand that meditation wasn't about achieving special states or having mystical experiences—though both sometimes occurred. It was about recognizing the ordinary awareness that was always present, that remained constant whether I was thinking or not thinking, feeling happy or sad, experiencing pleasure or pain.

This awareness felt like coming home to myself in the deepest possible way—not the self that was constructed through family conditioning, cultural expectations, or personal history, but the essential self that existed before all conditioning, that would remain after all stories ended, and was never actually touched by any of the experiences that had seemed so defining.

INTEGRATION OF EVERYTHING

Spirituality and meditation became something that not only my soul needed, but also my mental health and my body. The integration was profound and immediate—sitting in silence didn't just provide spiritual connection, but actually regulated my nervous system, processed traumatic material more gently than talk therapy alone, and created space for insights that my thinking mind couldn't access through analysis.

The meditation practice became a bridge between all the healing modalities I was using. The insights that emerged in therapy could be deepened through contemplative practice. The emotional releases from EMDR could be integrated through mindful awareness. The shadow work discoveries could be witnessed with compassionate attention rather than judgmental analysis.

What I discovered was that spiritual practice and psychological healing weren't separate projects, but different aspects of the same journey toward wholeness. The same awareness that could witness thoughts and emotions during meditation could also witness traumatic memories during EMDR processing, observe shadow aspects during inner work, and hold space for difficult emotions during therapeutic exploration.

Meditation taught me that healing wasn't about eliminating difficult experiences, but about changing my relationship to them. Pain could be witnessed with compassion rather than resistance. Fear could be met with curious attention rather than avoidance. Even shame—that most corrosive of emotions—could be held in awareness with the same unconditional acceptance I was learning to offer to all arising experience.

SACRED DAILY RITUAL

It has become a sacred ritual that I now practice daily, sometimes two to three times. Morning meditation to set intention and connect with presence before engaging with the world's bullshit. Afternoon meditation to reset and process whatever stress or stimulation the day had brought. Evening meditation to integrate experiences and release anything that didn't serve my highest good.

This wasn't meditation as spiritual performance or achievement, but as basic hygiene for consciousness—as essential as brushing teeth or eating meals, a fundamental requirement for maintaining psychological and spiritual health in a world that consistently pulls attention outward, that rewards reactivity over responsiveness, that values productivity over presence.

The practice didn't require perfect conditions or extensive time commitments. Five minutes of conscious breathing while sitting in my car before work could shift my entire day. Ten minutes of awareness practice before sleep could transform anxious rumination into peaceful rest. Brief moments of presence throughout the day—really tasting food, really listening to music, really feeling the sensation of water during a shower—became opportunities for sacred connection.

What I was really developing was the capacity to access peace and clarity regardless of external circumstances. This didn't mean becoming passive or checked out from life's challenges, but rather approaching those challenges from a centered, responsive place rather than a reactive, unconscious one.

WHERE THE ANSWERS LIVE

It's where I discover all the answers to my problems and where I can truly connect with my authentic self. The guidance that emerged in meditative silence was consistently wiser, more compassionate, and more aligned with my deepest values than any advice I could generate through worried thinking or external consultation. In that space of inner stillness, solutions arose organically, perspectives shifted naturally, and the artificial problems created by ego identification dissolved into the deeper peace that was always available.

It keeps me present and at peace—not as temporary states to achieve, but as my natural condition when not distracted by mental noise and emotional reactivity. Meditation taught me that presence and peace weren't goals to attain, but my fundamental nature to return to—not rewards for good spiritual behavior, but my birthright as a conscious being.

The questions that had tormented me for years—*Am I worthy of love? What's my purpose? How do I forgive people who hurt me?*—didn't get answered through meditation so much as they became irrelevant. When resting in pure awareness, the very framework that created those questions dissolved. There was no separate self to be worthy or unworthy, no fixed purpose to discover, no past to forgive, because there was only this moment, this awareness, this perfect presence that needed nothing and lacked nothing.

THE RESISTANCE WAS REAL

I'll be honest with you—at first, just like everything else on this journey and with all the limiting beliefs I was carrying, I thought this was complete bullshit too. The resistance was intense and familiar. Sitting still felt like wasting time. Watching thoughts felt pointless. The whole enterprise seemed like new-age nonsense that wouldn't address my very real problems with family rejection, financial stress, and relationship challenges.

My Mexican machismo training kicked in hard—real men don't sit around contemplating their navels; they take action, solve problems, power through difficulties rather than sitting passively, hoping for mystical insights. The Catholic conditioning added another layer of skepticism—if this wasn't prayer directed toward an external God, what was the fucking point? How could self-examination lead to divine connection?

Given that I had explored meditation in the past during my Buddhist phase, I carried additional resistance from previous experiences that hadn't met my expectations. I'd tried meditation before, and it hadn't magically solved my problems or provided the instant peace that spiritual marketing seemed to promise. Why would this time be different?

The expectations I brought to meditation were part of the problem. I wanted it to work like medication—take the prescribed dose and experience predictable relief from psychological symptoms. When five minutes of sitting practice didn't eliminate decades of trauma conditioning, I concluded that meditation wasn't for me, that I was probably too damaged or too mentally chaotic for contemplative practice.

THIS TIME WAS DIFFERENT

But this time I was different, and my perception had shifted completely. The therapy work had created enough self-awareness for me to recognize when I was operating from ego-defense rather than authentic curiosity. The EMDR had processed enough trauma for me to access states of nervous system regulation that made stillness possible. The shadow work had integrated enough rejected aspects of myself that I could approach meditation without needing it to fix me or make me into someone different.

I started with five minutes—the longest five fucking minutes known to man. That first week of daily practice felt eternal, each session an exercise in tolerating mental chaos rather than experiencing transcendent peace. My mind raced, my body fidgeted, my attention scattered to every possible distraction rather than settling into present moment awareness.

But something was happening beneath the surface noise. Even those chaotic five-minute sessions were creating tiny gaps in the constant mental commentary—brief moments where I could observe thoughts rather than being completely identified with them, fleeting experiences of the witnessing consciousness that both Osho and Yogananda wrote about with such eloquent certainty.

I learned to measure success not by how peaceful or blissful my meditation sessions were, but by my increasing capacity to stay present with whatever arose—including restlessness, boredom, physical discomfort, or emotional turbulence. The goal wasn't to have perfect meditations, but to develop a more conscious, less reactive relationship with my moment-to-moment experience.

Gradually, I began to notice that the benefits of meditation weren't limited to the time I spent sitting in formal practice. The awareness I was cultivating during meditation began to infuse my daily activities. I was slightly less reactive during difficult conversations, slightly more present during routine activities, slightly more aware of the choices I was making rather than operating completely on autopilot.

BUILDING THE PRACTICE

Eventually, throughout the years, I learned to work my way up. The progression wasn't linear—some days I could sit for thirty minutes in profound stillness; other days, five minutes felt impossible. But gradually and consistently, my capacity for presence expanded, my tolerance for inner silence increased, and my ability to rest in awareness rather than being hijacked by mental activity developed into reliable skill.

Now I can easily do an hour or more without hesitation—not because I've become some superior meditator or achieved some advanced spiritual state, but because I've learned to recognize meditation not as doing something, but as stopping the habitual doing that keeps consciousness fragmented and reactive. An hour of meditation now feels like returning home rather than enduring spiritual discipline.

The practice evolved from sitting meditation to moment-to-moment awareness throughout the day. Washing dishes became meditation. Walking became meditation. Listening to music, having conversations, even dealing with difficult emotions became opportunities to practice the same quality of conscious attention I was developing during formal sitting practice.

I also learned to adapt the practice to my actual life rather than trying to force my life to accommodate some idealized version of spiritual practice. Some days I meditated in my car before work. Some days I practiced awareness while exercising. Some days the only meditation I managed was three conscious breaths during a bathroom break. All of it counted. All of it contributed to the gradual transformation of consciousness that was occurring beneath the surface of daily routine.

FOR THE SKEPTICS

If you're a skeptic like I was, I say let those fucking walls down and give this a try. The skepticism itself isn't wrong—there's plenty of spiritual bullshit in the meditation world, plenty of teachers promising results they can't deliver, plenty of practices that substitute spiritual materialism for genuine transformation. But beneath the commercial spirituality and new-age marketing, the core practice of conscious stillness remains one of the most reliable technologies for accessing inner wisdom, emotional regulation, and direct spiritual experience.

The scientific research on meditation's benefits is overwhelming at this point. Regular practice has been shown to reduce anxiety and depression, improve immune function, increase emotional regulation, enhance creativity, and even change brain structure in ways that support psychological health. But these benefits are side effects of the real purpose: discovering your true nature beneath the conditioned patterns of thought and emotion.

Don't take my word for it—or anyone else's. Try it for yourself, with the same systematic approach you'd bring to any experiment. Commit to a daily practice for at least a month, starting with just five or ten minutes. Notice what changes in your life—not just during meditation but throughout your day. Pay attention to how you respond to stress, how present you are during conversations, how much mental energy you spend on unnecessary worry or rumination.

THE SILENCE THAT SPOKE

The silence that had once felt empty and pointless revealed itself as fullness beyond description, as the pregnant void from which all experience emerges and to which it returns. In learning to sit with silence, I had found not just spiritual practice but spiritual homecoming—not just a meditation technique but direct access to the divine presence that both pervaded and transcended all religious interpretation, all cultural conditioning, all inherited beliefs about what spirituality should look like for someone like me.

The God I met in meditation felt nothing like the demanding deity of institutional religion and everything like the unconditional awareness that had always been my deepest nature. This wasn't conversion to Eastern spirituality any more than my previous explorations had been conversion to Western religions—this was coming home to myself, to the divine consciousness that was both my essence and the essence of all existence, available not through belief or behavior but through the simple, revolutionary act of conscious presence.

That silence had been speaking to me all along. I just finally learned how to fucking listen.

In that listening, I discovered what I'd been seeking through all those years of spiritual wandering—not a God who would accept me if I changed, but recognition that I was already an expression of divine consciousness, perfectly imperfect as I was. Not a spiritual home that would tolerate my presence, but the understanding that I was already home, that the awareness reading these words was itself the sacred presence I'd been seeking everywhere else.

The road back to myself had led through every religious tradition I could find, not because any of them contained the complete truth, but because each one contributed something to my understanding of the vastness that can't be contained in any single framework.

The spiritual journey hadn't been about finding the right tradition, but about developing the capacity to recognize the sacred in whatever form it appeared—including, especially, in the authentic expression of who I truly am.

RECLAIMING MY INNER SANCTUARY

When practiced regularly, meditation can not only help with anxiety and depression but also train the mind stay present and stop running around like a fucking hamster on a wheel. Through my meditation and breathwork journey—which we'll explore in the next chapter, I've learned to create my own sacred space, something I've longed for since I was a kid and lost my abuelito. It's a space where I can connect with my authentic self without all the bullshit masks and performances.

The sacred space I created through meditation wasn't just a physical corner of my bedroom with a cushion and candles—it was a sanctuary of consciousness, an internal refuge that remained accessible regardless of whatever external bullshit was happening around me. For the first time since my abuelito's workshop, I had found a place where I could exist without performance, without adaptation, without the constant vigilance required to navigate a world determined to convince me I was fundamentally flawed.

This space felt familiar in ways that surprised the hell out of me. The same acceptance I'd experienced in my grandfather's presence, the same permission to exist authentically without apology, the same sense of unconditional belonging—all of it was available in the stillness of meditation. But instead of depending on another person's love to create this sanctuary, I was learning to access it directly through a conscious relationship with my own awareness.

The practice became my daily return to the truth of who I was beneath all the conditioning, trauma, and adaptive strategies I'd developed to survive in a hostile world. In those minutes of conscious stillness, I could remember that I was not broken, not deficient, and not requiring external validation to be worthy of love and belonging. I was the awareness itself—vast, peaceful, and never actually touched by any of the experiences that had seemed so defining.

That's where I came to realize that about ninety percent of my thoughts at the beginning of this journey were just repeating patterns that allowed me to self-sabotage. At the same time, I realized the internal conflicts we create in our minds—conflicts we convince ourselves are real. We build narratives that are complete fiction, just to prove a point or move through this life on an ego high. Through these practices, I've learned how to reconfigure and reconstruct my subconscious, breaking down those limiting beliefs and false narratives. I've also learned to control my ego and try to live day-to-day as present as fucking possible.

The spiritual seeking that had consumed my twenties and thirties wasn't wasted time or evidence of spiritual ADD—it was necessary preparation for developing the kind of faith that could actually sustain me. All the disappointment with various religious traditions, all the conversations with other spiritual refugees, all the books I'd read and teachers I'd encountered, had contributed to my ability to distinguish between authentic spiritual experience and religious programming, between divine truth and human interpretation, between faith and dogma.

What I discovered wasn't a new religion but a way of being that could embrace the wisdom of all traditions while being trapped by none of them: a spirituality that honored my sexuality as an expression of divine creativity rather than treating it as an obstacle to overcome, a faith that included my anger, my questions, and my refusal to accept easy answers about complex realities.

The God I finally met through meditation and authentic spiritual seeking wasn't the judgmental father figure of my religious upbringing but the unconditional love that I am at my deepest level, that you are at *your* deepest level, and that underlies all existence when perceived through clear awareness rather than conditioned fear.

That silence had been calling me home all along—not to some distant heaven but to the sacred presence that was never actually absent, just overlooked in the noise of spiritual seeking. In learning to be still, to listen, to trust my own direct experience of the divine, I had found what I'd been searching for in every church, temple, and spiritual community I'd ever visited.

The road back to myself had required leaving every spiritual tradition I'd ever tried—not because they were all wrong, but because none were big enough to contain the vastness of authentic spiritual experience. True faith, I discovered, wasn't about believing the right things but about trusting the relationship itself—the intimate, ongoing dialogue between human consciousness and the divine mystery that creates and sustains all existence.

BUILDING YOUR OWN FUCKING SANCTUARY

So here's the thing: after all that spiritual wandering, all those failed attempts to find God in other people's frameworks, I had to learn to build my own sacred space—not the physical kind (though that matters too), but the internal sanctuary that no religious authority could contaminate, no family rejection could destroy, no cultural conditioning could infiltrate.

This practice I'm about to share isn't some ancient wisdom I discovered in a monastery, nor a technique I learned from a guru who charges $500 for "enlightenment weekends." This is the practical, no-bullshit approach I developed through years of trial and error, designed specifically for people like us—the spiritual refugees, the family black sheep, the ones who need healing but can't stomach any more spiritual bypassing or religious performance.

If you're reading this and thinking, "meditation sounds like hippie bullshit," I get it—I thought the same thing. But I'm not talking about transcending your humanity or achieving some blissed-out state where nothing bothers you. I'm talking about creating a daily practice that helps you stay connected to your authentic self in a world that's constantly trying to convince you that you're broken.

This isn't about becoming a perfect meditator. It's about reclaiming your inner sanctuary—the place where you can exist without masks, without apologies, without the exhausting performance of being who others think you should be.

SIMPLE AT-HOME MEDITATION PRACTICE

Important Note: This practice is designed to be gentle and accessible for beginners, but let's be real—sometimes shit gets intense when you start sitting with yourself. Start small and build gradually. If you feel overwhelmed, simply return to normal breathing and open your eyes. Don't be a hero about it.

GETTING STARTED: CREATING YOUR SACRED SPACE

Physical Setup:

- Find a quiet corner where you won't be interrupted for ten to thirty minutes (tell people to fuck off if necessary)
- Choose a comfortable position—sit in a chair, on a cushion, on the floor, or lie down on your bed or a yoga mat—whatever works for your body
- If sitting, keep your spine naturally upright but not rigid, like you're in the military
- If lying down, make sure you're fully supported with pillows where needed
- Place a small table or shelf nearby for meaningful objects, if that's your thing
- Dim the lights or use natural lighting—harsh fluorescents will kill the vibe
- Turn off phone notifications (seriously, the world can survive without you for twenty minutes)

Your Meditation Space:

- A simple cushion, comfortable chair, or your bed with supportive pillows

- Optional: candle, small plant, photo of your abuelito, or whatever spiritual object speaks to you
- Timer or meditation app
- Light blanket if you get cold (nobody meditates well when they're shivering, whether sitting or lying down)
- Journal for post-meditation insights

WEEK 1-2: BUILDING THE FOUNDATION

Basic Breath Awareness (5-10 minutes)

The STOP Technique:

- Sit or lie down comfortably in your chosen position
- Take three deep breaths to transition from daily bullshit
- Observe your natural breathing without trying to change it
- Presence—simply be with whatever arises

Simple Instructions:

- Position yourself comfortably—spine straight if sitting, fully supported if lying down
- Close your eyes or soften your gaze
- Breathe naturally through your nose
- If lying down, you can place hands on your chest and belly to feel the breath
- Notice the sensation of breath entering and leaving
- When your mind wanders (it absolutely will!), gently return to the breath

- No judgment—wandering is normal and expected, so don't beat yourself up

What to Expect:

- Your mind will be very active at first—like a caffeinated monkey
- You'll forget to focus on breath repeatedly
- Physical discomfort or restlessness is normal; adjust your position as needed
- If lying down, you might get sleepy—that's okay; your body knows what it needs
- Some days will feel "better" than others
- Progress isn't always obvious day to day (trust the fucking process)

Remember, this isn't about spiritual achievement or proving you're evolved enough to sit still. This is basic fucking maintenance for your consciousness—like brushing your teeth, but for your mental health. Some days you'll feel like you're communing with the divine. Other days, you'll spend the entire time thinking about what you're going to eat for lunch. Both are perfect.

WEEK 3-4: DEVELOPING WITNESSING CONSCIOUSNESS

The Observer Practice (10-15 minutes)

Watching Thoughts:

- Begin with breath awareness for two to three minutes in your comfortable position
- Shift attention to observing thoughts as they arise

- Don't try to stop thoughts—just watch them like Netflix
- Imagine thoughts as clouds passing through the sky of awareness
- Notice the space between thoughts
- Return to the breath when you get caught up in the mental drama

Mental Noting Technique:

- When thoughts arise, gently label them: "thinking," "planning," "worrying about stupid shit"
- When emotions come up, label them: "feeling sad," "feeling anxious," "feeling excited"
- When body sensations occur, note them: "tension," "warmth," "tingling," "sleepiness"
- Always return to breath awareness after noting

MONTH 2: DEEPENING PRACTICE

Expanded Awareness Meditation (15-20 minutes)

The Four Foundations:

- **Body Awareness (5 min):** Scan from head to toe, noticing sensations (especially accessible when lying down)
- **Breath Awareness (5 min):** Focus on natural breathing rhythm
- **Mind Awareness (5 min):** Observe thoughts and emotions without getting hooked
- **Open Awareness (5 min):** Rest in spacious consciousness that contains all experience

Loving-Kindness Practice (For healing familial and cultural wounds):

- Begin with breath awareness (3 minutes) in whatever position feels most open
- Bring yourself to mind and repeat:
  - "May I be happy and peaceful"
  - "May I be free from suffering"
  - "May I be safe and protected"
  - "May I live with ease"
- Extend these wishes to loved ones, neutral people, difficult people (even your homophobic family), and all beings

ADVANCED PRACTICES (MONTH 3+)

Silent Sitting/Lying (20-60 minutes)

Pure Awareness Practice:

- Rest in complete stillness in your most comfortable position
- Rest in the awareness that is aware of all experience
- Don't try to achieve any particular state
- Simply be present with whatever arises
- This is closest to what Osho and traditional masters taught

POSITION-SPECIFIC PRACTICES

For Lying Down Meditation:

- **Body Scan:** Start at the top of your head and slowly move your attention through each part of your body

- **Yoga Nidra Style:** Systematically relax each body part while maintaining awareness
- **Heart-Centered Practice:** Place both hands on your heart and breathe into that space
- **Leg Elevation:** Elevate legs against a wall for nervous system calming

For Sitting Meditation:

- **Traditional Postures:** Cross-legged, chair, or kneeling with support
- **Walking Meditation:** Alternate between sitting and slow walking
- **Gazing Practices:** Soft gaze at a candle flame or natural object

DEALING WITH COMMON CHALLENGES

"My Mind is Too Busy." Listen: if your mind were not busy, you probably wouldn't need meditation in the first place. The chattering monkey brain isn't a meditation problem—it's a human condition. I spent years thinking I was "bad at meditation" because my mind wouldn't shut the fuck up. Turns out, noticing that your mind is busy *is* the meditation. You're not trying to lobotomize yourself into some zombie-like peace. You're learning to observe the chaos with some compassion instead of getting completely hijacked by it.

- This is normal and doesn't mean you're failing at meditation
- The goal isn't to stop thoughts but to change your relationship to them
- Sessions with a busy mind are just as valuable as peaceful ones

- Keep returning to your anchor (breath, body, awareness)

Physical Discomfort:

- Adjust your position mindfully during practice—sitting, lying down, or switching between
- Use chairs, pillows, or back support if needed—you're not trying to be a spiritual martyr
- Notice the difference between pain and mere discomfort
- Sometimes discomfort dissolves with patient attention

Falling Asleep (When Lying Down):

- This is often exactly what your nervous system needs
- Don't judge it—sleep can be deeply healing
- If you want to stay awake, try sitting up or opening eyes slightly
- Consider it "yoga nidra" style practice—conscious rest

DIFFERENT APPROACHES FOR DIFFERENT NEEDS

For Trauma Survivors:

- Lying down can feel safer than sitting upright
- Keep eyes slightly open if closed eyes feel unsafe
- Focus on external sounds or physical sensations rather than internal awareness
- Have grounding objects nearby (a soft blanket or meaningful item)

For Chronic Pain/Disability:

- Use whatever position minimizes pain—lying down, supported sitting, reclining
- Props and support are meditation tools, not cheating
- Pain can be part of the meditation—observing without resistance
- Shorter sessions with full comfort beat longer sessions with suffering

For Anxiety:

- Lying down can activate the parasympathetic nervous system faster
- Try the "legs up the wall" pose while meditating
- Focus on lengthening exhales
- Use weighted blankets or gentle pressure for grounding

CREATING SUSTAINABLE PRACTICE

Position Rotation:

- Monday/Wednesday/Friday: Sitting practice
- Tuesday/Thursday: Lying down practice
- Weekend: Whatever your body needs
- Listen to your body's wisdom about what serves you each day

WHY THIS ACTUALLY WORKS (FROM SOMEONE WHO TRIED EVERYTHING ELSE)

Look, I spent two decades searching for spiritual home in every tradition I could find. I prayed to the Catholic God, studied with Jehovah's Witnesses, tried to detach from desire through Buddhism, cast spells in occult circles, and read every spiritual book I could get my hands on. All of it contributed something, but none of it gave me what this simple practice has given me: the ability to come home to myself daily, regardless of what external bullshit is happening.

This isn't about replacing your spiritual seeking or dismissing the wisdom you've found in other traditions. It's about developing a foundation of inner stability that can hold whatever spiritual understanding you discover. It's about creating a sanctuary of consciousness that belongs to you—not to your family's religion, not to whatever guru or teacher you're following, but to your own authentic relationship with the sacred.

When I sit in meditation now, I'm not trying to become someone different. I'm remembering who I actually am beneath all the conditioning, trauma, and adaptive strategies I developed to survive in a world that told me I was wrong for existing. In that remembering, I've found the God I was searching for in every church, temple, and spiritual community I ever visited.

REMEMBER:

- There's no "perfect" meditation position—every position can lead to awakening
- Your body's needs change daily—honor those changes
- Lying down meditation is just as legitimate as sitting meditation
- Comfort supports presence; discomfort distracts from it
- Meditation is coming home to yourself, not performing spirituality for others

THE REAL GOAL

The goal isn't to become some perfect meditator sitting in lotus position for hours. It's to develop an intimate, compassionate relationship with your own consciousness—whatever position allows that relationship to flourish. In that relationship, you'll discover that the sacred space you've been seeking has always been available within you.

Your meditation practice becomes a daily return to the workshop of consciousness—the inner sanctuary where your authentic self can exist without performance, where healing happens through gentle attention, where the divine presence that transcends all religious interpretation reveals itself as your own deepest nature.

This is your spiritual inheritance—not the conditional love of religious institutions, but the unconditional awareness that you already are enough; not the God who judges your sexuality, but the consciousness that celebrates your authentic expression; not the faith that requires you to change, but the recognition that you were never broken in the first place.Start with five minutes. Show up daily in whatever position serves you. Trust the fucking process. Let the silence teach you what words never could—whether you're sitting like a Buddha or lying down like someone who's been through enough to know that sometimes horizontal is the most honest position of all.

And stop making excuses—your mental health depends on this shit, your spiritual freedom requires it, and your ancestors, who never had the luxury of questioning religious authority, are counting on you to break the cycle and find the peace they couldn't access in their lifetimes.

This is how you build your own bridge to the divine—not through external validation, but through the simple, revolutionary act of coming home to yourself, exactly as you are, every single day.

CHAPTER 6

The Magic of Breathing

Do you ever catch yourself not fucking breathing? Hyper-focused on bullshit that shouldn't—and doesn't—deserve your full attention, and when you finally come back to yourself, you realize you haven't taken a proper breath? Next thing you know, you're anxious as hell, stressed out, and feeling overwhelmed by things you have absolutely no control over? You don't have to tell me—I already know. That was me for years, living like I was suffocating myself one shallow breath at a time.

Until the day my heart started screaming at me to pay attention. Until the day I could have—and almost did have—a full-blown heart attack. That's the day I realized I wasn't actually breathing; I was just surviving on fumes. My body had been keeping score from all the years of self-abuse and abuse I'd allowed from others, including family and past relationships. When I realized I could have died—or spent the rest of my days half-paralyzed—my world shifted completely, as did my perspective. Why the fuck did I wait so long to listen?

THE SELF-BLAME SPIRAL

At first, in those early days of therapy, I went straight into self-guilt and blame mode—because that's what I did with everything. Through my therapist, I realized I couldn't change the past, but I could accept it, make peace with it, and grow from it. Be a better person, a better partner to the love of my life, a better son, a better brother, and actually be of service to the world instead of just taking up space. My rock bottom didn't wake me up until it almost cost me my goddamn life.

The last tool I discovered on my journey to healing was breath work, and let me tell you—it came right on fucking time. Through breath work, I learned to really dive into all the trauma I had carried for years and work through it, process it, and finally—finally—let that shit go.

BREATHING: THE MOST BASIC THING WE FORGET

Breathing is the first thing we do when we arrive in this world and the last thing we do when we leave. Yet somewhere between birth and the moment I nearly lost everything, I had forgotten how to truly breathe. I had reduced this sacred act to the bare minimum—shallow, anxious gasps that kept me alive but never allowed me to actually live.

The breath carries way more than oxygen through our bodies; it carries our life force, our emotions, our stored trauma, and our capacity for healing. When we breathe consciously, we access a power that has been available to us every moment of our lives, yet most of us never fully tap into its transformative potential because we're too busy being anxious about stupid shit.

I had been living like a person underwater, taking quick sips of air when I absolutely had to, but never allowing myself the luxury of breathing deeply. My chest had become a fortress, my diaphragm a locked door, my entire respiratory system a monument to holding back rather than letting in.

Growing up in a household where emotional expression was dangerous, where showing vulnerability could trigger violence, where being "too much" in any way invited punishment, I had learned to breathe carefully—not just around my father's explosive moods, but around life itself. Deep breathing meant deep feeling, and deep feeling meant potential devastation in a world that seemed determined to punish authenticity.

The irony wasn't lost on me: in trying to protect myself from emotional pain through shallow breathing, I had created physical conditions that almost killed me. The anxiety attacks, the chest pain, the chronic fatigue—all of it was my body's way of saying, "If you won't breathe consciously, I'll force you to pay attention through crisis."

THE BODY KEEPS SCORE THROUGH BREATH

Bessel van der Kolk wrote about how the body keeps score of our traumas, but what he didn't fully explain is how the breath becomes the prison warden of our pain. Every unprocessed emotion, every swallowed word, every moment we made ourselves small gets locked away in the pattern of our breathing. We literally hold our breath against life—against feeling, against truth, against the possibility that things could be different.

I had spent decades breathing around my pain rather than through it. My chest had become a vault of unspoken truths, unexpressed grief, and unprocessed rage. My shallow breathing was my body's way of saying, "If we don't breathe too deeply, we won't feel too much." But in protecting myself from feeling, I was slowly suffocating my soul.

The tension in my shoulders wasn't just from sitting at a desk all day. The knot in my stomach wasn't just from stress eating. The constant fatigue wasn't just from poor sleep. These were all symptoms of a respiratory system compromised by years of emotional suppression, a nervous system stuck in perpetual fight-or-flight mode, and a heart that had learned to beat cautiously rather than boldly.

Through my therapy work, I began to understand the science behind what I'd been experiencing. When we're in chronic stress or trauma response, our breathing automatically becomes shallow and rapid. This activates the sympathetic nervous system—the part responsible for fight, flight, or freeze responses. Over time, this pattern becomes so habitual that we forget how to access the parasympathetic nervous system—the part responsible for rest, digestion, healing, and emotional regulation.

My breathing had been stuck in survival mode for decades. Every shallow breath was my nervous system's way of staying alert for the next threat, the next rejection, the next moment when I might need to defend myself or run away. I'd been living in a state of chronic hypervigilance, which manifested in my respiratory system as perpetual breath-holding.

What I didn't understand until I started working with breath work was that the breath is bidirectional medicine. Just as trauma and stress can restrict our breathing, conscious breathing can heal trauma and regulate the nervous system. The same mechanism that had kept me trapped in survival mode could become the key to accessing deeper states of healing and presence.

MY BODY'S FINAL PLEA

The heart attack—or what could have been one—wasn't just a medical event. It was my body's final fucking plea for attention. As I sat in that emergency room, electrodes attached to my chest, watching the erratic rhythm of my heartbeat on the monitor, I realized I had been so focused on everyone else's needs, everyone else's dramas, everyone else's expectations that I had literally forgotten to breathe for myself.

The cardiologist said my stress tests looked like those of someone who had been holding their breath for years. He was more right than he knew. I had been holding my breath against my father's anger, my mother's depression, my ex-partners' emotional unavailability, and my own feelings of unworthiness. I had been living in a constant state of braced impact—waiting for the next blow to fall, never fully exhaling, never fully relaxing, never fully alive.

"When did you last take a really deep breath?" he asked me as he reviewed my charts. I couldn't fucking remember. That's when I knew something had to change—not just in my lifestyle or my stress management, but in the very way I inhabited my body.

I had to learn how to breathe again—not just to survive, but to actually live. That journey back to my breath became the journey back to myself, back to my life, back to the possibility that maybe—just maybe—I deserved to take up space in this world after all.

The magic wasn't in some complicated technique or ancient secret—it was in remembering how to do the most basic thing humans do to stay alive. But doing it consciously, intentionally, like my life depended on it. Because, as it turned out, it fucking did.

The cardiologist's question haunted me for weeks: "When did you last take a really deep breath?" The honest answer was that I couldn't remember ever breathing deeply without it being connected to panic, anxiety, or some form of crisis. Deep breathing had become associated with hyperventilation during panic attacks, not with relaxation or healing.

This realization led me to examine not just how I breathed, but when I allowed myself to breathe fully. I noticed that I held my breath during any conversation that might lead to conflict. I breathed shallowly when walking past groups of people who might judge me. I barely breathed at all when having to be vulnerable or authentic in any way.

The breath-holding was a full-body armor system that I'd developed to protect myself— from feeling too much, from being seen too clearly, from taking up too much space in a world that had consistently told me I was too much of everything: too sensitive, too dramatic, too gay, too different.

THE DISCOVERY OF BREATH WORK

When my therapist first mentioned breath work, I'll admit I was skeptical as fuck. How could something as simple as breathing be the key to healing trauma that therapy, meditation, and years of personal development work had only begun to touch? But desperation is a powerful motivator, and I was desperate to feel whole again instead of like a walking collection of broken pieces held together by sheer stubbornness.

My first breath work session was nothing short of revolutionary—like someone had finally given me the keys to my own goddamn healing. The facilitator, a gentle woman with knowing eyes that had clearly seen some shit, explained that we would be doing "conscious connected breathing"—a practice that would allow suppressed emotions and memories to surface safely so they could finally be processed and released instead of festering in my body like emotional poison.

She explained that unlike traditional therapy, which engages the thinking mind that often wants to analyze and rationalize our pain into neat little boxes, breath work bypasses the mental defenses and speaks directly to the nervous system. It accesses what the body knows that the mind has conveniently forgotten or buried under layers of "I'm fine" bullshit.

The science behind it made sense in ways that surprised me. When we breathe in specific patterns—particularly circular breathing without pauses between inhale and exhale—we change the chemistry of our blood and brain. This can induce non-ordinary states of consciousness that allow us to access memories, emotions, and insights that our normal waking consciousness keeps locked away.

What appealed to me most was that breath work didn't require me to tell my story, to explain my trauma, or to make sense of my experience for anyone else. The breath itself would guide the process, and my body's wisdom would determine what needed attention and in what order. After years of feeling like I had to perform my healing for therapists, this felt like a relief.

THE WALLS COME TUMBLING DOWN

As I lay on that mat in a room full of strangers, following the rhythm she guided us through, something began to shift in my chest. The protective walls I had built around my heart started to vibrate, then crack, then crumble entirely like they were made of fucking cardboard instead of steel. For the first time in decades, I felt my breath reach the deepest parts of my body—places that had been numb for so long I had forgotten they existed.

The breathing pattern was deceptively simple: inhale through the nose, exhale through the mouth, with no pause between breaths. But maintaining this rhythm for an extended period created profound physiological changes. Within ten minutes, I felt energy moving through my body in ways I'd never experienced. Within twenty minutes, emotions began rising like pressure that had been building for years behind a dam that was finally cracking.

Waves of emotion began to rise like a tsunami I couldn't stop. First came the anger—decades of swallowed rage at being diminished, dismissed, and disrespected by pretty much everyone in my life. This wasn't the surface irritation I was familiar with, but primal fury that seemed to come from my bones, from cellular memory of every time I'd been told to be smaller, quieter, more acceptable.

Then came the grief—for all the years I had spent sleepwalking through my existence, for the dreams I had abandoned because they seemed "impractical," for the love I had been too afraid to fully receive or give. This grief felt ancient, like it belonged not just to me but to generations of ancestors who had also been forced to abandon their authentic selves for survival.

Finally came something I hadn't felt in years: relief. The kind of relief that comes when you finally set down a burden you didn't even realize you'd been carrying around like a backpack full of rocks. The relief of finally feeling my emotions fully instead of keeping them at a safe distance. The relief of discovering that I could handle feeling everything I'd been so afraid of.

What surprised me most was how natural this emotional release felt. There was no shame, no self-consciousness, no need to explain or justify what was coming up. The breath created a container that felt completely safe for whatever needed to emerge. Other people in the room were having their own experiences—some laughing, some crying, some making sounds I'd never heard humans make—and it all felt perfectly normal.

NATURE'S PERFECT HEALING TECHNOLOGY

Breath work taught me that the breath is nature's most perfect healing technology—no pills, no side effects, no insurance copays required. Unlike talking therapy, which engages the thinking mind that often wants to analyze and rationalize our pain into neat little boxes, breath work bypasses the mental defenses and speaks directly to the nervous system. It accesses what the body knows that the mind has conveniently forgotten or buried under layers of "I'm fine" bullshit.

Through conscious connected breathing, I learned to breathe into the pain instead of around it like I'd been doing my whole life. Instead of contracting when difficult emotions arose, I learned to expand my breath and create space for everything I was feeling. The pain didn't disappear—that would be too fucking easy—but it transformed from something solid and stuck into something fluid that could move through me instead of setting up permanent residence.

The beauty of breath work is that it doesn't require you to understand or analyze what you're feeling. The breath itself is the healer. It creates a safe container for whatever needs to emerge, and it provides the energy necessary for transformation to occur. Your body's wisdom guides the process; you simply provide the breath to fuel it and trust that your system knows what it's doing.

This was radically different from my experience with traditional therapy, where I often felt pressure to make sense of my experience, to find meaning in my trauma, to extract lessons from my pain. With breath work, understanding could come later—or not at all. The healing happened at the level of sensation and energy, not through mental comprehension.

I learned that trauma isn't just stored in our minds—it lives in our bodies, in the tension of our muscles, in the shallowness of our breath, in the areas we unconsciously avoid feeling because they hurt too much. Each held breath is a held emotion, each restricted exhale a blocked expression. Through breath work, I gained access to these hidden places and, more importantly, the tool to heal them without needing to understand every fucking detail.

EMOTIONAL RELEASE VALVE

I discovered that breath could be used as an emotional release valve for all the shit I'd been storing in my body. Years of suppressed anger, grief, and fear had been locked in my muscles and organs like pressure in a cooker about to explode. Through breath work, these emotions found their natural exit through conscious exhalation. I learned that feelings aren't permanent visitors—they're temporary guests that need to be welcomed, witnessed, and then allowed to leave instead of being told to shut up and stay hidden.

The first few breath work sessions were like opening floodgates that had been sealed for decades. Rage that I'd never been allowed to express came pouring out in sounds that seemed to come from a wounded animal rather than a civilized human being. Grief that I'd been carrying since childhood emerged in waves of sobbing that felt like they might never stop. Fear that had been frozen in my nervous system began to move and release through trembling and shaking that my body seemed to do automatically.

What shocked me was how good I felt after these intense releases. Instead of feeling depleted or traumatized by the emotional intensity, I felt cleaner, lighter, more present. It was as if my body had been waiting years for permission to discharge all the accumulated stress and pain it had been holding.

I learned that emotions have a natural lifecycle—they arise, peak, and then naturally subside if we don't interfere with the process. But most of us learned to interrupt this natural flow through distraction, suppression, or premature analysis. Breath work taught me to ride the wave of emotion from beginning to end, trusting that no feeling lasts forever and that my body knew exactly how to process whatever came up.

Most importantly, I reconnected with my life force. I had been running on empty for so long that I had forgotten what it felt like to be truly alive—to feel energy coursing through my veins, to experience the simple joy of being embodied instead of just enduring existence. Through breath work, I remembered what vitality actually feels like.

This wasn't the temporary high of stimulants or the forced energy of caffeine. This was organic aliveness—the natural state of a human being whose energy isn't blocked by trauma, whose breath isn't restricted by fear, whose nervous system isn't constantly braced for the next threat. I felt as if I were meeting my body for the first time, discovering capacities for pleasure, joy, and presence that I'd never known existed.

MY DAILY BREATHING PRACTICE

The breath work practice that became my daily anchor was surprisingly simple, yet profoundly transformative. Each morning, before the world could demand my attention and drag me into its chaos, I would spend twenty minutes breathing consciously—not the mindful breathing of meditation, but the active, intentional breathing that moves energy and releases what no longer serves.

I would lie down on my bedroom floor, place one hand on my chest and one on my belly and begin a rhythm of connected breathing—no pause between the inhale and exhale, breathing in through the nose and out through the mouth. The breath became circular, continuous, like a river flowing without interruption or apology.

As I breathed, I would scan my body for places that felt tight, numb, or disconnected, and I would consciously direct my breath into those spaces like sending healing energy to wounded parts of myself. Sometimes my lower back would begin to release tension I didn't even know I was carrying. Other times, my throat would open and sounds would emerge—sighs, moans, even occasional sobs as old grief finally found its voice after years of being silenced.

The practice evolved as I became more comfortable with the process. Some days I would focus on breathing into my heart, allowing whatever emotions lived there to surface and move. Other days I would breathe into my belly, connecting with my power and strength. Still other days I would send breath into areas of my body that felt numb or disconnected, inviting feeling and aliveness back into spaces that had been shut down for protection.

What emerged during these sessions was often surprising. Memories would surface that I'd completely forgotten—not dramatic traumatic events, but smaller moments that had shaped my understanding of safety, love, and belonging. Insights would arise about current relationships or life situations. Sometimes I would have profound spiritual experiences, feeling connected to something vast and loving that seemed to exist both within and beyond my individual consciousness.

But most importantly, these daily sessions taught me that I had agency over my internal state. Instead of being a victim of whatever emotions or anxieties happened to arise during the day, I could actively participate in my own regulation and healing. The breath became my way back to center, my tool for processing stress before it accumulated, my daily practice of coming home to myself.

ARCHAEOLOGICAL DIG OF THE SOUL

What emerged during these sessions was extraordinary—and sometimes terrifying. Memories I had forgotten surfaced and were finally processed instead of being shoved back down. Emotions I had been carrying for decades found their expression and release. The chronic tension in my shoulders, the knot in my stomach, the weight on my chest—all of it began to dissolve through the alchemy of conscious breath.

Each breath work session became an archaeological dig into my own psyche. The breath would take me exactly where I needed to go, often to places I never would have chosen to visit consciously because they were too fucking painful. One day I might breathe through the rage I had never expressed to my father. Another day, the grief of relationships that ended badly. Sometimes I would breathe through the fear of not being enough, the shame of past mistakes, or the sadness of dreams I had let die.

The process was neither linear nor predictable. Some sessions would take me deep into childhood memories, while others would focus on recent experiences that had triggered old wounds. Sometimes I would process trauma that wasn't even mine—ancestral pain that seemed to flow through my bloodline, collective wounds that belonged to my community or culture.

What made these experiences different from therapy was the embodied nature of the healing. Instead of talking about my trauma, I was breathing through it. Instead of analyzing my patterns, I was feeling them shift in real time. The insights that emerged weren't mental understandings but cellular knowing—changes that occurred at the level of my nervous system and energy body.

I learned to trust whatever came up during breath work sessions, even when it didn't make logical sense. Sometimes I would have experiences that felt spiritual or mystical—encounters with deceased relatives, visions of healing light, or sensations of being held by a benevolent presence. Other times, the experience was purely physical: energy moving through my body, tension releasing, or areas that had felt numb suddenly coming alive with sensation.

The key was learning to stay present with whatever arose without trying to control or direct the experience. The breath was the guide, and my job was simply to keep breathing and trust the process. This required letting go of the need to understand everything that was happening and, instead, learning to feel my way through the experience.

THE BREATH KNOWS WHAT TO DO

The beauty of this practice is that it doesn't require you to understand or analyze what you're feeling. The breath itself is the healer. It creates a safe container for whatever needs to emerge, and it provides the energy necessary for transformation to occur. Your body's wisdom guides the process; you simply provide the breath to fuel it and trust that your system knows what it's doing.

This was perhaps the most liberating aspect of breath work for someone like me, who had spent years trying to think my way out of trauma. I didn't need to remember every detail of what had happened to me. I didn't need to forgive people who hadn't earned forgiveness. I didn't need to make sense of experiences that were fundamentally senseless. I just needed to breathe and let my body do what it naturally knows how to do—heal.

The intelligence of the body became apparent through this work in ways that humbled my mental arrogance. My body knew exactly which memories needed attention and in what order. It knew how much emotion I could handle in a single session without becoming overwhelmed. It knew when to go deep and when to stay at the surface, when to process and when to integrate.

This bodily wisdom operated according to principles that my mind couldn't grasp. Sometimes I would enter a session wanting to work on a specific issue, only to have my body take me somewhere completely different. I learned to trust this redirection, understanding that my conscious mind didn't always know what needed healing most urgently.

Breath became my teacher in ways that no book or guru ever could. It taught me patience: some sessions were intense and cathartic, others were gentle and subtle. It taught me trust: I could surrender to the process without knowing where it would lead. It taught me presence: the only way to work with breath effectively was to be completely here, now, in this moment.

Most importantly, the breath taught me that healing doesn't require perfection or the elimination of all pain. It requires the willingness to feel what's present, to breathe through rather than around difficulty, and to trust that whatever arises can be met with consciousness and compassion.

EVERYTHING CHANGED

As my breathing deepened, everything in my life began to change. My relationship with my partner became more intimate because I was no longer afraid to breathe deeply in their presence. When you can breathe fully, you can feel fully, and when you can feel fully, you can love fully without holding back any part of yourself.

My work became more creative and fulfilling because I was accessing parts of myself that had been shut down for decades. Ideas flowed more freely, decisions came more easily, and I found myself taking risks I never would have considered when breathing from a place of fear and constriction.

My relationships with family members improved because I was no longer carrying their emotional baggage in my body like some kind of unpaid therapist. When you learn to breathe through your own emotions, you stop absorbing everyone else's drama. Boundaries became easier to maintain because I could literally feel when something wasn't mine to carry.

The changes weren't immediate or dramatic—healing rarely is, despite what social media would have us believe. But gradually and consistently, I noticed that I was more present in conversations, less reactive to stress, and more capable of handling difficult emotions without falling apart or shutting down completely.

My nervous system began to shift from chronic hypervigilance to a more balanced state where I could access both activation and relaxation as needed. I could get excited about good things without waiting for the other shoe to drop. I could feel sad without being consumed by depression. I could experience anger without exploding or turning it against myself.

Most significantly, I began to trust my own inner wisdom. When you breath fully, you're connected to your intuition, your gut feelings, your inner knowing that cuts through all the mental bullshit. The breath became my compass, guiding me toward choices that honored my authentic self rather than my adapted, people-pleasing persona.

I started making decisions based on how they felt in my body rather than how they looked on paper. I could sense, through my breath, whether a situation was good for me, whether a person was trustworthy, or whether an opportunity aligned with my deeper values rather than serving as another distraction from what really mattered.

THE DEEP DIVE: HOLOTROPIC BREATH WORK

Through the magic of holotropic breath work (HB) specifically, I was able to release past traumas and pain that I had been carrying around like fucking baggage for years. I was able not only to process my abuelito's passing but also the horrible abuse brought on by my father at an early age, as well as all the trauma from my twenties and thirties that had been festering inside me like poison.

HB was developed by psychiatrist Stanislav Grof, and it goes way beyond simple conscious breathing. It's an intensive practice that uses accelerated breathing, evocative music, and focused energy work to access nonordinary states of consciousness—basically like taking a trip without drugs. Where gentle breath work had opened the door to my healing, HB kicked that door wide fucking open and invited me to walk through the fire of my deepest wounds.

The theoretical foundation of HB was compelling to my scientific mind. Dr. Grof had spent decades researching consciousness and healing, first through psychedelic therapy and later through breath work when psychedelics became illegal. He discovered that the same non-ordinary states of consciousness that could be accessed through substances could also be achieved through specific breathing techniques, music, and bodywork.

The word *holotropic* means "moving toward wholeness"—the idea that our psyche has an innate drive toward healing and integration, and that, given the right conditions, we can access states of consciousness that allow for profound transformation. This concept resonated with everything I'd learned about the body's natural healing capacity through my other therapeutic work.

THE JOURNEY BEGINS

The first time I experienced a full HB session, I wasn't prepared for the journey my psyche would take me on. Lying on a mat in a room filled with other seekers, breathing to the rhythm of drums and haunting melodies, I felt my consciousness expand beyond the boundaries of my everyday awareness. What emerged was both terrifying and liberating—like finally facing the monsters under the bed and realizing they were just scared parts of myself.

The session began with what seemed like simple instructions: lie down, close your eyes, and breathe faster and deeper than normal for an extended period—usually two to three hours. The facilitator explained that the breath would be our vehicle for the journey, the music would provide emotional support and direction, and trained assistants would be available if we needed physical support during intense moments.

As I settled onto my mat and began the accelerated breathing pattern, I felt skeptical about whether anything significant would happen. The first twenty minutes felt mechanical—just breathing faster than normal while listening to carefully curated music that ranged from tribal drumming to soaring orchestral pieces to modern ambient soundscapes.

But then something shifted. The boundary between my individual consciousness and the larger field of awareness began to dissolve. I felt like I was expanding beyond the confines of my body, becoming part of something vast and interconnected. The music wasn't just something I was hearing—it was moving through me, shaping my experience and carrying me into territories of consciousness I'd never imagined existed.

The breath took me first to the source of my deepest pain—the abuse from my father that had shaped my entire understanding of masculinity, power, and worth. In that expanded state of consciousness, I wasn't just remembering the trauma; I was experiencing it from a place of adult strength and wisdom instead of the helpless terror I'd carried for decades.

I could feel the frightened little boy I had been, cowering in corners and learning that love came with conditions and that safety was never guaranteed. But now, through the power of my breath, I could also feel the protective presence of my adult self holding that child, telling him that he was worthy of love, that the abuse was never his fault, and that he didn't deserve any of that shit.

CONFRONTING THE SOURCE

The session became a confrontation decades in the making. In my expanded consciousness, I found myself face-to-face with my father—not as the helpless child

I had been, but as the man I had become. I was able to feel and express the rage I had never been allowed to voice, the hurt I had never been permitted to acknowledge, the love I had never felt safe to expect from him.

Through breathing, I experienced what felt like a cellular release. The fear that had been lodged in my nervous system since childhood began to shake loose like old plaster falling from walls. The hypervigilance that had kept me constantly scanning for danger started to dissolve. The voice inside my head that sounded exactly like his—critical, dismissive, and never satisfied—began to quiet the fuck down for the first time in my life.

What surprised me was that this confrontation didn't feel vengeful or destructive. The expanded state of consciousness created by the breath work included both the wounded child who needed to express his pain and the wise adult who could see the bigger picture. I could feel my father's own wounds, his limitations, the generational trauma that had shaped his capacity for love and connection.

This didn't excuse his behavior or minimize the impact of his abuse. But it allowed me to separate his actions from my worth, his limitations from my potential, his pain from my responsibility. The rage I felt was clean and necessary—not the toxic resentment I'd been carrying, but healthy anger that served as fuel for setting boundaries and reclaiming my power.

The session also allowed me to grieve the father I'd never had—the one who could have seen my sensitivity as a gift rather than a weakness, who could have celebrated my creativity instead of trying to crush it, and who could have offered protection instead of being the primary source of danger in my young life. This grief was profound but healing, creating space for the possibility that I could become the kind of man I'd needed him to be.

GRIEVING MY ABUELITO

The breathing also took me to a place of profound grief—the loss of my grandfather, my abuelito, who had been the only source of unconditional love in my childhood. His passing had left a wound in my heart that I had never properly tended, a grief so deep I had buried it beneath layers of busyness and distraction because it hurt too much to feel.

In the holotropic state, I was able to feel the full weight of that loss without the usual defenses my mind employed to protect me from pain. I cried tears that had been waiting years to fall. I felt the devastating emptiness of losing the one person who had seen me as worthy of love exactly as I was, flaws and all.

But something miraculous happened in that space of raw grief. As I breathed through the pain, I began to feel my abuelito's presence—not as a memory, but as a living energy that had never actually left me. Through the expanded awareness that the breath provided, I could feel his love surrounding me, his pride in the man I was becoming, and his gentle encouragement to keep healing and stop punishing myself.

The session became a reunion and a final goodbye rolled into one. I was able to express gratitude for all he had given me, to ask for his forgiveness for the ways I had abandoned his teachings in my darkest years, and to promise him that I would carry his love forward in how I treated myself and others, instead of continuing the cycle of self-destruction.

This encounter felt as real as any conversation I'd ever had with him while he was alive. The skeptical part of my mind wondered whether I was just creating a fantasy to comfort myself, but the part of me that had been transformed by the experience knew that it didn't matter whether it was "real" in a conventional sense. What mattered was the healing it facilitated, the peace it brought, and the way it reconnected me to the love that had shaped my capacity for goodness.

THE LIFE REVIEW

The breathing also guided me through the labyrinth of trauma from my twenties and thirties—the toxic relationships I had accepted because I believed I deserved nothing better, the self-destructive behaviors I had used to numb the pain of feeling unworthy, the opportunities I had sabotaged because success felt foreign and dangerous to someone who'd been taught he was worthless.

In one particularly powerful session, I experienced what felt like a complete review of those decades. I could see clearly how the wounds from my father had created patterns that played out in every relationship, every job, every major life decision—like some fucked-up programming I couldn't escape. But rather than the self-judgment that usually accompanied such realizations, I felt profound compassion for the wounded man who had been doing his best to survive with the tools he had.

I breathed through the shame of choices I had made from places of pain rather than wisdom. I felt and released the anger at people who had taken advantage of my wounded state. I grieved the years I had lost to depression, addiction, and the endless cycle of seeking validation from sources that could never fill the void my father's abuse had created.

But most importantly, I felt forgiveness—for myself, for the people who had hurt me, even for my father. Not the kind of forgiveness that excuses harmful behavior or pretends it didn't happen, but the kind that sets the forgiver free from the prison of resentment and perpetual victimhood.

This forgiveness wasn't something I decided to feel—it arose naturally as a byproduct of seeing the whole picture with compassion rather than just my piece of it with bitterness. When you can see how everyone involved in your story was doing their best with their level of consciousness and the tools they had available, blame begins to dissolve, and understanding takes its place.

INTEGRATION: WHERE THE REAL WORK HAPPENS

The work didn't end when the breathing stopped. Each HB session was followed by hours of integration—drawing, sharing, and reflecting on what had emerged. This was where the real healing happened, as I learned to make meaning of the experiences and weave the insights into my daily life instead of just having some trippy experience and going back to the same old bullshit.

I drew pictures of the inner child I had reconnected with, the protective father figure I was learning to become to myself, and the ancestral strength I had inherited from my abuelito. I wrote letters to people who had hurt me—not to send, but to complete conversations that had been left unfinished for decades.

The drawing was particularly powerful because it engaged parts of my brain that words couldn't access. Often, I created images that surprised me—symbols and scenes that seemed to come from some deeper wisdom than my conscious mind. These drawings became talismans of my healing journey, visual reminders of the profound experiences and insights I'd accessed through the breath.

The sharing circles after sessions were equally important. Hearing other people's experiences helped me understand that the territories I'd explored weren't unique to me but were part of the human experience. The courage of others to speak their truth gave me permission to acknowledge my own experiences without shame or self-doubt.

Through this integration work, I began to understand that healing isn't about forgetting the past or pretending it didn't happen. It's about changing your relationship to what happened, reclaiming the parts of yourself that got lost in the trauma, and choosing to write a different story moving forward instead of staying stuck in victim mode forever.

THE GRADUAL TRANSFORMATION

The changes that emerged from this deep breath work were profound and lasting, but they didn't happen overnight like some fucking miraculous cure. The chronic anxiety that had been my constant companion for decades began to fade. The depression that had colored my worldview for so long started to lift. Most significantly, I began to experience myself as worthy of love—not because I had earned it through performance or perfection, but simply because I existed.

The transformation wasn't a single moment of change—it was a gradual awakening that unfolded in layers, each breath, each insight, each moment of courage adding to the shift. What I experienced wasn't a dramatic before-and-after scenario but rather a gentle metamorphosis that happened so gradually, I sometimes questioned whether anything was really changing at all.

The first changes were subtle: sleeping more deeply, feeling slightly less reactive to stress, noticing moments of spontaneous joy that had been absent for years. My nervous system began to shift from chronic hypervigilance to a more balanced state, in which I could access both activation and relaxation as needed.

Over months of regular HB sessions, patterns that had dominated my life for decades began to loosen their grip: the compulsive need to please everyone, the automatic assumption that I wasn't good enough, the fear of abandonment that had sabotaged relationships. All of these began to transform through the alchemy of conscious breathing and emotional release.

Physical changes accompanied the emotional and psychological shifts. The chronic tension I'd carried in my shoulders and jaw began to release. My digestion improved as my nervous system learned it was safe to rest and restore. The headaches that had been my constant companion became rare occurrences.

Most importantly, I began to trust myself in ways I had never experienced before. The inner critic that had dominated my mental landscape for decades began to quiet, replaced by a more compassionate inner voice that could offer guidance without condemnation. I started making decisions based on my authentic desires rather than on what I thought others expected of me.

THE ULTIMATE IRONY

The irony wasn't lost on me: the very thing that had almost killed me became the very thing that saved my life. My inability to breathe under stress had nearly cost me everything, yet learning to breathe consciously gave me everything I had been searching for: peace, vitality, authentic connection, and a sense of coming home to myself after decades of feeling like a stranger in my own body.

Every conscious breath became an act of rebellion against the forces that had taught me to make myself small, to hold back, to play it safe, and never rock the boat. Each deep inhale was a declaration of my right to take up space, to feel my feelings, to be fully alive instead of merely surviving. Each complete exhale was a release of everything that no longer served me—old pain, limiting beliefs, the need to be anyone other than exactly who I am.

I realized that I had been living my entire life like someone who had forgotten they could breathe underwater, gasping and struggling on the surface when an ocean of life-giving breath had been available to me all along. The breath had always been there, waiting patiently for me to remember its power and stop being a fucking martyr to my own suffocation.

The journey from shallow, survival-driven breathing to conscious, life-giving breath became a metaphor for my entire healing journey. Just as I had learned to breathe more fully, I was learning to live more fully—to feel more deeply, to love more openly, to exist more authentically in a world that had spent decades trying to convince me I was too much of everything.

THE IMPORTANCE OF PROPER GUIDANCE

I will always recommend you seek a breath work specialist just like you would a therapist. Someone who can help guide you through the journey of breath work before you try to do this shit on your own and potentially fuck yourself up in the process.

This isn't just a suggestion—it's a necessity born from understanding the profound power of this practice and not wanting you to go through what I went through trying to figure it out alone. Breath work, especially intensive practices like HB, can unlock doors in your psyche that have been sealed for damn good reason. While this unlocking is ultimately healing, it needs to happen in a safe, supported environment with someone who understands the terrain you'll be navigating—not in your bedroom, where you might lose your shit with no one to help you.

A qualified breath work facilitator is like a skilled mountain guide leading you through treacherous but rewarding terrain. They know the landscape of consciousness like the back of their hand. They can recognize when someone is moving too fast or getting lost in the journey, and they have the tools to help you integrate whatever emerges safely, instead of leaving you traumatized by your own healing process.

WHAT TO LOOK FOR IN A BREATH WORK FACILITATOR

Finding the right breath work practitioner is as important as finding the right therapist—maybe more so, because you'll be entering altered states of consciousness with this person. This person will be holding space for some of your most vulnerable moments, so trust and competency aren't just nice-to-haves—they're absolutely fucking essential.

Look for someone who has extensive training in the specific modality they practice. For HB, that means certification through the Grof Foundation—not some weekend workshop that now makes them think they're an expert. For other forms of breath work, look for practitioners who have completed comprehensive training programs and have real experience working with trauma—not just someone who watched YouTube videos and decided to hang up a shingle.

Your facilitator should have a solid understanding of trauma-informed care. They should know how to create physical and emotional safety, recognize signs of overwhelm or re-traumatization, and have techniques to help you ground and integrate after intense experiences. If they don't understand trauma, they have no business guiding people through processes that can unearth deep wounds.

Pay attention to how they speak about the work. A good facilitator will be honest about both the potential benefits and risks. They'll ask about your mental health history, any medications you're taking, and whether you've experienced trauma. They should be willing to refer you to additional resources if needed, rather than trying to be your everything.

The facilitator should also create what we call a "sacred container"—a space that feels safe enough for your deepest truths to emerge. This isn't just about the physical environment, though that matters too. It's about the energetic and emotional atmosphere they cultivate. And trust me, you can feel the difference between someone who knows what they're doing and someone who's just winging it.

BUILDING YOUR PRACTICE GRADUALLY

The path I recommend is to start with guided sessions to learn proper technique and understand your own patterns and responses. Most people benefit from attending several individual or group sessions before attempting solo practice—and honestly, even then, you should probably have someone on speed dial.

During these guided sessions, pay attention to how the facilitator manages the experience. Notice how they create safety, how they guide you through difficult moments, how they help you integrate afterward. Observing this will inform your own solo practice when the time is right, so you're not just flying blind.

As you become more experienced, you can gradually extend your solo practice while maintaining regular check-ins with your facilitator. Think of it like learning to drive—you wouldn't get behind the wheel without an instructor, but eventually, you develop the skills to drive safely on your own while still knowing when to ask for help.

The investment you make in proper guidance at the beginning pays dividends in the safety and effectiveness of your ongoing practice. Yes, working with a qualified breath work facilitator requires an investment of time and money. But consider what you're investing in—your mental health, your emotional freedom, and your capacity for joy and authentic connection.

A SACRED TECHNOLOGY

HB showed me that we carry within us a sacred technology for healing that requires no guru, no expensive treatments, no years of fucking analysis that goes nowhere. The breath itself is the medicine, the healer, and the gateway to the wisdom our bodies have been trying to share with us all along. We just forgot how to listen because we are too busy being practical and ignoring our inner knowing.

Through this practice, I learned that trauma isn't a life sentence; it's information. It's the psyche's way of preserving our authentic selves until we're strong and safe enough to reclaim them without getting destroyed in the process. The breath gives us access to that preservation system and the tools to gently coax our true selves back into the light, rather than leaving them buried under layers of protection and pain.

But like any powerful tool, breathing is best learned under the guidance of someone who knows how to wield it safely and effectively. You wouldn't hand a chainsaw to someone who has never used one and say "Figure it out." The same principle applies here. Once you've learned the fundamentals and built trust in your own capacity to navigate these inner landscapes without losing your shit, the breath becomes your constant companion and healer.

YOUR INVITATION TO LIVE AGAIN

This is an invitation to stop holding your breath against life and to start breathing yourself back to wholeness, one conscious breath at a time. But please, don't walk this path alone; find a guide who can help you navigate the territory safely until you're ready to trust your own inner compass and not end up more fucked up than when you started.

The magic isn't in some complex technique or ancient secret that only special people can access—it's in the simple, revolutionary act of remembering how to breathe as if your life depends on it—while being held and witnessed by someone who understands the sacred nature of your healing journey and won't let you drown in the process.

Because here's the thing—your life does depend on it. Maybe not in the dramatic, immediate way mine almost did with that near-heart attack, but in the deeper sense of truly living instead of just surviving, of feeling instead of numbing, of being present instead of constantly running from yourself.

The breath has been there all along, waiting patiently for you to remember its power. It's been there through every panic attack, every sleepless night, every moment you felt like you couldn't handle what life was throwing at you. It's ready to help you process, release, and transform whatever you've been carrying.

You don't need to be special or spiritual or have your shit together to do this work. You just need to be willing to breathe consciously, to feel what wants to be felt, and to trust that your body knows how to heal itself when you give it the proper tools and support.

Your breath is your birthright. Your healing is your birthright. The wholeness you seek isn't something you have to earn or achieve; it's something you get to remember and reclaim.

Stop making excuses. Stop waiting for the "right time." Stop convincing yourself you're too broken to heal. Find a qualified guide, show up to the work, and start breathing like your life depends on it.

Because it fucking does.

LEARNING TO BREATHE AGAIN: YOUR FOUNDATION PRACTICE

After decades of shallow survival breathing and that wake-up call from my heart, I had to learn how to breathe all over again—not just to avoid another medical crisis, but to actually fucking live instead of just surviving on fumes. What follows isn't some complicated, ancient technique that requires years to master. This is the practical, accessible foundation that taught me to reconnect with my breath and, through it, with my life force itself.

These aren't the intensive HB practices I described earlier—those absolutely require professional guidance, and I stand by that. What I'm sharing here are the daily, foundational breathing practices that created the stability and body awareness necessary for the deeper work. Think of this as learning to walk before you run; in this case, we're learning to breathe consciously before we dive into the more profound altered states.

This foundation practice literally saved my life by teaching me that I had agency over my nervous system, that I could shift from anxiety to calm, from shallow survival mode to deep presence, just by changing how I breathed. It's the practice that taught me breathing is medicine—not metaphorically, but literally physiologically and immediately effective medicine.

SIMPLE AT-HOME BREATH WORK PRACTICE

CRITICAL WARNING: True HB should only be practiced under the supervision of a certified facilitator—I can't stress this enough. What I'm sharing here are gentler, holotropic inspired techniques that can safely introduce you to this powerful modality without you losing your shit or ending up in the ER. These practices will give you a taste of the transformative potential while keeping you in a safe zone for solo practice.

Absolute Prerequisites Before You Begin:

- You must be in good physical and mental health
- No history of cardiovascular issues, seizures, or severe mental illness
- Not pregnant or taking medications that affect breathing or consciousness
- Have a completely private space where you won't be interrupted
- Someone available by phone if you need support
- Clear understanding that if anything feels overwhelming, you stop immediately—no heroics

Foundation Practice:

Learning to Breathe Like Your Life Depends on It (10-15 minutes)

This is where I started after my heart scare—simple but profound practices that taught me the difference between survival breathing and life-giving breath.

Setup:

- Lie down on a comfortable surface with pillows for support
- Place one hand on your chest and one on your belly
- Ensure you won't be interrupted for fifteen minutes
- Have water nearby

The Practice:

1. **Awareness Phase (3 minutes):** Just notice your natural breath without changing anything. Feel

how shallow or deep it is, where it goes in your body, how your nervous system responds.
2. **Expansion Phase (5 minutes):** Begin by breathing deeply into your belly, then expanding into your chest. Make each breath longer and fuller than your natural breath, but do not force or strain.
3. **Conscious Connected Breathing (5 minutes):** Breathe in a gentle circle—no pause between inhale and exhale. Inhale through the nose, exhale through mouth, with a slight opening.
4. **Integration (2 minutes):** Return to natural breathing and notice any changes in your body, emotions, or mental state.

What This Addresses:

- Chronic anxiety and shallow breathing patterns
- Nervous system regulation
- Reconnecting with your body's wisdom
- Building confidence in your ability to self-regulate

Listen, this basic practice alone was life-changing for me. After years of breathing like I was constantly braced for impact, learning to breathe fully again felt like meeting my body for the first time. On some days, this simple practice was all I needed to shift from anxious and overwhelmed to present and grounded.

HOLOTROPIC-INSPIRED BREATHING (15-20 MINUTES MAXIMUM)

This is a gentler version of the circular breathing pattern used in full holotropic sessions—think of it as breath work training wheels that won't launch you into the stratosphere without a guide.

Setup:

- Lie down on a comfortable surface with pillows for support
- Use evocative music (instrumental, rhythmic, building in intensity)
- Have water, tissues, and a journal nearby
- Set a timer so you're not watching the clock like a crazy person
- Tell someone trusted when you're doing this practice

The Breathing Pattern:

- Breathe in a circular pattern—no pause between inhale and exhale
- Inhale through the nose deeper and faster than normal
- Exhale through the mouth with a slight opening
- Focus on making the inhale active and the exhale a natural release
- Breathe into your belly first, then let it expand into your chest
- Maintain this rhythm for ten to fifteen minutes maximum (start with five to seven minutes if you're new to this)

What May Happen:

- Tingling in hands, feet, or around the mouth (totally normal)
- Emotional releases—crying, anger, joy, or whatever wants to come up

- Body sensations or the urge to move
- Memories or insights arising
- Feeling of energy moving through your body

How to Navigate:

- If tingling becomes uncomfortable, slow your breathing slightly
- Allow emotions to flow without trying to stop or analyze them—just let that shit out
- Let your body move if it wants to—stretch, shake, or change positions
- Stay with whatever arises rather than trying to control the experience
- Trust your body's wisdom to guide the process

The first time I practiced this, I cried for what felt like hours—but it was probably only five minutes. Grief I hadn't realized I was carrying just poured out of me. It wasn't scary or overwhelming; it felt like finally letting out a breath I'd been holding for decades.

THE TRAUMA RELEASE VARIATION (10-15 MINUTES)

This focuses specifically on releasing stored trauma from the body—the stuff you've been carrying around like emotional baggage that your nervous system has been trying to discharge for years.

Setup:

- Same as above, but place extra pillows around you for comfort
- Choose music that feels protective and supportive

- Have a stuffed animal or comfort object nearby if helpful (no judgment)

The Practice:

- Begin with two to three minutes of the circular breathing pattern
- Scan your body for areas of tension, numbness, or holding
- Direct your breath toward these areas
- Breathe into the tension as if you're breathing space into tight places
- If emotions arise connected to these areas, breathe through them
- Make whatever sounds want to come—sighs, moans, even screams into a pillow
- Let your body shake, tremble, or move if it wants to
- End with three to five minutes of gentle, natural breathing

Integration Notes:

- This work specifically targets trauma stored in the body
- Shaking and trembling are natural trauma-release mechanisms—don't fight it
- Don't try to understand what's happening mentally—let the body lead the show
- Some sessions may feel intense, while others are gentle—both are perfect

The first time I deliberately breathed into my chronic shoulder tension, my whole upper body started shaking like I was cold—but I wasn't. I was finally releasing decades of braced-for-impact energy that had been locked in my muscles since childhood.

THE ANCESTRAL HEALING BREATH (15-20 MINUTES)

This variation focuses on healing generational patterns and connecting with ancestral wisdom—basically addressing the family shit that got passed down to you through bloodlines and cultural conditioning.

Setup:
- Create a small altar with photos of loved ones who have passed
- Use music that feels sacred or connected to your heritage
- Light a candle if it feels appropriate

The Practice:
- Begin with the circular breathing pattern
- Call to mind your ancestors—grandparents, great-grandparents, those who came before
- Breathe with the intention of healing patterns that no longer serve your lineage
- If pain arises (generational trauma, family wounds, etc.), breathe through it
- Breathe in the strength, wisdom, and love of your ancestors
- Feel yourself as a bridge between past and future generations
- Send healing back through your family line and forward to future generations

What This Addresses:

- Inherited trauma patterns
- Family system dysfunction
- Cultural or generational wounds
- Connection to ancestral strength and wisdom

This practice connected me to my abuelito in ways I hadn't experienced since his passing. I could feel his presence, his love, and his strength flowing through me as I breathed. It wasn't woo-woo bullshit; it was a lived experience of the love and resilience that run through my bloodline.

THE INNER CHILD CONNECTION (10-15 MINUTES)

This practice helps heal childhood wounds and reconnect with your authentic self—the kid you were before the world told you to be different, smaller, and more acceptable.

Setup:

- Have a photo of yourself as a child nearby
- Choose gentle, nurturing music
- Wrap yourself in a soft blanket for comfort

The Practice:

- Start with the circular breathing while looking at your childhood photograph
- Breathe with the intention of connecting with your younger self
- If pain, fear, or sadness arises, breathe love toward your inner child

- Let yourself feel protected and safe in this moment
- Speak internally to your younger self, offering comfort, validation, and protection
- Allow any grief about lost innocence or childhood pain to flow through you
- End by placing your hands on your heart and breathing love to yourself

When I first did this practice with a photo of myself at age seven, I felt such overwhelming love and protection for that little boy who had been so scared and alone. I found myself saying aloud, "You're safe now. You're loved now. You don't have to be afraid anymore." And for the first time in decades, I actually believed it.

CRITICAL SAFETY GUIDELINES

Stop Immediately If You Experience:

- Severe dizziness or feeling faint
- Chest pain or difficulty breathing normally
- Overwhelming panic that doesn't subside
- Dissociation or feeling completely disconnected from your body
- Traumatic memories that feel too intense to handle alone

After Each Session:

- Return to normal breathing for at least five minutes
- Drink water and eat something light if needed
- Journal about your experience without trying to analyze it to death

- Rest and be gentle with yourself for the remainder of the day
- Avoid making major decisions for several hours

Integration Practices:

- Draw, paint, or create something to express what you experienced
- Take a warm bath or shower
- Spend time in nature if possible
- Avoid alcohol or substances for twenty-four hours
- Get adequate sleep and nourishing food

BUILDING YOUR PRACTICE SAFELY

- **Week 1-2:** Practice basic conscious breathing for five to ten minutes maximum
- **Week 3-4:** Add the circular breathing pattern for short periods
- **Month 2+:** Choose specific variations based on what you're working on

RED FLAGS TO WATCH FOR:

- Needing longer or more intense sessions to feel "normal"
- Using breath work to avoid dealing with practical life issues
- Becoming isolated or disconnected from relationships
- Persistent anxiety or emotional instability after sessions
- Physical symptoms that don't resolve quickly

WHEN THIS POINTS TO PROFESSIONAL WORK

These home practices should eventually point you toward working with a certified holotropic facilitator for the full experience. If you find yourself drawn to this work, if significant material is arising, or if you want to go deeper, seek professional guidance.

The full holotropic experience in a supported setting can take you places these gentle versions cannot—and that's by design. These practices are meant to introduce you to the possibility while keeping you safe, not to replace the profound work that happens in proper therapeutic settings.

WHY THIS FOUNDATION MATTERS

What I'm giving you here isn't just breathing exercises—it's a way back to your body, your life force, your capacity for self-regulation and healing. After my heart scare, these practices taught me the difference between existing and living, between surviving and thriving.

Every conscious breath became an act of choosing life over the slow suffocation I'd been accepting as normal. Every deep inhale was a declaration that I deserved to take up space, to feel my feelings, to be fully alive. Every complete exhale was a release of everything that was killing me slowly: stress, trauma, and the accumulated weight of decades of shallow breathing.

You can stop holding your breath against life and start breathing yourself back to wholeness. Not through some esoteric practice that demands perfection, but through the simple, revolutionary act of remembering how to breathe consciously, with intention, like the sacred practice it has always been.

THE SACRED NATURE OF THIS WORK

Even these gentler versions connect you to something profound: your body's innate wisdom, your psyche's drive toward healing, your connection to something larger than your everyday consciousness. Treat this work with reverence and respect, not as a casual breathing exercise you do while checking email.

Your breath is a bridge between your conscious and unconscious mind, between your individual healing and your connection to all life. Even in these simplified forms, you're engaging with ancient wisdom and powerful medicine that have the potential to change your life.

Remember: this is not just breathing. This is a sacred dialogue with your deepest self, conducted through the language of breath, witnessed by your own compassionate awareness, and held by your commitment to your own healing.

Start gently, proceed slowly, and trust that your inner wisdom will guide you toward exactly what you need for your healing journey. Your breath has been waiting your entire life for you to remember its power.

And for fuck's sake, be safe about it. Find professional guidance when you're ready to go deeper. Your healing is too important to risk by being careless or trying to be a hero.

This is how you stop suffocating yourself one shallow breath at a time and start living fully—one conscious breath at a time.

CHAPTER 7

The Road Back to Me

Through my own journey of self-healing and discovering these six tools along the way—shadow work, generational trauma healing, EMDR, journaling, meditation, and breath work—not only was I able to heal the PTSD that I'd been carrying around like a fucking backpack for over thirty-five years, but I also broke generational curses and healed wounds that had been passed down like toxic heirlooms. These six sacred tools allowed me to do the work on this healing journey; they allowed me to pave the path to a much healthier, happier life instead of the half-life I'd been surviving.

The road that I built led me back to me. The answer was always with in me—not some external savior, not a perfect partner, not a magical cure, but me. I no longer needed to outsource my happiness like I was some kind of emotional contractor. I no longer needed to outsource love, validation, acceptance, and worth to people who couldn't even give those things to themselves. With these six magical tools, I found that, in the end, I needed to find all those things within myself, where they'd been waiting all along.

THE PERFECT PATH

Looking back, I can see how each tool I discovered wasn't random; each was a stepping stone on a path my soul guided me toward, even when my conscious mind was fighting the process every step of the way. Each one prepared me for the next, revealing a different aspect of the healing puzzle, and together they created something far more powerful than any single modality could achieve alone.

Shadow Work taught me to stop running from the parts of myself I had deemed unacceptable—the angry parts, the sensitive parts, the parts that didn't fit into neat little boxes that made other people comfortable. It showed me that wholeness meant embracing all of who I am, not just the parts that others found palatable or "appropriate." Through facing my shadow, I reclaimed the energy I had been wasting on hiding, suppressing, and pretending to be someone I wasn't.

But shadow work did more than just help me accept rejected aspects of myself; it revolutionized my entire understanding of human psychology and healing. I learned that what we judge most harshly in others is often what we've disowned in ourselves, that our triggers are invitations to reclaim lost parts of our wholeness, that the very traits we've learned to see as weaknesses might actually be our greatest strengths in disguise.

The process of befriending my shadow transformed my relationships in ways I hadn't expected. When I stopped projecting my disowned anger onto others, I could see their behavior more clearly and respond rather than react. When I embraced my own sensitivity instead of trying to toughen up, I became more compassionate and better able to hold space for others' pain. When I owned my need for attention and validation instead of pretending I didn't care what people thought, I could ask for what I needed directly rather than manipulating for it indirectly.

EMDR gave me a way to process the trauma without drowning in it, as I'd been doing for decades. It taught me that my nervous system could learn new responses, that the past didn't have to control my present like some kind of emotional puppet master, and that healing was possible even when the wounds felt permanent and defining.

The breakthrough moments in EMDR weren't just about remembering traumatic events differently—they were about discovering that my adult self had resources and strength that my traumatized child self couldn't access. I could revisit scenes from my childhood with the wisdom and power of my current age, offering protection and comfort to younger versions of myself who had felt completely alone and helpless.

This process taught me that trauma isn't just what happened to us, but what happened inside us as a result of what happened to us. The events themselves couldn't be changed, but my relationship to those events could be completely transformed. Instead of being haunted by the past, I could reach back and offer my younger selves what they'd needed but never received—love, protection, and the acknowledgment that they deserved better.

FINDING THE REAL ME

Journaling became my daily practice of truth-telling. It gave me a safe space to be honest about my experience without judgment, to track my growth, and to engage in dialogue with the parts of myself that needed attention.

Through writing, I learned to be my own witness and my own guide instead of constantly seeking validation from people who couldn't even figure out their own shit.

But journaling offered something beyond just emotional release—it became my laboratory for experimenting with different ways of being. On the page, I could try on new perspectives, explore possibilities I was too scared to consider in real life, and practice conversations I needed to have but hadn't yet found the courage for. I could be simultaneously the scientist and the subject of my own transformation.

The daily practice of writing taught me to listen to my own voice instead of the chorus of other people's opinions, expectations, and judgments that had been running my life for decades. In the quiet space where pen met paper, I could hear what I actually thought about things—what I wanted and what mattered to me beneath all the conditioning and people-pleasing patterns.

Meditation showed me that beneath all the noise of my thoughts and emotions was a vast, peaceful awareness that had never been touched by trauma. It taught me that I was not my thoughts, not my feelings, not my story—I was the consciousness experiencing all of these things, the awareness that remained constant even when everything else was chaos.

This wasn't just a philosophical concept but a lived reality that I could access through practice. In meditation, I discovered the part of myself that had never been damaged, never been rejected, never been abandoned. This awareness didn't deny or minimize my human experiences, but it provided a stable foundation from which to relate to them without becoming completely identified with them.

The space between thoughts that meditation revealed became my refuge during difficult times. When anxiety threatened to overwhelm me, I could rest in the awareness that was witnessing the anxiety without being consumed by it. When sadness arose, I could feel it fully while knowing that it was a temporary weather pattern in the sky of consciousness—not a permanent statement about reality.

Breath work became my bridge between the conscious and unconscious, between the mind and the body, between the individual and the universal. It gave me access to healing energies and wisdom I didn't even know existed within me—like discovering I had superpowers I'd never used.

Through breath work, I learned that the body holds wisdom the mind can't access through thinking alone. My breath became a direct line to information about what I needed, what was ready to heal, what wanted to be released. It taught me to trust my body's intelligence and to work with, rather than against, my natural healing processes.

Generational trauma healing became the missing piece that finally made everything else make sense. For years I'd been trying to understand why certain patterns felt so deeply embedded, why some wounds seemed to come from nowhere, and why healing certain aspects of myself felt like I was fighting against invisible forces. This tool taught me that I wasn't just carrying my own pain—I was carrying the unhealed trauma of my entire lineage.

Through generational trauma work, I learned that many of the beliefs I thought were mine weren't actually mine at all. The fear of being too much, the shame around my queerness, the terror of abandonment—these were inherited survival strategies passed down through generations of family members who had learned to hide, adapt, and survive in hostile environments. Understanding this didn't minimize my pain, but it helped me see that my healing could break cycles that had been repeating for decades—maybe centuries.

This work also helped me understand that my queerness wasn't a deviation from my family line—it was evolution. I was the one chosen to break patterns of emotional unavailability, rigid gender roles, and fear-based living. My difference wasn't a mistake; it was medicine for my entire lineage.

THE TOOLS DANCING TOGETHER

Each tool had its own gifts, but the real magic happened when they began working together like some kind of healing orchestra. Shadow work would reveal a hidden aspect of myself; generational trauma healing would show me how that pattern had been passed down through my family line; EMDR would help me process both the personal and ancestral trauma; journaling would help me integrate the insights; meditation would give me the space to hold it all with compassion; and breath work would help me embody the changes at a cellular level.

This wasn't a linear process—healing never is, despite what the self-help books promise. Some days I would start with meditation and end up in deep shadow work. Other days, a journaling session would reveal something that needed EMDR processing. Sometimes breath work would unlock ancestral memories that required generational trauma healing. The tools began to dance together, each one informing and enhancing the others in ways that created exponential rather than additive effects.

For example, shadow work might reveal that I had disowned my anger, but generational trauma healing would show me how that rejection was learned from watching my father suppress his rage—which he had learned from his father, and so on. EMDR would help me process both my personal trauma around anger and the inherited fear of emotional expression, while journaling would help me make meaning of the patterns. Meditation would provide spacious awareness to hold both my anger and my family's fear with compassion, and breath work would help me embody healthy anger and emotional expression at a cellular level.

This integrated dance of tools isn't just some mystical concept—it's exactly what you'll experience when you do the deep work. When you sit down for your weekly deep dive, you'll feel shadow work revealing family patterns, generational trauma healing illuminating personal wounds, breath work moving ancestral energy, and EMDR helping you process both individual and inherited shit simultaneously. It's messy, it's powerful, and it works in ways that single-tool approaches just can't match.

I learned that healing isn't about perfection—it's about integration. It's about bringing all the scattered parts of yourself home, accepting the totality of your experience, and learning to love yourself not despite your wounds but because of how you've grown through them. The goal wasn't to eliminate all pain or challenge from my life, but to develop the capacity to meet whatever arose with presence, wisdom, and compassion.

Each tool taught me something essential about this integration process. Shadow work taught me that wholeness includes darkness as well as light. Generational trauma healing taught me that my wounds weren't just mine—and my healing wasn't just for me. EMDR taught me that painful experiences could be metabolized rather than just endured. Journaling taught me that my story belonged to me and I could choose how to tell it. Meditation taught me that I was much vaster than any single experience or identity. Breath work taught me that healing happened in the body, not just the mind.

BREAKING THE GENERATIONAL BULLSHIT

But perhaps the most profound realization was that my healing wasn't just about me. As I worked through my own trauma, I began to understand that I was carrying wounds that weren't originally mine. The anxiety, the depression, the patterns of dysfunction—many of these were inherited, passed down through generations of family members who had never had the tools or opportunity to heal their own pain.

My father's rage wasn't just his—it was his father's, and his fathers before him, like some fucked-up family tradition nobody wanted but everyone kept passing along. The family patterns of emotional unavailability, of using alcohol to numb pain, of believing that vulnerability was weakness—these were generational strategies for survival that had outlived their usefulness, but nobody had bothered to update them.

Through my healing work, I wasn't just changing my own life—I was changing the trajectory of my entire family line. Every pattern I broke, every wound I healed, every limiting belief I transformed was a gift not just to myself but to the generations that would come after me—kids who wouldn't have to carry the same emotional baggage I'd been lugging around.

I could feel it happening in real time. As I healed my relationship with my father through shadow work and EMDR, I noticed changes in how he related to me during our rare interactions. The charge between us began to dissipate. I no longer felt triggered by his limitations, and he seemed less defensive about my differences. As I processed my generational trauma through breath work, I felt lighter—as if ancestral burdens were being lifted from my shoulders like invisible weights I'd been carrying.

The understanding that I was healing for more than just myself gave my work a sense of purpose that sustained me through the difficult phases. When the shadow work felt too painful, when the EMDR sessions stirred up more than I thought I could handle, when the breath work took me to places that scared the shit out of me, I could remember that I wasn't just doing this for me. I was doing it for my ancestors who never had these opportunities and for descendants who would inherit a different legacy because of the work I was willing to do.

This understanding also helped me approach my family with more compassion. Instead of seeing them as the villains in my story—which felt satisfying but kept me stuck—I could finally see them as wounded people passing along wounds they never got the chance to heal. Their parents had fucked them up, and their parents' parents had fucked them up—going back generations of people doing their best with the tools they had, which weren't nearly enough.

The practice that follows this chapter will show you exactly how to do this generational healing work—not through wishful thinking or burning sage, but through practical tools that address the trauma living in your nervous system. You'll learn to talk with your lineage, release inherited patterns through breath work, and quite literally feel the weight of ancestral burdens lifting from your shoulders.

THE SEARCH OUTSIDE MYSELF

For most of my life, I had been looking outside myself for the things I needed most, like some kind of spiritual beggar asking everyone else for what I already had. I sought validation from relationships, tried to find worth through achievements, chased happiness through external circumstances, and looked for love in all the wrong places—basically, everywhere except the one place it actually existed.

This pattern wasn't conscious; I wasn't deliberately choosing to outsource my well-being. It was the natural result of growing up in a family system where my authentic self was consistently rejected, where love came with conditions, and where my worth was determined by how well I could perform the role everyone else needed me to play. I learned to look outside myself for validation because looking inside had only revealed a self that nobody seemed to want.

The deeper wound beneath all my trauma was the belief that I was fundamentally lacking—that what I needed to be whole existed somewhere out there: in someone else, in some future moment when I finally got my life together and stopped being such a mess. This core belief had driven every self-destructive pattern, every toxic relationship, every moment of settling for less than I deserved.

I had developed an elaborate system of external-validation seeking that operated like an addiction. I needed other people to tell me I was smart, attractive, worthy, lovable—and even when they did, it never stuck. The high would wear off within hours or days, and I'd need another fix. No amount of external validation could fill the internal void, because the void wasn't caused by a lack of love from others—it was caused by a lack of love from myself.

This realization was both devastating and liberating: devastating because it meant that all the energy I'd spent trying to get others to love me had been misdirected; liberating because it meant that the love I was seeking was actually within my control. I didn't need to wait for someone else to see my worth—I could learn to see it myself.

THE MOST RADICAL TRUTH

These six tools taught me the most radical truth of all: everything I had been seeking was already within me—not as some bullshit concept to understand intellectually, but as a living reality to experience directly.

Through shadow work, I found that the parts of myself I had rejected were often the keys to my wholeness. The sensitivity I had learned to see as weakness was actually my superpower for connecting with others. The anger I had tried to suppress was healthy, boundary-setting energy that I needed to protect myself. The creativity I had dismissed as impractical was the expression of my authentic self that brought me joy and purpose.

Through EMDR, I discovered that my nervous system could generate feelings of safety and calm without needing perfect external circumstances. The peace I had been seeking through controlling my environment and other people's behavior was available internally, regardless of what was happening around me. I learned that I could feel secure even when things were uncertain, loved even when I was alone, and worthy even when others didn't recognize my value.

Through journaling, I learned to be my own best friend, therapist, and guide. The wise voice I had been seeking in teachers and mentors and partners was my own voice—just covered over by years of conditioning that told me not to trust my own experience. On the page, I could access insights and perspectives that were more helpful than any advice I'd ever received from others.

Through meditation, I touched the unshakeable peace that existed beneath all my stories about myself and my life. This wasn't a temporary state to achieve but my fundamental nature to return to. The love, acceptance, and belonging I had been desperately seeking from others was what I actually was at the deepest level—not something I needed to earn or find, but something I needed to remember and embody.

Through breath work, I accessed the life force energy that had always been my birthright, but that I had learned to restrict through trauma and conditioning. The vitality, passion, and aliveness I had been trying to generate through external stimulation were available through simply breathing consciously and allowing my natural energy to flow.

The outsourcing stopped because I finally understood that I was not a broken thing needing to be fixed by someone else. I was a whole being who had temporarily forgotten my wholeness under layers of conditioning, trauma, and adaptation to a world that seemed determined to convince me I was fundamentally flawed.

THE TRANSFORMATION BEGINS

The changes that began to occur as I integrated these tools weren't dramatic or instantaneous—they were subtle shifts that accumulated over time into a completely different way of being in the world. I started noticing that I was less reactive to other people's moods and opinions. Criticism that would have devastated me before just bounced off like I was wearing invisible armor. Praise felt nice, but I no longer needed it to feel good about myself.

My relationships began to transform as I stopped trying to get from others what I could only give to myself. Instead of entering interactions with a hidden agenda of needing validation, approval, or emotional regulation, I could show up as I actually was and relate to people as they actually were, rather than as characters in my story about getting my needs met.

This shift was most obvious with my partner. For years, our relationship had been strained by my constant need for reassurance—that he still loved me, still found me attractive, still wanted to be with me. I would interpret his bad moods as evidence that he was losing interest, his need for space as rejection, and his focus on work or other interests as abandonment. I was exhausting to be in relationship with because I was constantly seeking external regulation of my internal emotional state.

As I learned to validate myself, regulate my own emotions, and find my own center regardless of what was happening around me, our relationship became lighter, more playful, more genuinely intimate. Instead of relating to him as a source of supply for my emotional needs, I could relate to him as a separate person with his own experiences, challenges, and journey. Instead of love being something I desperately needed from him, it became something I was overflowing with that I wanted to share.

This transformation happened gradually in all my relationships. Friendships became more authentic because I stopped performing and started showing up as I was. Family interactions became less charged because I wasn't seeking their approval or validation. Professional relationships improved because I wasn't constantly worried about what people thought of me.

THE PERSON I BECAME

Looking back at who I was before this healing journey feels like looking at a different person entirely—not because I became someone new, but because I finally became who I'd always been underneath all the trauma and adaptation. The angry, anxious, spiritually homeless gay man who first walked into therapy transformed, through thousands of hours of practice, into someone capable of finding peace, guidance, and authentic connection regardless of external circumstances.

The transformation wasn't about eliminating all negative emotions or achieving some state of perpetual bliss—that would have been spiritual bypassing, not authentic healing. Instead, it was about developing a completely different relationship to whatever arose in my experience. Fear could be felt without controlling me. Sadness could be honored without drowning in it.

Anger could be expressed without destroying relationships. Joy could be experienced without waiting for the other shoe to drop.

I became someone who could sit with uncertainty without needing to control outcomes. Someone who could be vulnerable without feeling like I was going to die from exposure. Someone who could set boundaries without guilt, ask for what I needed without shame, and say no without extensive justification.

Perhaps most significantly, I became someone who genuinely liked himself—not in an arrogant or narcissistic way, but with the simple appreciation you might have for a friend who had been through hell and come out the other side with wisdom, humor, and compassion intact. I could look in the mirror and see someone who had done the best he could with what he had, who had learned from his mistakes, and who was worthy of love and respect.

This self-acceptance wasn't conditional on perfect behavior or constant growth; it was unconditional acceptance of my humanity, including my flaws, limitations, and ongoing areas of growth. I no longer needed to be perfect to be worthy. I could be imperfect and still be enough.

WHEN HEALING CHANGES EVERYTHING

As I healed, everything around me began to change—not because I became someone new, but because I was finally showing up as myself. My relationship with my partner deepened because I was no longer trying to get from him what I could only give to myself. My friendships became more authentic because I stopped performing and started showing up as I am, messy parts and all. My work became more fulfilling because I was no longer seeking external validation for my worth like some kind of approval addict.

The changes in my work life were particularly dramatic. For years, I had been stuck in jobs that felt soul-crushing but provided the security and stability I thought I needed to feel saf in the world. I had prioritized financial security over creative fulfillment, thinking that pursuing my artistic interests was selfish or impractical.

As I healed and reconnected with my authentic self, I began to feel called to work that expressed my creativity and served others' healing. The book you're reading now is a direct result of that transformation—I never could have written about healing with such honesty and vulnerability before I had done the work myself. The courage to share my story, to be public about my struggles and growth, came from no longer needing to maintain a perfect image.

I also started offering support to other LGBTQ+ people of color who were facing similar challenges—not as some expert who had figured everything out, but as someone who had walked a similar path and was willing to share what I'd learned. This work felt infinitely more meaningful than any corporate job I'd ever had because it was aligned with my authentic purpose rather than just paying bills.

The transformation also affected my relationship with my family. While I couldn't change their beliefs or behaviors, I could change my response to them. Instead of being triggered by their limitations, I could feel compassion for the pain that drove their rejection. Instead of trying to convince them to accept me, I could accept myself fully and relate to them from that place of wholeness.

This didn't mean becoming a doormat or accepting abusive behavior—if anything, I became much better at setting boundaries. But the boundaries came from self-care rather than reactive anger, from clarity rather than confusion, from strength rather than defensiveness.

THE RIPPLE EFFECTS

Perhaps most importantly, I became a different presence in the world. Where once I had unconsciously passed on my wounds through my interactions—spreading anxiety, negativity, and dysfunction like some kind of emotional virus—I now had the capacity to offer healing. Not as someone who had figured it all out, but as someone who had done the work and was willing to be vulnerable about the journey.

I realized that every person who heals themselves changes the entire field of human consciousness. We're all connected, and when one person breaks free from patterns of suffering, it becomes easier for others to do the same. My healing wasn't just personal—it was transpersonal, touching the lives of everyone I encountered and creating ripple effects I may never fully know.

The transformation was evident in small, daily interactions. Cashiers at grocery stores seemed to light up when I approached—not because I was performing friendliness, but because I was genuinely present with them. Friends started seeking me out for advice about their own challenges, sensing that I had developed some capacity to hold space for pain without being overwhelmed by it.

I began to understand that healing is not a destination but a way of being—a commitment to consciousness, to growth, and to showing up authentically regardless of circumstances. The tools I had learned weren't just techniques for fixing problems but technologies for ongoing transformation: ways of engaging with life that supported continuous evolution rather than just temporary relief from symptoms.

THE CALL YOU RECOGNIZE

If you've read this far, something in you recognizes this journey. Something in you knows that you, too, are carrying burdens that aren't yours to carry—patterns that no longer serve you, wounds that are ready to be healed. Something in you is calling you home to yourself, and it's growing louder every day.

That something is your soul speaking—the part of you that has never forgotten your true nature, even when your mind was convinced you were broken beyond repair. It's the inner wisdom that drew you to this book, that keeps you awake at night knowing there's more to life than the patterns you've been living, that whispers in quiet moments that healing is possible even when everything feels hopeless.

The recognition you're feeling isn't coincidence—it's resonance. Your soul recognizes truth when it encounters it, even when your mind is full of doubt. The fact that you're here, reading these words and considering the possibility that another way exists, is evidence that you're ready for this journey, even if you don't yet feel ready.

Right now, as you read these words, pay attention to what's happening in your body. Is there a stirring?

A recognition? Perhaps a flutter of hope mixed with fear? That's your soul saying yes to the possibility of return, even though your wounded parts wonder whether it's safe to hope again after being disappointed so many times.

I want you to know: it is safe to hope. More than safe—it's fucking necessary.

THE COURAGE TO BEGIN

These six tools—shadow work, generational trauma healing, EMDR, journaling, meditation, and breath work—are available to you right now. Not as magic bullets that will instantly solve all your problems (because that's not how healing works), but as faithful companions on the journey back to wholeness. They require courage, commitment, and compassion for yourself as you navigate the terrain of your own healing—and your family's healing.

Let's be honest about what this courage looks like, because it's not the Hollywood version. It's the courage to feel emotions you've spent years avoiding because they hurt too much. It's the courage to look at parts of yourself you've hidden even from your own awareness. It's the courage to sit with discomfort without immediately reaching for distraction. And it's the courage to trust that you can handle whatever arises in your healing process, even when it feels overwhelming.

This isn't the courage of heroes in movies—it's quieter, more ordinary, more real. It's the courage to get out of bed on days when depression feels like a weighted blanket trying to suffocate you. It's the courage to breathe through anxiety instead of running from it. It's the courage to write one true sentence in your journal when lies feel safer. It's the courage to meditate for five minutes when your mind is screaming that you don't have time for this shit.

The commitment required isn't perfection—it's persistence. It's showing up for yourself even when you don't feel like it, especially when you don't feel like it. It's choosing growth over comfort, truth over convenience, healing over hiding in familiar dysfunction. Some days you'll feel motivated and inspired; on others, you'll need to rely on discipline and determination. Both are part of the process.

And the compassion—oh, the compassion you'll need for yourself. Compassion for how long it's taken you to get here. Compassion for the choices you made from wounded places when you didn't know better. Compassion for the parts of you that are still afraid to trust. Compassion for the slowness of healing, for the nonlinear nature of growth, for the days when you feel like you're going backward instead of forward.

WHAT YOU'LL DISCOVER

The road back to yourself won't be easy, but it will be worth every difficult step. Because at the end of that road, you'll discover what I discovered—that everything you've been searching for has been within you all along, waiting patiently for you to come home.

This road will have unexpected turns that'll catch you off guard. There will be days when you feel like you're making incredible progress, followed by days when old patterns resurface and you wonder whether you've learned anything at all. There will be moments of profound insight followed by periods of confusion. There will be times when healing feels like the most natural thing in the world—and times when it feels impossible.

Some days the road will feel like a gentle path through a beautiful garden. Other days it will feel like you're climbing a mountain in a fucking storm with no visibility. Both experiences are part of the journey. Both are necessary. Both are preparing you for the reunion with yourself that awaits.

You'll discover that courage isn't the absence of fear—it's feeling the fear and choosing love anyway. You'll learn that strength isn't about never falling—it's about getting back up, again and again, with more self-compassion each time. You'll understand that healing isn't about becoming perfect—it's about becoming whole.

You'll find that you are enough, you are worthy, you are love—not because of what you do or achieve, but because of who you are in your essence. This isn't a consolation prize or something you have to earn through good behavior or spiritual achievement. It is the fundamental truth of your being, the bedrock reality that exists whether you believe it or not.

When you were born—before you learned you were supposed to be different than you were—you knew this truth. You existed in a state of natural self-acceptance, natural joy, natural connection to life itself. That state didn't disappear; it just got covered by layers of conditioning, trauma, and adaptation to a world that often demanded you be smaller than you were.

The journey home is about excavating that original self, not creating something new. It's about removing what doesn't belong so that what has always belonged can shine through. It's about unlearning the lies you were taught about your worth and remembering the truth you were born knowing.

YOU ARE BOTH THE JOURNEY AND THE DESTINATION

These six tools can help you find your way, but ultimately you are both the seeker and the sought, the question and the answer, the road and the destination. This isn't some mystical bullshit—it's the most practical truth you'll ever encounter.

You are the seeker because you're the one choosing to embark on this journey, the one committing to your own healing, the one willing to do the hard fucking work of return when it would be easier to stay stuck in familiar dysfunction. But you're also what you're seeking—wholeness, love, acceptance, peace. These aren't destinations you arrive at like some spiritual vacation spot; they're the very ground of your being that you're learning to recognize and inhabit.

You are the question that life is asking: *How will this unique expression of consciousness choose to heal and grow and love?* But you're also the answer: *Through this particular combination of experiences, challenges, gifts, and choices that could only be lived by me—in my own messy, beautiful, completely fucked-up, and perfectly imperfect way.*

You are the road because every step of your healing journey becomes part of the path that others will follow. Your courage to face your shadow gives others permission to face theirs instead of pretending they don't have one. Your willingness to heal generational patterns shows others that family cycles can, in fact, be broken. Your commitment to processing trauma helps heal the collective wounds we all carry—because when one person heals, it creates ripples that touch everyone around them. Your dedication to authenticity makes it safer for others to be real instead of performing some acceptable version of themselves.

And you are the destination because what you're returning to was never actually lost—only forgotten, buried, and covered over by years of conditioning that convinced you that you needed to be someone else to be worthy of love. The wholeness you seek is your true nature. The love you crave is what you are. The peace you long for is the essence of who you've always been beneath all the noise and drama.

THE TIME IS NOW

So, here's my invitation, and I'm not going to sugarcoat it: stop waiting for the perfect moment, the perfect readiness, the perfect circumstance. Stop waiting until you feel brave enough, strong enough, worthy enough to begin. That day will never come if you keep waiting for it. The time is now because now is all we ever fucking have. The place is here because here is where your life is happening—not in some imaginary future when everything is easier.

Start where you are, with what you have, as you are—messy, scared, imperfect, and completely human. Choose one of these five tools and take one small step. Write one true sentence in a journal, even if your handwriting sucks. Sit in meditation for five minutes, even if your mind races the entire time. Take ten conscious breaths, even if you feel ridiculous doing it. Schedule an appointment with a therapist trained in EMDR, even if you're terrified of what might come up. Reflect on one shadow aspect you're ready to integrate, even if you'd rather pretend it doesn't exist.

And because I'm not going to leave you hanging with just inspiration and no instruction, what follows is a complete roadmap for integrating all six tools into one powerful practice. This isn't some gentle, light-touch bullshit—it's a comprehensive weekly practice that will kick your ass in all the right ways while honoring both your personal healing and your ancestral lineage. It's where all that beautiful theory about the six tools dancing together becomes a lived reality that'll transform you from the inside out.

The journey of a thousand miles begins with a single step, but even more importantly, the journey home to yourself begins with a single moment of choice—the choice to stop running from who you are and start running toward who you've always been beneath all the masks and performances and adaptations.

Your soul is calling you home. It's been calling for years, maybe decades, through every moment of dissatisfaction, every feeling of emptiness, every time you've looked in the mirror and felt like you were seeing a stranger. It's calling through your anxiety, your depression, your addiction, your relationship problems—all of it is your soul saying, *"Come home. Remember who you really are. Stop trying to be someone else."*

WILL YOU ANSWER?

The question isn't whether you're ready. The question isn't whether you deserve healing. The question isn't whether you're strong enough or brave enough or worthy enough.

The question is simple: Will you answer?

Will you take that first step, imperfect as it may be? Will you choose healing over familiar suffering? Will you risk discovering that you've been enough all along, that the love you've been seeking has been waiting inside you, that the peace you've been chasing has been your birthright from the beginning?

Your healing matters. Your wholeness matters. Your authentic self—the one you've been hiding and protecting and apologizing for—that self matters more than you can possibly imagine.

The tools are here. The path is available. You are worthy.

All that's left is to begin.

So, what are you waiting for? Your life is calling. Your soul is calling. The real you—the one you've been looking for everywhere except the one place it actually lives—is calling.

Answer the call. Take the step. Begin the journey home.

You've got this, and you've always had this. You just forgot for a while.

Now it's time to remember.

THE SACRED INTEGRATION PRACTICE: BRINGING ALL SIX TOOLS HOME

All right, you've read about the journey; now it's time to actually take it. This integrated practice is where the rubber meets the road—where all that beautiful theory about the six tools dancing together becomes a lived reality that'll transform you from the inside out.

Important Note: This isn't for spiritual beginners who want everything to be comfortable and easy. This practice is designed for those ready to do the real work of breaking generational cycles and reclaiming their authentic selves. If you're new to any of these tools, start with individual practices first and work with professionals when needed. Don't try to be a hero and jump into the deep end—you'll just end up drowning in your own shit and your ancestors' too.

This practice honors the truth I've been sharing throughout this chapter—that your healing and your family's healing are inseparable. Every shadow you integrate, every generational pattern you understand, every breath you take with consciousness is simultaneously personal revolution and ancestral liberation.

THE SACRED INTEGRATION PRACTICE

This practice weaves together shadow work, generational trauma healing, EMDR-inspired techniques, journaling, meditation, and breathwork into a cohesive healing session. It honors the truth that your healing and your family's healing are inseparable. Every shadow you integrate, every generational pattern you understand, every breath you take with consciousness is simultaneously personal revolution and ancestral liberation.

Time Required: 2-2.5 hours

Frequency: Weekly

Note: This isn't for beginners who want everything comfortable. If you're new to these tools, start with individual practices first and work with professionals when needed. Don't jump into the deep end—you'll drown in your own shit and your ancestors' too.

Preparation:

Choose a quiet, private space. Gather a journal, pen, cushion or mat, blanket, tissues, and water. Set up meaningful objects—photos of ancestors, candles, whatever supports your practice. Turn your phone off. Have contact info for a trusted friend or therapist available if needed.

Light a candle to mark the beginning of sacred time. Take three deep breaths and set an intention. Remind yourself: "I am safe to explore my family patterns. I have the strength to heal what needs healing. I am supported by all who came before me."

PHASE 1: CENTERING MEDITATION (10-15 MINUTES)

Sit comfortably with your spine straight but relaxed. Close your eyes and begin with natural breathing. Feel your connection to the earth beneath you and your ancestors before you. Bring awareness to your body, starting from your feet and moving up. Notice any areas of tension, numbness, or holding without trying to change them—just notice and breathe.

As you settle into stillness, acknowledge that you are about to enter sacred space. This isn't just self-improvement—this is ancestral work, lineage healing. Ask yourself: "What aspect of my healing most needs attention today—personal shadows or family patterns?" Listen for the first response that arises, without judgment. Hold this intention as you continue.

PHASE 2: SHADOW WORK INQUIRY (15-20 MINUTES)

Explore these questions: What am I avoiding looking at in my life right now? What pattern keeps repeating that I'm ready to understand differently? What part of myself am I rejecting or trying to hide? What would I never want anyone to know about me?

When you identify a shadow aspect, don't judge it—it developed to protect you. Get curious: "How has this part been trying to protect me?" Imagine it as a character and give it a voice. Ask: "What do you need me to know? What do you need from me?" Listen without judgment; this part developed for good fucking reasons.

PHASE 3: GENERATIONAL TRAUMA HEALING PRACTICE (25-30 MINUTES)

Safety Note: This can bring up intense emotions related to family patterns and ancestral wounds. Start slowly and have support available if needed.

Generational trauma consists of the emotional and psychological wounds that get embedded in families, showing up in how we love, fight, survive, and self-destruct—generation after generation until someone finally breaks the cycle. For LGBTQ+ people of color, we're often carrying multiple layers: historical trauma, cultural trauma, family trauma, and personal trauma from rejection.

Family Pattern Recognition: Complete these sentences quickly, writing the first thing that comes to mind: "In our family, emotions are..." "In our family, being different means..." "Love in our family looks like..." "To be safe, I learned to..." "People like us don't..."

For each message, ask: How does this belief still control my choices? How has this served my family's survival? How is it limiting me now?

Ancestral Dialogue: Place both hands on your heart and say: "I honor all my ancestors who survived so I could be here. I see your strength, your sacrifice, your love." Then write about one family pattern you're ready to heal—how it served your ancestors' survival, how it's limiting you now, what the healthy version would look like.

Healing Conversation: Write a brief letter: "Dear ancestors, I understand you did the best you could. I see how trauma shaped the patterns you passed down. I am breaking the cycles of pain while keeping your gifts of resilience and love. The healing begins with me."

Integration: Take several deep breaths. Feel the support of healed ancestors around you. Say aloud: "I break these cycles not just for me, but for all of us. The trauma stops here. The healing begins now."

PHASE 4: EMDR-INSPIRED SELF-PROCESSING (15-20 MINUTES)

Safety Note: This is a gentler, self-administered version. If intense trauma arises, stop immediately and seek professional support. Don't try to be a hero—some wounds need professional care.

EMDR works by using bilateral stimulation to help your brain process stuck traumatic material. When we experience trauma, especially repeated trauma, memories can get stuck in fragmented, unprocessed forms. This is why a smell or tone of voice can send you right back to feeling twelve years old and rejected.

Bilateral Stimulation Options: Choose one—Butterfly Hug (cross arms over chest, alternately tap shoulders), Knee Tapping (alternately tap left and right knees), or Eye Movements (slowly move eyes left and right while keeping head still).

The Process: Bring to mind a family pattern from earlier work—start small, not your biggest trauma. Notice where you feel it in your body. Rate disturbance 1–10. Begin bilateral stimulation for 15–30 seconds. Pause and notice what arose—images, feelings, ancestral memories. Repeat 4–6 sets, letting whatever wants to arise come forward. Continue until disturbance decreases.

PHASE 5: CONSCIOUS BREATH WORK (15-20 MINUTES)

Breathwork is one of the most powerful tools for releasing trauma stored in the body. For communities that have experienced generations of survival-mode living—holding breath, bracing for danger, swallowing grief—learning to breathe fully again is literally learning to live fully again.

Lie down comfortably with knees supported. Practice connected circular breathing—inhale through nose, exhale through mouth, no pause between breaths. Breathe slightly deeper and faster than normal, but not to strain. Direct breath to areas activated during earlier phases.

The Process:
Minutes 1–5: Establish the rhythm.
Minutes 5–10: Allow whatever wants to arise—emotions, sensations, ancestral memories.

Minutes 10–15: Breathe into and through whatever is present, imagining you're breathing healing back through your family line. Final minutes: gradually return to natural breathing.

Safety: If overwhelmed, slow down or return to natural breath. Let your body move, shake, or make sounds if it wants to—you might be releasing ancestral energy that's been stuck for generations. You are safe, and this too shall pass.

PHASE 6: INTEGRATIVE JOURNALING (25-30 MINUTES)

Without editing or censoring, write continuously about your experience. What came up during each phase? What emotions, sensations, or insights arose? What felt challenging? What felt healing?

Reflection Questions: What did you discover about the shadow aspect you explored? How does it relate to family patterns? What family patterns did you recognize today? What ancestral gifts are you ready to reclaim? What shifted during the bilateral stimulation? What did the breath reveal? What's one thing you can do this week to honor your healing? How can you be an ancestor that future generations will be proud of?

PHASE 7: CLOSING INTEGRATION (5-10 MINUTES)

Return to meditation. Sit quietly and breathe naturally. Notice how your body feels now compared to the beginning. Thank yourself for showing up to this healing work. Thank your ancestors for their survival and your descendants for inspiring your healing. Set a gentle intention for integrating today's insights.

Closing Ritual: Blow out your candle mindfully. Take three deep breaths. Say aloud: "I honor my courage to heal generational patterns. I embrace all parts of myself and my heritage. I am breaking cycles and creating new legacies. I am exactly where I need to be."

POST-PRACTICE CARE

Immediate: Drink water, eat something nourishing, take a warm shower if desired. Avoid alcohol or substances for the day. Be gentle with yourself—generational trauma work is intense. Spend time in nature if possible.

Integration: Review journal entries over the following days. Notice any dreams or shifts around family relationships. Practice extra self-compassion. Reach out for support if family trauma feels overwhelming.

WEEKLY VARIATIONS

- **Week 1:** Foundation: Gentle shadow work, light generational work. Just learn the flow.
- **Week 2:** Emotional Release: Emphasize breathwork. Let ancestral grief and anger move through.
- **Week 3:** Deeper Work: More time on generational healing. Explore cultural patterns.
- **Week 4:** ntegration: Focus on journaling. Celebrate cycles broken, envision your legacy.

WHEN TO MODIFY OR SEEK SUPPORT

Reduce intensity if: overwhelmed by family trauma or ancestral grief, shadow material feels too intense to handle alone, you're in conflict with family about your healing, nervous system feels overstimulated, or you're questioning your cultural identity in destabilizing ways. Seek professional support if: intense trauma memories feel unmanageable, you experience suicidal thoughts or feeling like you don't belong anywhere, family members become hostile about your healing work, or you feel completely disconnected from your cultural identity.

BUILDING YOUR PERSONAL PRACTICE

This practice is a template, not a prison. As you become familiar with the flow, adapt it to your needs. If you only have 90 minutes, shorten each phase proportionally while maintaining the sequence. Some days, focus more on personal shadows; other days, on family patterns. Let your system guide you toward what needs attention.

- **Month 1:** Learn the flow and build safety.
- **Month 2:** Deepen shadow work and pattern recognition.
- **Month 3:** Process deeper family trauma.
- **Month 4+:** Let intuition guide which areas need attention.

THE SACRED NATURE OF THIS WORK

Remember that you are engaging in sacred work—not just returning home to yourself, but healing your entire lineage. Each time you show up, you choose courage over inherited fear, integration over fragmentation, healing over perpetuating cycles of harm. This is not small work. This is the work that changes everything.

You are not just healing yourself—you are healing backward through your family line and forward into future generations. When you break a cycle, you free the ancestors who were trapped in that pattern. They may have passed on, but on some level they are still waiting for someone to do what they couldn't do. You are that someone.

And when you break the cycle, you create a new legacy for all the descendants who won't have to carry it—who will get to start from a different place, a freer place, because you did this work.

Trust the process. Trust your wisdom. Your healing is revolutionary. Your wholeness is an act of love for everyone who came before you and everyone who will come after. The trauma stops with you. The healing begins with you. And that is the most powerful fucking thing you can do.

So take a breath. Light your candle. Open your journal. And begin the work that will change everything. You—brave, beautiful, broken-open you—are exactly the right person to do this work.

CHAPTER 8

A Love Letter to My Community

Look, I need to start by saying thank you for taking this wild fucking ride with me. I'm writing this book because I know damn well I'm not the only first-generation queer person of color who's been drowning in this shit. When I first started researching generational trauma, trying to make sense of why I felt so broken, you know what I found? Nothing. Absolutely nothing that spoke to someone like me—gay, Mexican, carrying family wounds that go back generations while also dealing with the fresh trauma of being rejected for who I love.

I kept searching, piecing together whatever scraps of information I could find, making my own path through the wilderness of healing because I had no other choice. If someone had handed me a book like this one when I was at my lowest point, when I was convinced I was too fucked up to ever be whole? I would have thrown my money at them so fast it would have made their head spin.

Before I go any further, though, I need to pause and thank the people who made this transformation—and this book—possible. Because healing doesn't happen in isolation. My journey would have been impossible without the guides who saw my potential when I couldn't see it myself.

THANK YOU TO THE PIVOTAL PEOPLE I MET ALONG THE ROAD

Drew Olsen, my therapist—the man who created the first truly safe space I'd ever experienced in my life. Drew, you allowed me to open up completely and heal in ways I never thought possible. When I walked into your office five years ago, I was a broken mess of rage, fear, and self-hatred. You saw through all that bullshit to the whole person underneath. More than that, you saw this book in my future when I was still convinced I had nothing valuable to offer the world. You believed in my story before I even knew I had one worth telling. Your patience, your wisdom, and your refusal to let me hide from my truth changed the entire trajectory of my life. Thank you from the bottom of my heart for seeing me when I couldn't see myself.

Diane Collard, my spiritual advisor—the woman who saw my full potential and gave me the sacred space to continue healing after therapy had opened the doors. Diane, you created a container where I could vent, process, and integrate all the transformation happening inside me. You saw this book as part of my story and healing journey long before I understood that my pain could become medicine for others. You knew that I needed to create a space of love and authenticity to spread my knowledge and my story to help others. Your guidance helped me understand that my healing wasn't just personal—it was meant to be shared. Thank you for holding space for my evolution and for always believing in my capacity to transform pain into purpose.

Stephen Cervantes, my husband, my anchor, my home—I could not have done any of this without your unconditional love and support from day one. For eleven years, you've loved me through every breakdown, every breakthrough, every moment when I wanted to give up on healing because it hurt too much. You've celebrated my victories and held me through my failures. You've never asked me to be smaller, different, or easier to love. You've just loved me—fiercely, completely, without conditions. Cheers to eleven beautiful years together and to many more memories we'll create as the people we're becoming. You are living proof that chosen family can love better than blood family ever could.

These three humans—Drew, Diane, and Stephen—didn't just support my healing—they made it possible. They saw things in me that I was too wounded to see in myself, and they refused to let me settle for the half-life I thought was all I deserved.

THE BRUTAL REALITY WE FACE

Here's the brutal truth: as queer people of color, we're not just playing life on hard mode—we're playing on expert level while everyone else gets the fucking tutorial. Most of us don't make it past forty or forty-five, and that's not an exaggeration—that's reality. When our families disown us for being who we are, when we're cut off from the very support systems that are supposed to keep us alive, we turn to whatever we can find to numb the pain: drugs, meaningless sex, alcohol—anything to quiet the voice in our heads that says we're worthless, anything to fill the void where family love used to live.

Research backs up what we already know in our bones: generational trauma affects more than eighty-three percent of LGBTQ+ people. We can't keep pretending this isn't happening. We can't keep acting like this is just "normal" struggle.

THE STATISTICS THAT BREAK MY HEART

When I tell you that LGBTQ+ youth are four times more likely to attempt suicide than their heterosexual peers, when I share that forty percent of homeless youth identify as LGBTQ+ despite being only seven percent of the general population, these aren't just numbers—these are our brothers and sisters, our children, our community members. These are real people whose lives were cut short or derailed because the world couldn't handle their authenticity.

Let me break down what we're really dealing with here, because the numbers paint a picture that should make every single person in this country lose sleep at night.

When it comes to suicide and mental health, the numbers tell a brutal story. LGBTQ+ youth are four times more likely to attempt suicide than their straight peers. Transgender youth face suicide attempt rates of fifty to sixty percent. LGBTQ+ adults are twice as likely to experience a mental health disorder and two and a half times more likely to experience depression, anxiety, and substance abuse than the general population.

The homelessness crisis in our communities is staggering. Nearly seventy percent of LGBTQ+ homeless youth report that family rejection was a major factor in their housing instability, and we're 120 percent more likely to experience homelessness than our straight counterparts.

Violence and discrimination follow us everywhere. One in four LGBTQ+ people experience discrimination based on sexual orientation or gender identity. Transgender people face unemployment rates twice the national average, and LGBTQ+ people of color experience higher rates of violence than white LGBTQ+ individuals. We're more likely to be victims of hate crimes than any other marginalized group.

But here's what those cold statistics don't capture—they don't show the daily microaggressions that wear us down like water on stone. They don't measure the exhaustion of code-switching between our authentic selves and the versions we perform for safety. They don't quantify the psychological toll of hypervigilance, of constantly scanning environments to determine which parts of ourselves are safe to reveal.

They don't capture the specific trauma of being rejected by the very people who brought you into this world, who are supposed to love you unconditionally but instead decide you're too shameful to claim. They don't show the ripple effects of family rejection—the lost holiday traditions, the absence from family photos, the cousins who grow up not knowing you exist because your parents erased you from the family narrative.

THE DOUBLE-BIND THAT'S KILLING US

Being queer comes with its own particular flavor of trauma. Being a person of color comes with another. But existing at the intersection of both? That creates a special kind of hell that most healing spaces don't even acknowledge, let alone know how to address.

We're carrying wounds that aren't even ours—the trauma of slavery, colonization, genocide, all that ancestral pain living in our DNA like some kind of inherited poison. We're carrying our families' struggles with poverty, discrimination, the exhaustion of trying to survive in a world that was literally designed to destroy us. And then, because life apparently has a sense of humor, we add our own layer of rejection—being cast out for whom we love, how we move through the world, our refusal to squeeze ourselves into boxes that were never meant to fit us anyway.

Most of us grew up in communities where being queer wasn't just frowned upon—it was seen as a betrayal of everything sacred. Coming out didn't just mean losing a relationship or two; it meant risking the complete obliteration of our support systems.

In Latino families, machismo culture teaches that being a "real man" means being aggressive, emotionally closed off, and sexually dominant over women. Being gay doesn't just violate these expectations—it obliterates them completely. You're not just failing to be the right kind of man; you're being the wrong kind of human. The shame isn't just personal—it's cultural, generational, and spiritual.

This constant shape-shifting, this exhausting hypervigilance about which parts of ourselves are safe to reveal and when, creates a bone-deep tiredness that goes way beyond anything a single marginalized identity experiences. We're not just tired; we're soul-exhausted from never being able to just exist without calculation.

We learn to be one version of ourselves with family (if we're lucky enough to still have contact), another with our communities of origin, another in predominantly white queer spaces where we're the only brown face in the room, and yet another in professional settings where both queerness and culture have to be carefully managed so we don't make anyone "uncomfortable."

The psychological toll of this constant navigation is staggering. We develop hypervigilance as a survival skill—constantly reading rooms, assessing threats, and calculating which aspects of our identity are safe to reveal in any given situation. This hypervigilance burns enormous amounts of mental and emotional energy, leaving us exhausted before we even begin to deal with the normal stresses of life.

THE SILENCE THAT'S LITERALLY KILLING US

For too damn long, our communities have treated mental health, trauma, and healing like dirty secrets. We've been raised with the toxic belief that therapy is for "locos," that vulnerability is weakness, that talking about our pain is somehow betraying our families or our cultures. "Don't air our dirty laundry," they say. "Be grateful for what you have." "Pray harder, work harder, try harder—anything but actually deal with the shit that's eating you alive."

This silence is murdering us. Not metaphorically—literally.

In Latino families, mental health is often understood through a spiritual lens. Depression is interpreted as a failure to pray enough, anxiety as not trusting God enough, struggle as ingratitude for your blessings. Seeking professional help is seen as a lack of faith, an admission that God isn't sufficient to handle your problems.

In immigrant families across cultures, there's often the belief that since previous generations survived war, poverty, and displacement without therapy, current generations should be able to handle modern problems without "special treatment." There's survivor guilt—who are we to complain about our problems when our ancestors faced so much worse?

When we can't name our pain, we can't heal it. When trauma becomes this thing we're not allowed to discuss, it rots inside us like emotional cancer. When we're told to just "get over" being abandoned, abused, or discriminated against, those experiences don't disappear—they go underground where they fuck with our nervous systems, destroy our self-worth, and make healthy relationships feel impossible.

Substance abuse in LGBTQ+ communities isn't just partying or poor choices—it's often self-medication for untreated trauma. When you can't afford therapy, when your family won't acknowledge your pain, when the world tells you that your very existence is wrong, alcohol and drugs become medicine for emotional wounds that no one will help you heal.

Risky sexual behavior isn't just about promiscuity or moral failure—it's often about seeking connection and validation in a world that denies your worth. When you've been told you're unlovable, when your family has rejected you, when society treats your sexuality as deviant, any form of physical intimacy can feel like proof that you're not completely worthless.

Self-harm and suicide attempts aren't attention-seeking or manipulation—they're the logical result of being told repeatedly that the world would be better without you. When your own family would rather pretend you don't exist than accept who you are, when religious institutions tell you that God hates you, when society treats your love as an abomination, death can start to feel like mercy rather than tragedy.

BUT WE'RE ALSO FUCKING RESILIENT

The statistics are absolutely heartbreaking, but you know what those cold numbers don't capture? They don't capture the fact that we're also the most resilient, creative, joy-filled motherfuckers on the planet. They don't show how we've learned to build chosen families that love us better than the ones we were born into. They don't measure how we've transformed our pain into art that moves people, activism that changes laws, healing practices that serve entire communities.

Every Pride parade is a celebration of our refusal to disappear. Every LGBTQ+ business is a declaration that we deserve economic power. Every same-sex couple raising healthy children is proof that love makes families, not genetics. Every openly queer person of color in a position of leadership is evidence that we can transform systems from the inside out.

We've created entire cultural movements that have changed how the world understands gender, sexuality, love, and family. We've pioneered new forms of art, music, literature, and performance that express truths the mainstream couldn't handle. We've developed healing practices that integrate Western psychology with indigenous wisdom, creating therapeutic approaches that honor both individual trauma and collective healing.

Our communities have always been laboratories for social innovation. Long before mainstream society accepted the idea that families could be chosen rather than biological, we were creating kinship networks based on love and mutual support rather than blood relations. Before the broader culture understood that gender is a spectrum rather than a binary, we were living and expressing gender fluidity as a natural part of human diversity.

THE SUPERPOWERS NOBODY TALKS ABOUT

Our experiences at the intersection of multiple marginalized identities have given us insights into healing that others completely miss. We understand that trauma isn't just personal—it's systemic, generational, and cultural. We know that healing can't happen in some isolated therapy bubble; it has to happen in community, with people who get it, who've walked similar paths.

We know what it means to mother ourselves when our actual mothers couldn't or wouldn't. We know how to create sacred rituals from whatever spiritual scraps we can gather—a little Catholicism here, some indigenous wisdom there, whatever speaks to our souls when traditional religion has slammed the door in our faces.

We've learned to trust our gut because external authorities failed us so spectacularly. We've learned to question everything because the rules we inherited were designed for our oppression, not our liberation. We've learned to love fiercely—ourselves and others—because we know how rare and precious real love actually is.

Our emotional intelligence is off the charts because growing up having to read every room for potential danger develops extraordinary sensitivity to mood shifts, unspoken tensions, and hidden motivations. This hypervigilance—while exhausting—makes us incredibly skilled at understanding human psychology and navigating complex social dynamics.

Our adaptability is unmatched because constantly switching between different cultural codes makes us incredibly flexible. We can speak multiple "languages"—not just linguistic but cultural, social, and professional. This skill makes us invaluable in workplaces, relationships, and communities that need bridge-builders and translators between different worlds.

Our creativity emerges from necessity because when you can't find yourself reflected in mainstream culture, you learn to create your own representation. LGBTQ+ people of color have always been cultural innovators—creating new forms of art, music, fashion, and expression that eventually influence mainstream culture. Our creativity isn't just talent—it's a survival skill, a way of making ourselves visible in a world that prefers us invisible.

Our resilience runs deeper than most people can imagine because surviving family rejection, cultural discrimination, and systemic oppression requires a level of strength that most people never have to develop. This isn't just individual fortitude—it's collective wisdom about how to endure, how to find hope in hopeless situations, how to create joy in the midst of suffering.

These aren't consolation prizes for all the shit we've endured. These are actual superpowers, forged in the fire of adversity, refined through the alchemy of survival. And now it's time to use them—not just for ourselves, but for our communities, for the generations coming behind us, and for the world that desperately needs what we have to offer.

CREATING THE RESOURCES WE NEEDED

I wrote this book because I was tired of searching for healing resources that actually understood my experience and coming up empty-handed. I was tired of reading self-help books written by people who'd never had to choose between their family and their truth, who'd never had to navigate being brown in white spaces or queer in straight spaces or poor in rich spaces.

I wanted queer people of color to pick up a book and see themselves reflected in the healing journey, not just as footnotes or special case studies, but as the central story. I wanted people to know that our particular brand of complex trauma isn't some exotic disorder that requires specialized treatment—it's valid, it's treatable, and it's actually more common than anyone wants to admit.

But more than just representation, I wanted to document a real path through the wilderness that others could follow. Not the exact same path—because everyone's healing journey is as unique as their fingerprint—but proof that there is a way through. Evidence that it's possible to heal from the kind of complex, intersectional trauma that therapists sometimes don't even know how to name, let alone treat.

I wanted to create something that held space for both our pain and our power—something that didn't minimize the real impact of systemic oppression or ask us to just "think positive" our way out of structural inequality, but also didn't leave us stuck in victim mode forever. Something that said, "Yes, the world has been brutal to you, and yes, you still have the power to heal and thrive and create a life worth living."

The six tools I've shared throughout this book—shadow work, generational trauma healing, EMDR, journaling, meditation, and breathwork—aren't just techniques I happened to stumble upon. They're the result of years of searching for healing modalities that could address the specific ways trauma shows up in our communities. Each tool addresses a different aspect of the complex trauma we carry.

Shadow work helps us reclaim the parts of ourselves we've learned to reject based on cultural messaging about what's acceptable. For LGBTQ+ people of color, this often means reclaiming our sensitivity, our creativity, our emotional expressiveness—all the things that made us targets for discrimination but are actually our gifts.

Generational trauma healing addresses the inherited wounds that live in our family systems and our bodies. This is crucial for our communities because we're often carrying not just our own trauma, but ancestral trauma passed down through bloodlines that have experienced slavery, colonization, war, and displacement.

EMDR processes the specific traumatic memories that created our survival patterns. This helps us rewrite our nervous system's responses to triggers and develop new ways of relating to our past experiences.

Journaling gives us a way to process our experiences without having to make them palatable for others. In a world that constantly demands we translate our pain into language that makes others comfortable, journaling is where we can tell our truth in our own words.

Meditation connects us to the part of ourselves that was never damaged by oppression. Beneath all the conditioning and trauma, there's an essential self that remains whole and worthy regardless of external circumstances.

Breathwork helps us release trauma that's stored in our bodies, not just our minds. For communities that have experienced generations of survival-mode living, learning to breathe fully again is literally learning to live fully again.

What I discovered in my healing journey is that there's an entire underground network of healers, teachers, and wisdom keepers who understand our specific needs. They might not be in mainstream psychology journals or featured on wellness podcasts, but they're out there—often other LGBTQ+ people of color who've done their own healing work and are now serving their communities.

TO THOSE STILL FINDING THEIR WAY

If you're reading this and you're still drowning in the thick of it—if you're still using whatever you can get your hands on to numb the pain, if you haven't spoken to your family in years because loving yourself means losing them, if you wake up some mornings wondering if it's worth staying alive—I need you to hear something: you are not broken beyond repair. You are not too damaged to heal. You are not the lost cause your inner critic keeps telling you that you are.

The fact that you picked up this book means something is still fighting for your life inside you. The fact that you're curious about healing, even if you don't believe it's possible for someone like you, means there's still a spark of hope that hasn't been extinguished by all the shit you've been through. That spark—however small, however flickering—is everything. That's the seed your entire transformation can grow from.

Listen to me: you don't have to heal perfectly. You don't have to do it quickly or follow anyone else's timeline or meet anyone else's expectations of what recovery should look like. You don't have to forgive people who haven't earned forgiveness or make peace with systems that are still actively trying to destroy you. You don't have to be grateful for trauma that should never have happened to you in the first place.

You just have to keep breathing. You just have to keep choosing life, one messy day at a time, one imperfect breath at a time, one small act of self-care at a time. Some days, survival is the victory. Some days, getting out of bed is heroic. Some days, not hurting yourself is the most radical act of self-love you can manage—and that's enough. That's more than enough.

Your healing doesn't have to look like anyone else's. It doesn't have to be linear or pretty or Instagram-worthy. It just has to be yours, and it just has to keep you moving forward, even if forward looks like standing still some days.

I know the world has given you every reason to believe you're worthless, unlovable, too damaged to deserve good things. I know your family's rejection feels like proof that there's something fundamentally wrong with you. I know the discrimination you've faced makes it hard to believe you matter. But all of that is lies—lies told by people who were hurt themselves, lies perpetuated by systems that profit from our pain, lies that have nothing to do with your actual worth.

You matter because you exist. You deserve love because you're human. You have gifts the world needs because you've survived shit that would have destroyed people with less resilience. Your difference isn't a mistake—it's medicine for a world that desperately needs the perspective that can only come from someone who's been where you've been.

TO THOSE WHO HAVE FOUND HEALING

If you're reading this and you've already walked through the fire and come out the other side—if you've done the hard fucking work of breaking generational cycles, if you've found some semblance of peace with your family situation or made peace with the fact that peace isn't possible, if you've built a life that actually feels worth living—first of all, thank you. Thank you for not giving up when everything in you wanted to. Thank you for choosing to heal instead of just surviving. Thank you for being living, breathing proof that transformation is possible, even when it feels impossible.

But here's the thing: our work isn't done. Not even close.

As we heal, we become something precious and powerful—we become lighthouses for people who are still lost in the storm. Our very existence becomes a form of activism, a middle finger to every system that expected us to stay broken, stay silent, stay small. Every day we wake up whole and healed and choosing joy over bitterness is an act of revolution against forces that profit from our pain.

So share your story when it's safe to do so. Don't let anyone guilt you into sharing before you're ready or in spaces that aren't safe, but when you can, let people see what's possible. Create art that tells the truth about what it's like to heal from the inside out. Write songs, paint pictures, write poetry, make TikToks—whatever medium speaks through you, use it to show others that healing isn't just some fantasy for privileged people with perfect lives.

Mentor the younger queer people of color who are just starting to realize they deserve better than the hand they were dealt. Be the person you needed when you were drowning. Share resources, offer guidance, hold space for their anger and their fear and their confusion. Remember what it felt like to believe you were alone in this shit and make sure they know they're not.

Your healing isn't just personal—it's political as fuck. It's revolutionary. Every pattern you break weakens the systems designed to keep us traumatized and powerless. Every boundary you set teaches someone else that boundaries are possible. Every time you choose self-love over self-destruction, you're not just healing yourself—you're healing all of us.

THE FUTURE WE'RE CREATING

I have dreams about the future we're building together, and they keep me going on the days when the world feels too heavy and the work feels too slow.

I dream of a world where young queer people of color don't have to spend the first three decades of their lives unlearning trauma before they can start actually living. Where they don't have to choose between honoring their heritage and honoring their truth. Where being different isn't dangerous—it's celebrated as the gift it actually is.

I dream of families who don't mourn when their kids come out, but celebrate. Parents who say, "Thank you for trusting us with your truth" instead of "How could you do this to us?" Abuelas who brag about their gay grandkids instead of pretending they don't exist. Communities that see our queerness as adding richness to the culture, not threatening it.

I dream of healing resources that actually understand our experience—therapists who get why coming out isn't just individual courage but community risk, treatment centers that understand how racism and homophobia compound each other, healing spaces that don't ask us to choose between our queerness and our culture because they understand that we are whole people deserving of whole acceptance.

I dream of a world where being queer and being a person of color aren't sources of shame and trauma but sources of pride and power. Where our intersectional identities are recognized as the superpowers they actually are—the wisdom that comes from navigating multiple worlds, the resilience that comes from surviving multiple forms of oppression, the creativity that emerges from having to invent ourselves when the world gives us no models.

This future isn't some pipe dream that'll magically appear if we wait long enough. We have to build it, brick by fucking brick, choice by choice, healed life by healed life.

Every time we choose therapy over self-medication, we're building it. Every time we set a boundary with family instead of accepting toxic love, we're building it. Every time we choose vulnerability over isolation, even when it's scary as hell, we're building it. Every time we choose to love ourselves fiercely instead of accepting the scraps others are willing to offer, we're building this future for ourselves and everyone who comes after us.

HEALING FOR THE ANCESTORS WHO COULDN'T

Here's something I truly believe: when we do this healing work, we're not just fixing ourselves. We're healing for all the ancestors who never got the chance. We're healing for the abuelas who swallowed their pain because survival was more important than processing. We're healing for the abuelos who drowned their trauma in alcohol because that was the only coping mechanism available to men in their generation.

We're healing for all the queer ancestors who lived and died in closets, who never experienced the freedom of being fully themselves, who carried the crushing weight of hiding their truest selves from the very people they needed love from most. We're healing for all the people of color who endured discrimination and violence without having words for systemic oppression, without having communities that understood their specific struggles.

Every cycle we break, every boundary we set, every wound we heal—it doesn't just change our lives. It changes the trajectory for everyone who comes after us. The kids being born today into families touched by our healing won't have to carry the same emotional baggage we inherited. They'll get to start from a different place, a place where wholeness is possible, where being different isn't dangerous, where love doesn't come with impossible conditions.

Our ancestors survived unimaginable hardships so that we could be here today, doing this work. They endured slavery, war, genocide, displacement, and persecution without the tools and resources we have access to. They carried trauma in their bodies, their genes, their family systems because they had no other choice.

They passed it down to us not because they wanted to harm us, but because they didn't know how to heal it.

Now we have the opportunity to be the generation that says, "This stops here." We have access to healing modalities our ancestors couldn't even imagine. We have language for experiences they had to suffer in silence. We have communities of support they could only dream of. We have the legal protections and social acceptance that they died fighting for.

Using these advantages to heal ourselves isn't selfish—it's sacred work. It's honoring their sacrifice by breaking the cycles they couldn't break. It's taking the foundation they built with their suffering and using it to construct something beautiful and life-giving for future generations.

A PRAYER FOR OUR COMMUNITY

May we never forget that we come from a long line of badass survivors—people who endured shit that would break most humans so that we could be here today, living and loving and healing in ways they could only dream of.

May we honor their sacrifice by keeping the parts of their legacy that make us strong while having the courage to say "fuck no" to the parts that keep us small. May we take the resilience and leave the trauma. May we inherit their strength without inheriting their silence.

May we build chosen families that love us so completely, so unconditionally, that we finally understand what we were missing all along. May we create homes where authenticity is celebrated, where difference is treasured, where love doesn't come with impossible conditions or expiration dates.

May we find healing that doesn't just help us cope with our pain but transforms us into people who can experience genuine joy without waiting for the other shoe to drop. May we discover peace that isn't fragile, wholeness that doesn't require perfection, love that doesn't demand we shrink ourselves to receive it.

May we use all the wisdom we've gained from walking through hell to create more justice in this world. May our unique perspectives—forged in fire, refined through struggle—become tools for liberation, not just for ourselves but for everyone still fighting to be free.

May we remember that our queerness isn't some cosmic mistake or burden we have to bear with grace. It's a fucking gift—a superpower that lets us see the world differently, love more expansively, create more authentically. May we stop apologizing for who we are and start celebrating the magic we bring to this world.

May we remember that our cultures of origin aren't prisons to escape from but treasures to reclaim and transform. May we take the beauty and wisdom and leave the homophobia. May we honor our roots while growing in directions our ancestors never imagined possible.

May we live long, full lives that honor both the struggles that shaped us and the triumphs we've fought for. May we collect joy like we once collected wounds. May we die old and surrounded by love, having lived so authentically that our very existence inspired others to do the same.

May we become the ancestors that future generations look back on with pride. May they say, "Those were the ones who broke the cycles. Those were the ones who chose healing over harm. Those were the ones who made it possible for us to love ourselves from the beginning."

UNTIL WE ARE ALL FREE

The work continues, and it's beautiful and messy and hard as hell. The healing continues, sometimes in big breakthrough moments and sometimes in the quiet choice to treat ourselves with kindness when the world hasn't been kind. The love continues—imperfect, fierce, revolutionary love that refuses to accept anything less than full acceptance.

We're not just surviving anymore, though survival was its own form of resistance. We're thriving in ways that would blow our younger selves' minds. We're not just healing ourselves—we're healing entire family lines, entire communities, the collective wounds that have been festering for generations.

We are the ones we've been waiting for. We are the answer to our ancestors' desperate prayers whispered in the dark. We are the beginning of the future our descendants will inherit—a future where being different isn't dangerous, where love isn't conditional, where healing is possible for everyone.

So keep going, even on the days when going feels impossible. Keep healing, even when it hurts worse before it gets better. Keep loving—yourself, your chosen family, your community, this broken beautiful world that needs what only you can offer.

Keep being exactly who you are, unapologetically and fully and without asking permission from anyone. The world needs your light, your truth, your particular flavor of magic that could only come from someone who has walked your exact path and emerged not bitter but brilliant—not broken but beautifully whole.

Your healing is sacred work. Your love is revolutionary. Your very existence is proof that another way is possible.

Until we are all free, we keep walking each other home.

With infinite love, respect, and solidarity for this wild, beautiful journey we're on together,
Peter J Cervantes

"We are not going to be some fragile people. We are going to be a people who have been through fire and came out whole." —James Baldwin

"Your silence will not protect you. Your healing will liberate us all." —Audre Lorde

"The most revolutionary thing you can do is heal yourself and love yourself fully." —Unknown

EPILOGUE

The Work in Real Time

I'm writing this sixteen days before my wedding and three months before my book releases.

My emotional support best friend has been laid to rest, and I'm supposed to be finalizing edits about trauma recovery while learning what grief actually feels like when you can't run from it.

Let me tell you about the mindfuck I'm living through right now:

I have a manuscript open on my laptop. The Road Back to Me: Six Sacred Tools for Queer Healing Through Shadow, Breath, and Truth. My debut self help/ memoir. The book I spent five years living and two years writing. The book that is being released early 2026 that will change my life and prove that the illiterate kid everyone gave up on actually had something worth saying.

I'm on my final round of edits with my editor. We're polishing chapters about Shadow Work and EMDR and breathwork. We're making sure my voice stays raw and real. We're refining sections about how to sit with difficult emotions, how to process trauma, how to do the brutal, necessary work of healing.

And I'm doing all of this while sobbing at my keyboard because my son just died.

Not my human son—my fur son. My eighty-pound white boxer with the prance walk and the heart-shaped spot on his face and the grunts that meant "I love you." The being who taught me more about unconditional love than any human ever did. The family member who was there for every single therapy breakthrough and every panic attack and every moment I wanted to quit the healing work because it was too fucking hard.

Ziggy Marley is gone. And I'm supposed to be finishing a book about healing while I'm actively using every single tool in it just to survive the day.

Here's the cosmic joke: I wrote an entire book about doing the work. About facing your shadow. About staying present with pain instead of running from it. About using tools like breathwork and EMDR to process trauma so it doesn't control your life anymore.

I wrote about transformation because I lived it. Because I survived five years of the hardest healing work I've ever done. Because I learned how to use these tools and they fucking worked—they saved my life, they changed my life, they gave me a life worth living.

And then life said, "Good. You learned the tools. Now let's see if you can actually use them when shit gets real. Let's see if this healing work holds up under the weight of acute grief."

The irony isn't lost on me. The universe has a fucked up sense of humor, and apparently I'm the final exam for my own book.

But here's what I need you to understand: The tools work. They're working right now. I'm using them in real time, and that's what this chapter is about—showing you that everything I wrote in this book is real and true and holds up when life breaks you open.

I'm literally editing chapters about staying present with difficult emotions while using breathwork to get through panic attacks about Ziggy. I'm reading my own words about Shadow Work while doing Shadow Work on the parts of me that feel guilty for putting him down. I'm polishing sections about processing trauma while sitting in the middle of the most acute grief I've ever experienced.

I'm not writing about healing from a theoretical place anymore. I'm not writing about trauma I processed years ago with the luxury of distance and perspective. I'm writing about it while actively living it. While proving—to myself, to you, to anyone who doubts that this work actually works—that everything in this book is real.

This is the test. This is the proof. This is me showing you that the tools I'm teaching you actually fucking work when you need them most.

This is what nobody tells you about writing a memoir about trauma recovery: The work never ends. You don't write the book and then you're done. You don't process your trauma and then live happily ever after with no more pain to work through. You don't graduate from healing.

Life keeps teaching you. Life keeps breaking you open. Life keeps handing you new lessons when you think you've learned enough.

And if you're me—if you write a book about healing and then have it scheduled to come out right as life decides to test whether you actually believe what you wrote—you get to prove in real time that the work holds up.

That's the mindfuck. Not that the tools don't work—they do. But that using them doesn't mean you're not in pain. It just means you know how to be in pain without running from it. You know how to sit with grief instead of numbing it. You know how to process loss instead of pretending it didn't happen.

I have every tool I need. I know exactly what to do. I'm doing it right now—breathwork, therapy, Shadow Work, meditation, sitting with the uncomfortable emotions instead of spiritually bypassing them, and writing. Always writing.

And it still hurts like hell.

Both things are true. The tools work AND it hurts. The healing is real AND the grief is real. I can be doing everything right AND still be shattered.

That's the lesson Ziggy is teaching me right now. That's what this chapter is about. That's what I need you to understand before you go thinking that doing the work means you'll never hurt again.

WHAT NOVEMBER 8TH TOOK FROM US

Let me be fucking clear about something: Ziggy Marley wasn't my dog. He was my son. Stephen's son. He was the family we built when the world was still deciding whether we deserved to be called a family. He was ours in a way that nobody questioned, nobody legislated, nobody voted on.

And now he's gone.

November 8th, 2025. That's the date my world split into before and after. Before Ziggy was laid to rest. After everything changed.

The vet's office had that smell—sterile and sad and like every goodbye that ever happened in a room with fluorescent lights and people trying to be gentle while your world ends. Ziggy's body was shutting down. Brain tumors we didn't know were there, growing in the dark like secrets, causing grand mal seizures that turned our beautiful boy into something we didn't recognize.

The seizures started a few days before. At first, we thought maybe he ate something weird, maybe it was just a one-time thing. But then they kept happening. And they got worse. And the vet did tests and scans and gave us the news that no pet parent ever wants to hear: inoperable brain tumors. Multiple tumors. Cancer that we couldn't see from the outside but was destroying him from the inside.

He looked healthy. That's what fucked with everyone. On the outside, he looked like the same goofy, prancing, beautiful boy he'd always been. But inside, his brain was betraying him. Inside, he was suffering in ways we couldn't fix.

The seizures were horrific. Watching someone you love seize—watching their body convulse and their eyes roll back and knowing there's nothing you can do to stop it—that's a special kind of hell. And knowing it was only going to get worse? Knowing that the seizures would become more frequent, more severe, that he'd eventually seize so hard he'd hurt himself or never come out of it? We couldn't let that happen. We couldn't let him suffer like that just because we couldn't imagine our lives without him.

We made the decision. Stephen and I. Together. We sat in the car and held each other and cried and made the hardest decision we've ever had to make as a couple.

We gave Ziggy the gift of eternal rest because that's what you do when you love someone—you don't let them suffer just because you can't imagine your life without them.

But here's the thing nobody tells you about making that decision: you'll hate yourself for it anyway. Even when you know it was right. Even when the alternative was watching him seize until his body gave out on its own. Even when every medical professional tells you there's nothing else to be done. You'll still wake up at 3 a.m. wondering if you gave up too soon, if there was one more treatment you didn't try, if he knew you were trying to help and not abandon him.

And this is where the Shadow Work comes in. This is where I use the tools.

I'm sitting with the guilt. I'm not running from it or numbing it or spiritually bypassing it with "everything happens for a reason" bullshit. I'm feeling it. I'm letting it be as ugly and uncomfortable as it is. I'm doing the Shadow Work on the parts of me that want to believe I failed him, that want to punish myself for making that decision.

And here's what the Shadow Work is showing me: The guilt is grief wearing a different mask. The guilt is my brain's way of trying to control something that was always beyond my control. If I can blame myself, if I can find something I did wrong, then maybe I can fix it. Maybe I can go back and make a different choice. Maybe I can get him back.

But I can't. Sitting with that reality—sitting with the absolute powerlessness of it—that's the work. That's what all those years of therapy prepared me for, not to avoid this pain, but to survive it.

The tools work. They're not making the guilt disappear. But they're helping me understand it. They're helping me sit with it without letting it become the story. They're helping me separate the grief from the self-blame.

This is what I need you to understand. The tools don't make the pain go away. They help you survive it without being destroyed by it.

We scheduled Ziggy's appointment for November 8th. We wanted a few more days with him. Days where he wasn't seizing, where we could love on him and tell him everything he meant to us and take a million pictures and try to memorize the feeling of his body against ours.

Those were the longest and shortest days of my life.

Every moment felt precious and painful. Every grunt felt like a gift. Every time he pranced or did a tigger jump or rested his head in my lap, I thought, "This might be the last time." And then I'd cry. And then I'd breathe. And then I'd be present with him instead of lost in my grief about losing him.

That's the work. Being present even when presence hurts. Showing up even when showing up means feeling everything. Using the tools to stay grounded instead of dissociating or running or numbing.

I did breathwork multiple times a day during those last moments with Ziggy. Four counts in, hold for four, six counts out. Ground myself. Feel my feet on the floor. Feel my body in the chair. Feel Ziggy's warmth against me. Stay here. Stay present. Don't go into the future where he's gone. Stay in this moment where he's still here.

The breathwork worked. It kept me present. It kept me from spiraling into panic about what was coming.

It let me actually be with him instead of drowning in anticipatory grief.

That's what the tools do. They help you stay in the moment instead of getting lost in the pain.

November 8th arrived. We took Ziggy to the vet. Stephen drove because I couldn't. I sat in the back seat with him, holding him, telling him stories about all our adventures together. The beach trips. The dog park. The walks. The way he used to steal food off the counter when he thought we weren't looking.

I told him he was the best boy. The best son. The best teacher. I told him we loved him more than anything. I told him it was okay to go, that we'd be okay, that he'd done his job and done it perfectly.

I lied about that last part. We weren't going to be okay. But I needed him to believe we would be. I needed him to go peacefully, without worrying about us.

The vet was kind. She gave us as much time as we needed. She explained the process—first a sedative to make him sleepy and comfortable, then the final injection that would stop his heart.

We held him. Stephen and I, on either side of him on the floor of the exam room, holding him between us like we could protect him from what was coming.

And here's what I need to tell you about that moment: I was using my tools the entire time. I was doing breathwork to stay present. I was grounding myself in my body so I wouldn't dissociate. I was feeling everything—the texture of his fur, the warmth of his body, the sound of his breathing, the weight of Stephen's hand on mine.

I was present for every single second of it, and that's because I had the tools to be present. That's because

I'd spent five years learning how to sit with unbearable things without running.

The sedative went in. Ziggy got sleepy. His eyes got heavy. He looked at me one last time with those big beautiful brown eyes, and I swear to God he knew. I swear he was saying goodbye. I swear he was telling me it was okay, that he loved me, that this wasn't my fault.

And then he closed his eyes. And then the vet gave him the final injection. And then his heart stopped. And then he was gone.

Just like that. One second he was here. The next second he wasn't.

The vet checked for a heartbeat and shook her head. "He's gone. I'm so sorry."

And Stephen and I sat on the floor of that exam room holding our son's body and sobbing like our hearts were being ripped out of our chests. Because they were.

But even in that moment—even in the absolute worst moment of my life—I was using my tools. I was breathing. I was grounding. I was letting myself feel everything without trying to make it smaller or more manageable.

That's what the tools gave me. The ability to be present for the worst moment of my life. The ability to show up for Ziggy until the very end. The ability to feel it all without breaking completely.

USING THE TOOLS IN REAL TIME

Here's what I'm learning: grief is healing work. All of it. Every tear, every rage scream into a pillow at 2 a.m., every moment I break down because I heard his collar jingle in my memory and then remembered he's not here—it's all part of the process.

And this is the first time in my life I'm actually doing it right.

For the first time in my forty-two years, I'm actually processing loss while it's happening. I'm not running. I'm not numbing. I'm not spiritually bypassing my way into "everything happens for a reason" before I've even let myself feel the unreasonableness of it all.

I'm sitting in the wreckage. I'm letting it hurt. I'm using every single tool I learned in five years of brutal therapy and healing work.

And I need you to understand this: I'm not telling you this to brag about how well I'm handling it. I'm telling you this to show you that the tools work. That everything I wrote in this book about healing and transformation and doing the work—it's all real. It's all true. And it holds up when life tests you.

Here's what using the tools in real time actually looks like:

Breathwork: I'm doing it multiple times a day. When the panic hits and my chest gets tight and I can't remember how to inhale properly. When I'm sitting at my computer trying to work and suddenly, I'm sobbing and can't stop. When I wake up at 3 AM and remember all over again that he's gone. Four counts in, hold for four, six counts out. Ground myself. Feel my body. Feel the chair. Feel my feet on the floor. Survive this moment.

Shadow Work: I'm sitting with every uncomfortable emotion that comes up. The guilt about putting him down. The anger at the universe for taking him now. The shame I feel for being sad about a dog when other people have "real" problems. The parts of me that want to perform strength instead of admitting I'm shattered.

I'm looking at all of it. I'm not running from any of it. I'm letting it teach me what it needs to teach me.

Writing: This chapter. This act of putting words to grief. This is my processing. This is how I make sense of things that don't make sense. This is how I transform pain into something I can hold instead of something that crushes me.

Meditation: I'm sitting in silence even when the silence is unbearable. I'm feeling the absence of him. I'm not filling the quiet with distractions. I'm just... sitting with what is.

These tools aren't making the pain go away, but they're keeping me functional. They're keeping me present. They're keeping me from drowning.

That's what I need you to understand about healing work. It doesn't immunize you from pain. It gives you the ability to survive the pain when it comes.

THE LANGUAGE WE SPOKE

Ziggy wasn't a barker. He was a grunter. He had this whole vocabulary of grunts and grumbles and sounds that weren't quite barks but weren't quite anything else either.

He'd grunt at me when he was hungry. He'd grunt when he wanted to go outside. He'd grunt just to tell me he loved me—these soft little sounds when he'd rest his head on my lap and look up at me with those big beautiful brown eyes.

Those grunts were especially for me. More frequent with me than with Stephen. Like he knew I needed the constant reassurance that he was there, that he loved me, that I wasn't alone.

I knew every single one of those grunts. I knew what each one meant. We had a whole fucking language together, the three of us.

And now there's silence where those grunts used to be.

The silence is the worst part. I'll be sitting at my computer working on edits, and I'll hear a sound—or think I hear a sound—that could be him, and for a split second, I forget. For a split second, my brain goes, "Oh, Ziggy needs something," and I start to get up before I remember.

He's not here. He's never going to grunt at me again.

Every time I remember that, it's like losing him all over again. Little grief grenades exploding throughout the day.

This is where the breathwork saves me. When those moments hit and I can't breathe and the panic starts—four counts in, hold, six counts out. Ground. Feel my body. Feel the pain. Let it move through me instead of getting stuck.

The tool works. Every single time. It doesn't make the pain disappear. But it keeps me from drowning in it.

I miss our daily walks. Those walks were my meditation. My moving therapy. The time when I could just be with him and not have to perform anything.

I'd use those walks to think through chapters in my book. I'd talk out loud to him about whatever I was working on, and somehow the act of talking to my dog helped me find the right words.

Now I walk alone, and it's not the same. Every familiar spot is a reminder. Every dog we pass is a reminder.

But I'm still walking. Because that's what the tools teach you—you keep the routines even when they hurt.

You show up even when showing up is painful. You don't let grief win by letting everything fall apart.

That's not toxic positivity. That's not spiritual bypassing. That's just survival. That's using the structure to hold you together when you feel like you're falling apart.

I miss the dog park. I miss watching him prance—and I mean actually prance, this goofy high-stepping walk like he was in a fucking parade. Eighty pounds of white boxer lifting his paws higher than necessary because he knew he was fabulous.

I miss the beach. I miss watching him run into the waves and then run back out like he was surprised every time that water moved. I miss those tigger jumps—all four paws off the ground—when he was so happy he couldn't contain it.

He lived a big, beautiful life. And for that, I'm grateful. We're grateful. Stephen and I gave him everything we had. He knew he was loved every single day of his seven years with us.

And I'm doing Shadow Work on the guilt that still tries to tell me I should have done more. I'm sitting with it. I'm acknowledging it. And then I'm letting it go. Because the truth is we loved him well. We showed up for him every single day. We gave him the gift of a peaceful death instead of prolonged suffering.

The Shadow Work helps me hold onto that truth. It helps me separate the grief from the guilt. It helps me see the guilt for what it is—my brain's attempt to control something that was always beyond my control.

WHAT ZIGGY CAME TO TEACH

Stephen and I talk about this late at night when we can't sleep and the grief feels too big to carry alone. We talk about why Ziggy came into our lives when he did and why he had to leave now.

And here's what we believe, what we've come to understand even though it doesn't make the pain easier:

Our pets come to us when we need them. They show up exactly when we're ready for what they have to teach us, and they leave when their work is done.

Ziggy came into our lives seven years ago, right when I was starting the hardest healing work I've ever done. Right when I was beginning to face the generational trauma, the childhood wounds, the PTSD that had been running my life from the shadows.

And he stayed through all of it.

He was there for every therapy session where I came home broken open. Every breathwork class where I sobbed so hard I thought I'd never stop. Every EMDR appointment where I had to relive the worst moments of my life so I could finally release them. Every morning, I woke up and didn't know if I could do another day of this work.

Ziggy was there, steady and present and unconditionally loving, showing me what it looked like to just fucking be. No performance. No pretending. Just existing and being loved for it.

He held space for Stephen too—through career changes and family shit and all the ways life tests you when you're trying to build something real.

And we believe—fuck, we have to believe—that Ziggy's purpose in this life was to make sure Stephen and I made it to the altar. To make sure we processed enough of our trauma to actually be ready for this commitment. To teach us how to love something completely without needing it to be anything other than what it is.

His work was to get us here. To November 24th, 2025, when we stand in front of the people we love and say the words we've been living for eleven years.

And once he knew we'd make it? Once his work was done?

He could go.

I hate that I understand this. I hate that there's a spiritual logic to it that makes sense even while my human heart screams that it's not fair.

He should get to see us get married. He should get to grow old with us. He deserves more time.

But maybe he'd already given us everything he came here to give. Maybe staying longer would have meant suffering he didn't need to endure just because we couldn't imagine letting him go.

Maybe the most loving thing he could do was leave when his work was finished.

I don't know if that's true. I don't know if I'm finding spiritual meaning or creating it to cope with loss. But I know this: Ziggy showed up when we needed him most, and he left when he'd taught us everything he came here to teach.

And one of those lessons—maybe the hardest one—is that love doesn't always get to stay as long as we want it to. Sometimes the beings we love most complete their purpose and move on, and the only way through is to honor what they gave us and keep going.

Even when it hurts. Even when the house is too quiet. Even when we're getting married without him.

We keep going because that's what he taught us to do.

THE WEDDING AND WHAT COMES NEXT

Sixteen days from now, Stephen and I are going to get married at the courthouse. Just us and about fifteen people who actually showed up when shit got hard.

I'm going to wrap Ziggy's name tag as a pin on my suit jacket. Our something old and something new, all at once.

Stephen is going to wear Ziggy's blue collar around his arm. Our something blue.

Ziggy won't be there in his body. But he'll be there in spirit. He'll be woven into every part of that day. He'll be in the fact that we made it there at all. He'll be in the love we learned from him. He'll be in the healing work we did that made us ready for this commitment.

And I'm using my tools to prepare for that day. I'm doing breathwork to manage the anxiety about getting married without him physically present. I'm doing Shadow Work on the parts of me that feel guilty for being happy when I'm also devastated. I'm sitting with the contradiction of joy and grief existing simultaneously.

The tools are working. They're helping me show up for this moment fully. They're helping me be excited about marrying Stephen while also making space to miss Ziggy. They're helping me understand that both things can be true—that I can celebrate this new beginning while grieving what ended.

Here's what Stephen and I also believe: We will get our son back.

Not the same body. Not the same vessel. But the same soul. The same energy. The same being who chose us once and will choose us again when the time is right.

We have trust and faith in the universe that Ziggy will return to us in a new form when we're ready and when he's ready.

I keep thinking about his face. That heart-shaped pattern created by the brown spot above his right eye and the brown spot on his right ear. Those big beautiful brown eyes. His lower baby teeth that never grew out. His prance walk. His tigger jumps. All his boxer goofiness.

And I trust that when he comes back, we'll recognize him. Maybe not in the exact same package, but in the energy. In the soul. In the way he looks at us and we just know—that's him. That's our boy.

This isn't denial. I know he's gone. I feel the absence every single day. But I also believe in something bigger than what I can see or touch or prove. I believe that the connection we had with Ziggy was too profound to just . . . end.

He'll come back. When we're ready. When he's ready. When the universe decides it's time.

WHAT THIS CHAPTER IS REALLY ABOUT

So here's what I need you to understand about this chapter:

This isn't a chapter about loss. This is a chapter about proof.

Proof that the healing work is real. Proof that the tools actually work when you need them most. Proof that you can do everything right and still experience devastating loss, and that doesn't mean you failed—it means you're human.

Proof that healing isn't about reaching some perfect state where nothing hurts anymore. It's about having the capacity to survive when life inevitably breaks your heart again.

I'm not okay. Let me be clear about that. I'm not healed. I'm not over it. I'm not at peace with Ziggy's death yet. I might never be at peace with it.

But I'm surviving it. I'm processing it. I'm using breathwork and therapy and Shadow Work and meditation and writing to make it through each day. Some days are better than others. Some days I'm functional. Some days I'm a mess.

But I'm here. I'm still showing up. I'm still writing. I'm still getting married. I'm still finishing this book.

I'm doing all of it while grieving my son. And that's proof that the work is real.

This is what I want you to understand: Having tools doesn't make you immune to pain. Doing the healing work doesn't mean you'll never experience trauma or loss or grief again. The road back to yourself doesn't end—it just keeps going, and sometimes it leads you through dark places you didn't know existed.

But the tools help you survive those dark places. They help you walk through the valley without setting up permanent residence there. They help you feel everything without being consumed by everything.

That's what I'm learning right now, in real time, while editing this book. I'm learning that healing is ongoing. That lessons never end. That transformation happens in the middle of everything else you're trying to do.

I'm learning that you can be the expert and the student simultaneously. You can write the book and still need to read it. You can teach healing while actively healing.

There's no contradiction in that. That's just what being human looks like.

So this chapter stays in the book. This raw, unfinished, in-the-middle-of-it chapter about losing Ziggy while trying to finish a book about trauma recovery.

This chapter that shows you what it actually looks like to use the tools in real time. What it looks like to survive the unsurvivable. What proof looks like that the work is real, even when—especially when—you're in the middle of the hardest part.

This is what you need to see. Not some polished version of healing where everything works out perfectly, but the messy truth. The contradictions. The both/and instead of either/or.

The truth that you can be devastated and grateful simultaneously. That you can grieve and celebrate. That you can be broken and whole. That you can use all your tools and still cry in parking lots. That you can do everything right and still hurt like hell.

And all of it—all of it—is part of the healing.

Ziggy was the unexpected teacher. He showed up when I needed him most and taught me lessons I didn't know I needed to learn. And now he's teaching me the hardest lesson—how to keep going when the being you love most is gone. How to honor what was while building what's next. How to carry loss without being crushed by it.

I'm learning. I'm using my tools. I'm showing up. I'm surviving.

Sixteen days from now, I'm going to marry the love of my life and I'm going to understand that love doesn't end when the body does.

It just transforms.

Just like I'm being transformed right now.

Just like everyone who reads this book and does the work will be transformed too.

Not perfectly. Not easily. But truly.

That's what matters. That's what Ziggy came here to teach. That's what this chapter—this whole book—is about.

The road back to yourself never ends. But with the right tools, you can walk it. Even when it hurts. Even when you're grieving. Even when you don't know how.

You walk it anyway.

Because that's what healing actually is. And the tools? They fucking work.

I'm living proof.

ABOUT THE AUTHOR

Peter J Cervantes is a healer, writer, and advocate dedicated to breaking generational cycles of trauma within LGBTQ+ communities of color. Drawing from his lived experience as a first-generation Mexican American gay man, Peter combines personal narrative with practical healing tools to create pathways toward wholeness that honor both cultural heritage and authentic identity.

After nearly losing his life to unprocessed trauma at 37, Peter embarked on an intensive healing journey that transformed his understanding of generational wounds, shadow work, and the specific challenges facing queer people of color navigating family rejection and systemic oppression. Through therapy, EMDR, breathwork, meditation, journaling, and ancestral healing practices, he not only survived but discovered his purpose: to share the tools that saved his life with others who are still searching for their way home.

With over 20 years of experience in healthcare management and as a professional makeup artist and stylist, Peter brings a unique perspective to healing work—understanding that transformation requires both inner work and outer expression. His writing reflects the raw honesty, dark humor, and fierce compassion that characterize his approach to breaking cycles that have limited families for generations.

The Road Back to Me: Six Sacred Tools for Queer Healing Through Shadow, Breath, and Truth is Peter's first book, born from his conviction that healing resources must speak directly to the intersectional experiences of LGBTQ+ people of color rather than treating their struggles as footnotes in mainstream narratives.

Peter currently lives in San Diego with his partner of 11 years and now husband, Stephen, where he continues his work supporting queer communities through writing, spiritual guidance, and advocacy for accessible mental health resources.

www.ingramcontent.com/pod-product-compliance
Lightning Source LLC
Chambersburg PA
CBHW021140160426
43194CB00007B/639